IT'S NO SECRET

REAL MEN WEAR APRONS

... the distinguishing badge of a Mason. It is more ancient than the Golden Fleece or Roman Eagle, more honourable than the Garter or any other Order in existence, being the badge of innocence and the bond of friendship.

– from the initiation ceremony
of the First or Entered Apprentice Degree

Published by
Masonic Care Limited (ACN 109 508 116) as trustee for
The Museum of Freemasonry Foundation
ABN 98 617 484 908
The United Grand Lodge of NSW & ACT
Sydney Masonic Centre
279 Castlereagh Street
Sydney NSW 2000
Australia
www.uglnsw.freemasonry.org.au

First printed in Australia in 2009 by Griffin Press
a member company of the PMP Limited Group

Copyright © Masonic Care Limited 2009

ISBN 978-0-646-52446-7

Page design and typesetting by Midland Typesetters, Australia
Printed and bound by Griffin Press

IT'S NO SECRET

REAL MEN WEAR APRONS

To Hilary
expert guide
and friend
with warm
good
wishes

Peter Lazar
Ian Lershmark ?
(the
last
word)

May 2010

FREEMASONS

THE STORY OF FREEMASONRY IN AUSTRALIA
EDITED BY PETER LAZAR AM

Peter Lazar wears an apron ...

Peter Lazar AM has been a dedicated Freemason for more than 50 years and has initiated three family members into the Craft. He is a director of the Royal Freemasons' Benevolent Institution which owns and operates, on a not-for-profit basis, 23 retirement villages around NSW & ACT.

He and his family escaped from Nazi persecution in Austria when he was eight. At Double Bay Public and North Sydney Boys' High School he learned to speak English, play cricket and football and how to become a 'dinkum Aussie'.

At Sydney University he co-edited the student newspaper, participated in sport and theatre. He wrote scripts and lyrics, produced and directed University Revues. Peter Lazar was one of Australia's earliest TV personalities appearing on ABC panel programs in the 1950s and again in the 1970s.

He was instrumental in promoting the fluoridation of community water supplies and oral health. Although not a dentist, he was honoured by the profession which made him a Fellow of the International College of Dentists.

He is founder and chairman of one of Australia's largest communication consultancies, a past president and Life Fellow of the Public Relations Institute and co-author of *The Australian and New Zealand Public Relations Manual.*

He and his consultancy have counselled many of Australia's well-known businesses, professional associations, government and not-for-profit organisations including agricultural industry bodies, charities and more.

On Australia Day 2007, Peter Lazar was made a Member of the Order of Australia for service to business, to communication and to the community through aged care, health, cultural and social welfare organisations.

CONTENTS

FOREWORD

FREEMASONS

 Freemasonry has been misunderstood for far too long. The history and traditions of this ancient fraternity have proved to be both good and bad for its reputation.

Some praise it for the great work that it does in developing good men into even more valuable members of the community. Freemasons tend to be good citizens, good family men, staunch friends and many are leaders and role models.

Some people question the purpose of the Craft. Some fear what they think of as 'secret men's business'. This book explains that the purpose of Freemasonry is to do good, to build better lives and to be of service to society.

What Freemasonry has done and is doing in Australia has never been compiled in quite this way before. *It's No Secret ... Real Men Wear Aprons* covers how carefully the Craft attracts its good men, how it teaches them valuable lessons of morality and virtue, of charity and brotherly love and of happiness. It stresses the fact that good men of all races, religions and walks of life can join together in harmony and peace within the Lodges of Freemasonry and in the broader communities in which we live and operate.

Freemasonry is all about belonging to and connecting with our community.

The book makes the point that today Freemasonry is not secretive, nor is it a secret. That's why the book is called *It's No Secret*. It talks of how Freemasonry began, why it has existed for so long, what a candidate can expect from it. Importantly it focuses on how Freemasonry works in and supports Australia.

At the same time it is true that there is a mystique about this ancient fraternity. The allegories which explain Freemasonry are of the greatest value in conveying moral lessons to its members. The book talks of these things and points out that for Masons these elements are of real interest and benefit.

It's No Secret tells of some great and famous Masons of the past and the present. It provides glimpses into the lives of our leaders, artists, scientists, explorers, entrepreneurs, heroes, sportsmen. What being a Freemason means to members, to both new and long-serving brethren, is presented in a number of snapshots by contributors. Women get a say in these pages also. Increasingly women have become involved in the work of the Craft and we welcome this.

It is my hope that the readers of this book will come away with a warm feeling towards the Craft and a better understanding of this great fraternity. I invite enquiries from those good men who are non-Masons and wish to know more. Freemasonry has great benefits and can share them with you. It has helped hundreds of thousands of Australians to live a better, happier, more useful life.

Dr Greg Levenston,
Grand Master, United Grand Lodge of NSW & ACT

The Secret is how to live

Dan Brown's Prologue to *The Lost Symbol* begins with the words, 'The Secret is how to die' … which *heaven* knows has to be a *hell* of a good first sentence for any thriller.

We learned of it just in time.

Nearly all of this book was in manuscript form when *The Lost Symbol* was released on 15 September 2009. The novel itself was heavily embargoed but a massive publicity campaign, and the popularity of its predecessor, *The Da Vinci Code*, ensured that *The Lost Symbol* would sell a million copies in the USA on the day of its release.

All we knew until that day was that it was about Washington and Freemasonry. Nothing more. What would this mean to those of us in Australia who were already working on a well-considered plan to open the doors of Freemasonry, explain what it was all about? What should we do now? Delay our own book until we could see what he said, and respond or correct if necessary? Would our book look like a copycat response? Should we change course and give it up?

We decided to carry on. Whatever Dan Brown said about Freemasonry, we would not argue with him. He is one of the world's most successful storytellers. His new book would no doubt be full of excitement and symbols and explanations and theories about myths both ancient and urban. If nothing else, it would lift awareness of the Craft of Freemasonry.

Great, we said! We couldn't be happier! Mr Brown's readers would learn more about us, and give us a platform from which to continue our efforts to reveal Freemasonry's purpose, its activities, its contribution to men and to our society here in Australia.

But if we wanted to benefit from that, we had to work quickly. At that stage, my contributors and I had been working on *It's No Secret ... Real Men Wear Aprons* for only a few weeks. Suddenly we had a very tight deadline. So I am hoping that those readers who find errors or omissions here will forgive us on the grounds that we tried to make our book available as close to the launch of Mr Brown's book as we could.

And here it is: everything you ever wanted to know about Freemasonry – the Degrees, their ceremonies and moral teachings. It's tempting to add some hoopla of our own – *'The Secret is Out'* or *'Unveiling the Mystery'* – but in fact much of this information has not been a real secret for generations. Many books and websites about Freemasonry contain most of the 'secrets' in great detail. For example you can read the excellent books of Grahame Cumming, one of Australia's foremost Masonic authors, whose work inspired us as we approached the daunting task of creating our own.

Later in this book you will find a section that suggests additional reading.

For the opening sentence to his Prologue, Dan Brown has drawn from the deep meaning and purpose of the Master Mason's Degree, the third Degree of Ancient Freemasonry. The object of that Degree is to reveal to the candidate that death holds no terrors for those who live their lives honestly, ethically and in the genuine service of the community.

Morality, virtue, values and the highest principles of how to live a good and happy life are what Freemasonry has always been about. So thank you, Mr Brown, for your opening sentence ... 'The Secret is how to die'.

We agree, but we add ... the *real* Secret is how to live. Get that right and death holds no terrors for you.

So this is really a book about how to live, drawing on the ancient teachings of the Craft of Freemasonry.

My own introduction to Freemasonry began more than 50 years ago, and I can say ... hand on heart ... that it has helped me to live in harmony, with my family, at work, in my community and to enjoy the mutual trust and friendship of a very large number of people in every walk of life.

My son Richard has been a Freemason for 24 years. I had the pleasure of initiating him into my Masonic Lodge in 1985. It was Richard who came up with the idea for this book when he began working with the United Grand Lodge of NSW to address its communication challenges and opportunities. He saw *It's No Secret ... Real Men Wear Aprons* as being one part of an ongoing program to assist anyone interested in the Craft to learn more.

While recognising that the myths and intrigue surrounding Freemasonry encourage discussion and debate, his desire, like mine, is that this be put into context, appropriately explained and that this might result in better knowledge and understanding. Many good ideas for the book were suggested by him.

Many others have also contributed, and they are included in the acknowledgements at the end of the book.

Being a Freemason means that you live life 'on the level', that you do your utmost to deal 'on the square' with everyone. It means that you believe in values and ethics, that you don't just 'tolerate' diversity but that you embrace it. And you rejoice in the fact that 'we are all sprung from the same stock, are partakers of the same Nature and Sharers of the same Hope'. That quote comes directly from the Second Degree ritual explaining the working tools of a Fellow Craft Freemason.

We have tried to include many examples of the wisdom of the Craft; wisdom that has stood the test of time for centuries and has guided literally millions of men around the world to develop a better understanding and participation in their life and times.

Masonic wisdom is just as relevant today as it was in the time of King Solomon the Wise, from which much of its ritual is drawn. The world has changed and will change a great deal more, but the need of humans to understand their lives, how best to live in harmony with others and with nature remains a challenge for us all.

That challenge exists for people of all races, all religions and for all Freemasons around the world. Until humans learn to live in peace and brotherhood, to value diversity and to appreciate our individual right to freedom and to happiness, there will always be room for Masonic wisdom, understanding and charity.

Australia is especially fortunate in that it welcomes diversity and celebrates multiculturalism. I have experienced what it is to be made welcome in this country. My own escape from the holocaust of World War II was the result of the foresight of my Uncle Ernst ... a Freemason and something of a futurist.

Ernst Lazar was a pilot for the Kaiser in World War I. He saw the writing on the wall soon after Hitler annexed our native Austria. He foresaw what was facing the Jews of Europe, migrated to Australia in 1937 and applied for the visas which saved my family and me.

On November 8th 1938, my father was arrested at gunpoint by the Gestapo and taken to jail in Vienna. Just two hours later the postman brought our Australian visas. My mother stood in a long line of wives and relatives for several days at the jail before she could show the Kommandant our visas. He released my father and gave us 48 hours to clear out. Twelve weeks later we landed in Australia.

The welcome I received here has been a constant reminder of the value of tolerance, of harmony and of peace. Freemasonry has added to that appreciation. It has provided a great many trusted friends ... friends who are like brothers. Indeed once a man becomes a Freemason he has 50 million 'brothers' who live in 164 countries around the world.

In this attempt to explain Freemasonry, chapters cover how Freemasonry began; how it is linked to ancient history and to the traditions of the stonemasons; and what it does to help and encourage good men to develop themselves into better men as citizens, husbands and fathers, carers, friends and wiser, more human beings. It encourages them to recognise and uphold the four cardinal virtues of Freemasonry: Temperance, Prudence, Fortitude and Justice. These words are featured in the four corners of most Lodge rooms in Australia.

The book also shows how the fraternity contributes to the communities of which it is a part. On the way, it tells the stories of many interesting Australians who chose to become Freemasons.

As the title suggests, we seek to demystify and to debunk the misinformation brought about, to some extent, by the traditional reluctance of Freemasonry to talk about itself. That secrecy, which has been misunderstood both within and outside the Craft, has resulted in undue suspicion, in some silly urban myths and even in conspiracy theories.

This book throws light on how Freemasonry values freedom, equality and fraternity; how it encourages every moral and social virtue. For many it has provided a real meaning to life, to the concept of living in harmony with humanity and with nature. It is about being happy and conferring happiness. The *real* secret is how to live.

– Peter Lazar

Freemasonry:
a definition

**'A peculiar system of morality veiled in
allegory and illustrated by symbols.'**

While this is one of the most common descriptions of the Craft,
it is seldom considered in depth. As a result, Freemasons and
non-Masons tend not to understand its full significance.

The word 'peculiar' is used not to suggest strangeness ...
something weird. It comes from the dictionary definition:

> peculiar: *belonging exclusively to some person, group, or thing*

So, the system of morality which is the cornerstone of the
beliefs and values of Freemasonry is one which *belongs
exclusively to the Craft*.

And it is 'veiled in allegory'. The Masonic system of
morality is hidden, shrouded in allegory, in abstract ideas.
I went again to the dictionary:

> allegory: *The representation of abstract ideas or principles
> by characters, figures, or events in narrative, dramatic, or
> pictorial form.*

Exactly! Masonry communicates its morals and values
by acting out stories, small dramas involving its members

as leading actors … stars in small pieces of theatre. These are like the morality plays of earlier times which provided lessons in how to behave.

The effect on candidates of the Masonic Degree ceremonies is much more powerful than any written encouragement. These allegories remain with Freemasons for the rest of their lives. They help them to remember the important things in life, to live in harmony with others, to have high principles, to be happy and to promote happiness.

The allegories are 'illustrated by symbols'. These are to be found in the stonemason's tools which are applied to teach moral lessons, reflected in the furniture of Lodge rooms, in our Degree work and repeated in many other ways during the Masonic experiences in the life of each Mason.

From the ceremony of the First or Entered Apprentice Degree, the candidate is encouraged:

> As a last general recommendation, let me exhort you to devote yourself to such further pursuits as will enable you to continue respectable in your station, useful to your fellow beings, and an ornament to the society of which you have become a member.

CHAPTER ONE

What *is* Freemasonry?

Freemasonry helps good men live better lives. That's the reason it began, centuries ago. That's what it will do for many years to come: help good men lead better lives.

So just what is a 'better life'? To Freemasons, it is a life with meaning, a life lived consciously, a life of happiness – and a life in which we care for others and help to make them happy.

Thinking people have always sought meaning in their lives. The search might begin in childhood and adolescence. Early adulthood brings some distractions, but the search returns with a vengeance in mid-life. Or it might arrive full-blown as the result of a powerful personal experience such as the death of a partner or close relative. Whenever and however it begins, this search for meaning is a core component of personal development.

For many years people have found meaning in religion, from ancient pagans to modern parishioners. Unfortunately the journey of religion itself has seen the growth of various kinds of fundamentalism which is a threat to peace. Many people growing up in today's multicultural, more interde-pendent world, are choosing not to commit to any religious dogma, but to seek alternative paths to spiritual growth.

Whatever path any individual may choose, the shared goal – across all peoples, across all times – is, of course, success. Where we differ, sometimes tragically, is in how we define 'success': exactly what do we mean when we use that word?

Today there is a growing challenge to accepted ideas of success. During the 20th century, in the west, success came to be associated with celebrity and wealth ... yet the personal stories of the rich and famous don't always have happy endings. The tragic mistake of many – perhaps whole societies – was in believing that wealth and renown would lead to happiness.

So is happiness, then, what we mean by success? The leading edge of contemporary learning suggests that it is. Even governments are now exploring this subject as they learn to measure the prosperity of their nations *and* the wellbeing of their citizens. Australia's Bureau of Statistics and many other organisations – including UNESCO and the International Institute of Management – are currently engaged in comprehensive studies of indicators that will serve as better measures of wellbeing than traditional economic measures. The Kingdom of Bhutan has even developed its own Gross National Happiness Index.

Meanwhile the literature on the science of happiness has grown rapidly in the past 20 years, with more and more modern researchers finding evidence to confirm the conclusions of ancient philosophers – like the early Masons – that happiness is a legitimate, indeed a vital, goal in human evolution.

This in turn raises the question: what do we mean by happiness? Again, both ancient and modern thinkers have explored this question and there are truckloads of books purporting to tell us the answers. One thing is clear: happiness is not simple pleasure. Nor is it the distraction and entertainment of the modern world. Leading psychologists and philosophers tell us, in fact, that true happiness comes when we transcend ourselves, when we find meaning in things beyond ourselves, and especially when we help others.

Freemasonry supports these two fundamental human needs – for meaning and for happiness – by providing a supportive structure to live by. It actively welcomes people from any religion, and respects their spiritual and cultural traditions. It doesn't tell anyone how to live their lives in any specific way: rather, it allows and encourages individual members to take their own meaning and instruction from its teachings, each in accordance with his personal needs and beliefs. The teaching of the Craft simply offers a framework, a set of enriching principles and philosophies that are taught through the powerful means of story, metaphor, symbol and ritual – many of these unchanged for hundreds of years.

Central to its teachings, Freemasonry urges adherence to *Prudence, Justice, Temperance* and *Fortitude*. These four words – the Cardinal Virtues – are displayed in most Lodge room in Australia, and are always closely linked to the three theological virtues – *Faith, Hope* and *Charity* – as taught to new Masons on their way to the first level of qualification, the Entered Apprentice Degree.

In France, the aims of Masonry were encapsulated in the words *Liberty, Equality, Fraternity*, first heard in the Age of Enlightenment and later made famous by the French Revolution.

As well as teaching principles like these, Freemasonry offers the opportunity to join in fellowship and friendship with others; to discover life-long paths of personal development; and to enjoy useful charitable opportunities. Using funds raised entirely within the Craft, the Freemasons have developed aged care facilities, supported orphans and widows and given help to people in need without consideration of whether they were connected to the Craft. And Freemasonry has supported public charities, helped in bushfire relief work and more.

Through fellowship, learning and mentoring, Freemasons choose to adopt ethical values of their own. Taking their example from the tools associated with the stonemason's Craft, Freemasons seek to treat people fairly ('on the level') in all their daily dealings, and to restrict their own excesses by keeping their emotions and their actions within acceptable limits – as though within a circle drawn by a compass or prescribed by the artisan's dividers.

The stonemason's square and compass together form the symbol of Freemasonry worldwide. But many of the other tools in the Craft are also central to the teachings and offices of modern Freemasonry. Each of the tools and symbols serves as a metaphor to help shape and smooth the individual's character in such a way as to benefit himself and society as a whole, in the same way as well-crafted stones can be laid together to build structures that are upright, square and durable.

Masons advance through gaining knowledge in stages called Degrees – with self-development based on the individual's interpretation and understanding of the Masonic allegories or guiding philosophies.

The origins of Freemasonry

The Freemason movement has ancient origins that stretch back to the building of the Temple of King Solomon in biblical times. Remarkably strong links are maintained between those early stonemasons and the Freemasons of today, through allegorical teachings based on the design and construction of ancient structures.

The name, Free Mason, first came into use in medieval times when stonemasons travelled through Europe building many of the great cathedrals, castles and palaces that remain today. At that time, most people were 'bonded' to the land on which they were born, meaning they couldn't leave without the specific permission of their master.

Being the high-tech professionals of their day, stonemasons were responsible for the design and construction of vital infrastructure such as city walls and defences, castles, keeps and later the soaring cathedrals of Europe. When they were needed, stonemasons were needed in large numbers. This made them one of the few Crafts to be granted the freedom to travel as their work demanded – thus 'Free Masons'.

Europe was relatively wild and lawless during medieval times. Few people could read or write, so the Free Masons used secret signs and words to identify themselves to fellow craftsmen on the road and on new building sites – receiving work and protection in return. The secret handshake told others they were Masons and the secret word for each Degree let others know their status in the Craft – whether Entered Apprentice, Craftsman, or Master Mason.

These three Degrees are still the first three steps in modern Freemasonry's Craft Lodges. Over several centuries, other steps have come into being in related orders which follow the first three Degrees but do not outrank them.

Today's Freemasons still use the secret handshakes and the words that identify their status in the Craft – and these are still secret. They are kept secret because of their historical importance to the Craft, because they still serve a purpose, and because they have been kept secret for so long that it would seem a shame to reveal them simply to satisfy the curious, but otherwise disinterested, bystanders who just 'want to know'.

Apart from identifying Masons and their position in the Craft, the secret handshake and the words have no other practical meaning or purpose. They do, however, have a symbolic meaning. The values of Freemasonry are deeply anchored in trust: trust in oneself, trust in one's word, trust in each other. By keeping the handshake and the word secret, Masons are showing they are trustworthy. This is important as trust is absolute, and a man who can be trusted with a small secret is demonstrating that his word and conduct can be trusted in other things.

These two things then, and only these two things – the handshakes and the words – are secret, to the extent that they are shared only with those members who have completed the necessary work and made the appropriate commitments.

There is nothing else about Freemasonry that cannot be found in libraries or on the web. Some jurisdictions in Australia, including the United Grand Lodge in Sydney, have welcomed public interest for many years. The UGL building is in fact a major conference centre and many people who work in Sydney will have attended one or more conferences held there.

The Museum of Freemasonry located on the third floor of that building is a public museum and is open to visitors in normal museum hours. It contains a number of display areas showing antique Masonic aprons and the actual Masonic regalia worn by the first Grand Master in Australia, Lord Carrington. The regalia collection also includes that of some related orders from around the world, such as the Knights Templar.

The comprehensive collection houses sections dedicated to leaders such as Sir Edward 'Weary' Dunlop, the 16 Australian Masons awarded the Victoria Cross, and the Lodge established by inmates of the Changi Prison Camp. Cricket legend, Sir Donald Bradman can be found among the sportsmen. Sir Robert Menzies is included as one of ten Masonic Prime Ministers of Australia, and Sir Charles Kingsford Smith is among the explorers. The Museum provides a complete survey of Freemasonry and Freemasons in Australia from its inception to the present day, honouring the founders of the Craft and the recently departed – including the much loved Australian actor, Charles 'Bud' Tingwell.

Freemasons have long used Tracing Boards (the first of these deals with Faith, Hope and Charity) as teaching aids to represent the first three Degrees of Masonic learning. The Museum has a significant collection of these, many dating from the 19th century and all created in a style that would later be described as surreal. They represent a major art form that has yet to be widely studied and will one day take its place in the narrative of western art history.

The Museum also houses an extensive collection of Masonic 'jewels' – badges in gold and silver worn by office bearers – from around the world, as well as the current Grand Master's sword and banner.

Tours include entry to one of the most recently refurbished Masonic Lodge rooms, where all the elements of Lodge design and symbolic items are explained. A Son et

Lumière presentation will be installed in this room to explain the Lodge furniture and symbols. (See script in Appendix C.) Visitors can also see and use the Masonic library for academic or general research, or just for their own interest. A visit to the Museum of Freemasonry provides a wealth of information on the Craft and its history in Australia.

The modern movement

Modern, or 'speculative' Freemasonry began with the formation of the Grand Lodge of England in 1717, and quickly grew to include men from all trades and professions in all parts of the world.

Most of the Lodge buildings one sees in Australian cities and towns provide the meeting place for several different Masonic Lodges – a Lodge being a group of Masons recognised by the United Grand Lodge. This is no different from the way in which a number of cricket clubs, all recognised by the regional authority, may meet in the same club house during the course of a week or weekend during which a number of games are played.

The organisation of a Masonic Lodge is also similar to the organisation of a sports or social club, with each Lodge having a President, Vice Presidents, and other officers or, as they are called in Freemasonry: a Master, Wardens, Deacons and others.

Most countries have a Grand Lodge to oversee and administer the Lodges in their territory. In Australia, where each of the states was independent prior to Federation, the states have maintained their own Grand Lodges. The United Grand Lodge in Sydney represents Freemasons in New South Wales and the Australian Capital Territory while the South Australian Grand Lodge also has jurisdiction over the Northern Territory.

More about the early history of Freemasonry in Australia can be found in Appendix A at the back of this book, with details about how each of the State Lodges was formed.

There is no national authority in Australia, and while most Lodges in England, the USA, Australia and New Zealand are historically related to the Grand Lodge of England, there is no single international authority that governs Freemasonry around the world, and thus no single Masonic leader.

Freemasonry is therefore practised in a co-operative democratic manner, with each jurisdiction being able to practise the Craft in a way that meets its own needs and objectives, without having specific rules and practices imposed on it by a world 'head office'.

The lack of centralised command and the absence of any predetermined 'answers' makes the journey offered by Freemasonry intensely individual, and the search for meaning all the more rewarding.

Freemasonry is not a religion nor a substitute for religion. While all intending Masonic candidates are required to express their belief in a Higher Power or a Supreme Being, their private religious beliefs are respected and protected.

Each Lodge displays a book of Sacred Law relevant to its members, and in many cases two or three, such as the Old Testament, the New Testament and the Koran, where a Lodge includes individuals from these religious groups. These 'Sacred Texts' are used by members only to confirm their acceptance of any undertaking they make as part of their Masonic progress.

To protect the religious privacy and the political views of members, any further discussion of religion or politics is banned in Lodge – making Freemasonry the birthplace of the common caution: never talk about religion or politics!

Far from being a 'sect', Freemasonry opposes zealotry in any form. In fact, it is so firmly opposed to proselytising that it has even been reluctant to promote itself, and the benefits Freemasonry offers to individuals. One of the founding principles of Freemasonry requires that men who seek to join the Craft should be free, and approach *of their own free will.* This view has been so rigidly applied that Freemasons have been reluctant to publicise their actions, or promote their fellowship through any kind of 'hard sell'.

Even the sons of Masons have often followed their father into the Craft only at the urging of their mothers, with many an exasperated mother telling their sons to 'ask your father about Freemasonry' ... Upon which many equally exasperated (but stoically silent) fathers have responded with words along the lines of: 'Well, finally ... I thought you were never going to ask!'

Today, Masons are being encouraged to speak about their membership, but are still not urged to invite others to join. By tradition the applicant must make the first approach, but a simple question about Freemasonry is enough to result in an invitation to become a candidate

This reluctance to speak about the Craft or invite others to join has unintentionally strengthened the impression that Freemasonry is a secret brotherhood, and that Lodges are secret societies. Now that's changing, as the need for Freemasonry to be more open and more practical in its dealings with the outside world becomes increasingly apparent to those who lead the Craft.

Who can become a Freemason?

Any man over the age of 18 may apply to become a Free-mason in Australia or New Zealand by asking an existing Mason or his local Masonic Lodge for membership. A Candidate needs to be nominated by two members and must prove, upon investigation, to be worthy of membership. Then all members of the Lodge are invited to vote on his candidacy using the traditional black and white balls ... two black balls, and the candidacy is rejected. In practice this rarely happens, because those whose background or behaviour would disqualify them from membership rarely take the trouble to apply.

For many years before television, long before colour television, and a very long time before the advent of the World Wide Web, many young men became Freemasons to demonstrate their worth in this way, to better themselves and to enjoy the fellowship of others. This interest in face-to-face fellowship and the voluntary adoption of more disciplined and meaningful lives now shows some small signs of revival as the age of conspicuous consumption and self interest starts to wane, and more people are looking for deeper meaning in their lives.

The value of Masonic fellowship is supported by the sharing of interests, an emphasis on equality, the sharing of a common journey through the Degrees, and the use of mentorships in Freemasonry. The social aspects of friendship and brotherhood are highlighted in the supper room (known as the South) after Lodge meetings.

Masonic meetings, whether formal or social, are convivial. Masons enjoy each other's company and are expressly encouraged to be happy and make others happy. Freemasons also have a solemn duty of care towards one another, and many men have found their spirits lifted and their lives made meaningful again through their association with their fellows, as 'brothers' in the Craft.

There are presently more than 45,000 active Freemasons around Australia, with some 14,000 in Victoria; 14,000 in New South Wales and the ACT; 9,000 in Queensland; 4,000 in Western Australia; 4,000 in South Australia and the Northern Territory, and 1,500 in Tasmania.

Dr Greg Levenston, currently Grand Master of the United Grand Lodge of New South Wales and the Australian Capital Territory, believes that Freemasonry needs to be more open to attract new members, particularly young members.

Since first being elected Grand Master in 2008, he has encouraged other Freemasons to be more open and has introduced a number of new initiatives including a 20/20 program for young members, and a men's health outreach program that draws parallels between Freemasonry and health.

In an address at the National Press Club, he pointed out that: 'Men's health is about trust, belonging, understanding, empathy and support. It's about information, learning, personal development, the understanding that life itself is a "journey". It's about spreading light into the lives of people. It's about men and their community … and so is Freemasonry.'

Australian Lodges welcome good men of all cultures and religions. The Masonic Degrees focus on personal life-ethics and the development and maintenance of high personal standards of behaviour towards oneself and others.

'Decision making will certainly be required along the way,' says Dr Levenston, 'Freemasonry provides the firm foundations required to help men make appropriate and successful decisions that improve their lives, the lives of their families and their community.

'But it also requires individuals to own the decisions they make, and to live with the outcomes, for this is also part of making good men better.'

Above all else, Freemasonry is about making good men better … being happy and conferring happiness.

MARK'S STORY

Like many others, I've lain awake many a night wondering what is this all about? What am I here for? What am I looking to do with myself? How can I contribute to society as a whole?

I am a young Mason: young by age (I'm 24) and young in terms of my time as a member of the brotherhood, 18 months.

My life is crazy. I keep the family house afloat. I am engaged to be married. I run a business. I go to Lodge.

Eighteen months ago, all I did was work, go to the pub and stumble home just in time to get a shaky night's rest. This wasn't the meaning I had searched for. This wasn't the way I wanted to be living. I'd never find what I was after at the bottom of a bottle.

I'd spoken with my mum and the answer was that I was 'growing through a phase'. My fiancée thought it was stress mixed with immaturity. I didn't feel that I could go to my mates and have this kind of discussion. I summoned the courage and asked my father. He suggested the Masons. He reminisced with me as to how he grew as a man and how attending Lodge filled a gap that was missing in his life.

My father has been my inspiration throughout my life. He is a self-made man who had a stack of responsibility thrown on his shoulders from a young age. I'd known he was a Mason but he never discussed anything with me about what happened inside a Lodge room. I recall sneaking into his room as a child one night and opening his briefcase. I was on the receiving end of a few smacks that night. 'Don't go through things that don't belong to you' was the moral of the punishment.

For him to talk about Lodge was something that I didn't expect. I looked at the Lions Club, Rotary, The Salvos and for a split second, thought about becoming a priest. Becoming a Mason didn't even cross my mind.

I went straight to the internet and began my research. After browsing a number of anti-Masonic sites, I came across a website called 'The Lodge of Australia #3' and 'UGLNSWACT'. I read about the charitable works and the promised 'brotherly love' and thought, this could be interesting. I sent a couple of emails and shortly after, was contacted over the phone by one and over email by the other. I went for a coffee with the phone guy, who seemed interesting enough but was double my age. I wanted to fraternise with men my age. There would be so much more that we have in common. When I told him about the other guy I was in touch with, I was advised that I was in safe hands and to proceed through them.

Soon enough, I was invited to a late night dinner. I met some cool guys who worked in the IT space. Because I am an IT recruiter, common ground was established straight away. I was asked why I was interested in the Masons. I mentioned my conversation with my father and my research. The 'brotherly love' aspect was still strong in my mind.

The guys were really open and honest. We shared and laughed together. It was great. The dinner ended so fast. A 'deep south' would commence, I was told. 'What the heck is a deep South??' 'Just come along and you'll see', was the reply. A group of 10 young Aussie guys and three rather loud Americans in military uniform left the Sydney Masonic Centre and walked down to one of the local bars. We ordered a couple of drinks, pulled up some chairs and the conversation began flowing. However, there was something different. We didn't speak about women, sports, politics or religion. These guys were asking each other what is going on in their lives.

Honest conversations flowed. I couldn't believe it. Why aren't they having the 'masculine' types of conversations I have with my mates? I sat, stunned, listening to these guys speak candidly and offer advice to one another. 'Wow!' is all I was thinking. My focus changed to these American blokes. They were in Australia with one of the large US freighters. Why were these guys having a couple of quiet drinks, instead of being in Kings Cross going crazy, spending money and 'stimulating our economy'? I was shocked to find out that they had come to the centre just to visit and have a look around, but were greeted with open arms and invited into the Lodge room, and into the function room for dinner. They had never met one another but were so open. Amazing!!

– Mark Mansour

13

SIR JAMES'S STORY
by John Tuffin

In my time I have interviewed some of the great and famous. Some have disappointed. Some have not. The very best all have one thing in common. They are interested in everything and everyone around them. They smile. They ask. They laugh. They enjoy life with an energy that warms all those around them ... but speak little of themselves.

In an age when fame comes in fractions and almost everyone's a star, Sir James Hardy lives, I discover, a quiet life. It's a life that may have gone unnoticed altogether (there is no biography in Wikipedia) if it was left to him to publicise it; for while many have a taste for celebrity, Sir James has none. He is more comfortable with 'Jim'.

We meet at his apartment in the inner eastern suburbs of Sydney. He's on the 9th floor of a red brick building with a lobby from a 1950s movie; swing doors, round columns, upright reception desk with rows of pigeon holes behind it on the wall. Turns out it was designed by an American, built in the late 1930s and justly claims to be one of Sydney's most iconic Art Deco buildings. The lifts are from the same era. They look old now but, as Sir James points out, they were the first self-opening and closing lift doors in Sydney.

Sir James lives for the moment and exhorts others to do the same; so it's no surprise that he talks about the architecture, or the lifts. He knows about them because he takes an interest; because he cares to know and wants to share such simple pleasures widely.

In a comfortable, maybe even snug, sitting room, he talks about his great-grandfather, Thomas, who grew up in Devon and was of yeoman farming stock. In 1850, when he was 20 years old and working for a general merchant in Gittisham, Devon, he made the decision to leave, to settle in the remote colony of South Australia. Here he found work near Adelaide, tending the cattle and vines of a gentleman farmer for a shilling a day. (His descendants were to buy this property many years later.)

The lure of gold soon took him off to Ballarat 'where he got pinged for digging for gold without a licence' and fined £1. When he heard of plans for a butchery to supply meat to the gold fields, Thomas offered to go and fetch the cattle they would need – from South Australia.

'He made three trips as a drover,' said Sir James, 'and came back to Adelaide with £500.'

He used the money to buy land for a winery at Underdale, in suburban Adelaide and 23 years later another property at Tintara in the McLaren Vale.

'When the winery at Underdale caught fire, they used the wine to try and put out the fire,' Sir James said. 'but it burned to the ground, and Tintara became the focus of attention.'

The summer-dry, winter-wet land approaching Adelaide from the south reminded Thomas Hardy of Portugal and Spain and he quickly saw the wine-growing potential. The Tintara vineyards he established in 1853 are now at the centre of Australia's most recognised Shiraz wine growing area – with Hardy's 'Eileen Hardy Shiraz' acknowledged as one of Australia's best.

Thomas Hardy – yeoman farmer, gold digger and cattle drover – had landed on his feet and the family's financial future was assured. So was its continuity … Thomas Hardy's first-born son Thomas, was grandfather to the young Jim. His eldest son, in turn, was Tom – Jim's father.

As World War I threatened a new generation, Tom fought in Palestine, invented a special sight for the Vickers machine-gun, survived the war and returned to Adelaide to start a family of his own. Of course his own first son, Jim's older brother, was named Thomas.

James Hardy was born to the happy sound of children playing tennis on the family's grass court – or at least to the sound of children being told to hush – 'there's a baby being born upstairs!'

For a while, the family's life was idyllic. Then there was an aircraft crash. It was a DC2 and it flew into Mt Dandenong in fog. Sir James' father, Tom Hardy, was killed when James was six.

'I don't remember my father all that well,' he said. 'But things went on, with my older brother, Tom, going into the business.'

Jim's father Tom and his uncle James were both Freemasons.

'After I left school I took up piano lessons. I wasn't too bad when I did it by rote, and my teacher was the Grand Organist at Grand Lodge in Adelaide.'

Our talk turned to membership of the Craft and how good men might be invited to join.

'Still ... as a Mason, you can't just go out and solicit others,' Jim said. 'We're not allowed to solicit and to make sure that we don't, there's a rule that says a new man must approach of his own free will – which means we're supposed to wait for people to ask us. So nobody asked me, and it wasn't until I asked my piano teacher about his time with my father, that I learned about Freemasonry. And it wasn't until I transferred to Sydney in 1962 that I became a Freemason.'

Now, after more than 47 years in the Craft, I asked Sir James what it meant to him.

'It provides a terrific blueprint for a man's life,' he said. 'There are no hidden mysteries, just great teachings. It's very moral. Very upright. It's about the quality of the way we live ... our standards of behaviour. It's about good manners.

'People may think it's old fashioned to open a car door for a lady. Some ladies may even resent it. But it's just good manners – and to me good manners provide the glue we need to build a good society. Morality begins with good manners.'

This interviewer is not a Freemason, nor a sportsman. I have never represented my country, nor directed anything as large as the team that finally took the America's Cup from the New York Yacht Club in 1983 – ending the longest winning streak in sport and creating one of the greatest celebrations in Australian history.

Sir James is all these things and more. He has lost against the New York Yacht Club too – three times – before Alan Bond, Ben Lexcen, John Bertrand and Sir James (as team director) won with Australia II. He has also, all the time, been a successful businessman. In 1993 he became the second Australian after John Bertrand to be inducted by the 'old enemy' into the America's Cup Hall of Fame. In 1994 he was Australian Father of the Year.

He's been awarded an OBE ... even been knighted by the Queen. And yet there's still another quality that makes him who he is, and it is this: Sir James is a gentleman – through and through – all the time, in everything he does.

For the record then: Sir James Hardy represented Australia in the Olympic Yachting Team at the 1964 Olympic Games in Japan and the 1968 Games in Mexico. He won the 505 Class World Yachting Championships in Adelaide in 1966, and captained three America's Cup challenges in 1970 (on Gretel II*), in 1974 (*Southern Cross*) and in 1980 (*Australia*). All three were unsuccessful.*

Freemasonry encourages self-respect and charges its members to be happy, and to confer happiness on others.

At the end of the first America's Cup challenge in 1970, Gretel II looked threatening.

'I suddenly began to feel that we could win it. We were leading in thick fog – but when the final gun was fired, we had lost to Intrepid,' he said.

'I was so exhausted, I couldn't lift my arms. We were all exhausted. The crew on Intrepid were laughing and cheering while most of us were close to tears.

'So I said to my guys: "Just look at that. Just look at all that joy. Don't be downhearted. We made that possible!"'

James Hardy's services to the community, to the wine industry and yachting were first recognised when he was made an officer of the Order of the British Empire (OBE) in 1975, and again when he was knighted by Queen Elizabeth in 1981.

In 2006 he retired from ocean racing – on a high – by winning the Blue Water Classic, a 150 nautical mile race from Adelaide to Port Lincoln, on Geoff Boettcher's Hardy's Secret Men's Business.

He now spends his time between Sydney and the company's head office at Chateau Reynella Winery south of Adelaide – the property where his great-grandfather first worked for a shilling a day.

NOHA'S STORY

In 1992, we had three boys under the age of three. I decided to go back to Uni for a double degree, which meant four years of full time study.

My husband's mother had just passed away and he decided to join Freemasonry in order to fill a gap in his life and pursue something that his father had shown interest in, before he had his stroke.

I told my mother what Garry had done. She became very worried as she whispered to me that 'they are a secret Jewish Cult and they are powerful and dangerous. Garry will never be allowed to leave, they can destroy governments and make men who tell their secret disappear.'

My mother compared this 'cult' to a communist group that my father had joined back in Lebanon around 1964. He was being brainwashed against God and Islam ... 'as will Garry'. My father left the communist group two weeks after joining, because he got bashed by a group of Muslim Democrats who discovered his secret meetings.

I laughed as my mother spoke and thought to myself how exciting and romantic this would be; Garry knowing 'the Secret' and me standing by him, packing bags in the middle of the night, relocating, changing identities in case 'they' find us.

Garry started attending Lodge Sir Joseph Banks. He was enjoying it but wouldn't share information. I was getting cranky and curious; I wanted to see what he was up to.

A few months later, I got invited to a social night. I was 30 years old. I organised a babysitter, got dressed up and off we went.

I remember walking into the room and feeling like I'd just entered a nursing home. Everyone was old and Garry looked like a child playing dress-ups. I went up to Garry and said very seriously 'See that man over there in the suit, the old man in grey hair and glasses?' He looked around and replied 'Which one?' I said 'Exactly! What are we doing here?'

Freemasonry stole my husband away from me. I was only invited twice a year: ladies' night and kids' Christmas party.

I never wanted to be a Mason but I wanted to help. I could see that in a few years there'd be no one left. Something had to be done. I kept on nagging at Garry about this group and demanding to go with him and organise functions. I thought they were sexist male chauvinists who truly believed that a woman's place is in the kitchen. Something had to change.

First time Garry became Master, I was allowed to stand in the kitchen and wait till it was time to cut the cake, then join him. At the end of his term, I was given a $50 cheque for my services! What services? All I did was give up my husband twice a month.

The second time Garry became Master I put on a black tux and white shirt, Garry gave me his black bowtie to wear and I was allowed upstairs in the temple for part of the ceremony. I got so many dirty looks that I needed a bath at the end of the night! Old men all over the place told Garry out loud that we shouldn't change the old ways, Freemasonry was set in stone and that women had their place in the background, cutting sandwiches! They had no business discussing men's business.

I had just started on a mission to change the old ways and bring in something new and exciting that would increase membership and attract young people … people more our age group.

We started inviting women more and more to the South. We took away the organising of all functions from the men and gave it to their partners. We introduced younger music and dancing, after failing miserably at every attempt to learn ballroom dancing steps!

Christmas parties became events for the whole family, not just the kids.

We started to see younger people from the community joining the Lodge. We were on a roll.

Not everything was changing: members still complained about paying $5 for the South and I felt a need to improve quality and educate members about the importance of making the Lodge as much about family and friends as it is about the men.

I still fought about women's rights to become Freemasons if they so wished and argued with almost every member about my desire to know what 'the Secret' is.

After reading many pages about the Craft and after processing and evaluating so much of the information available, I came to the conclusion that, as much as I believe that every human being on this earth (regardless of their sex, colour, religious following or sexual orientation) has an equal right to be whatever they want, some things are the way they are, because there is a greater, more just system that operates above all systems.

As a Muslim woman, I accept and respect that although God created all as equals, women cannot be Imams in Mosques, nor can they ever lead a prayer amongst men. That is God's way, and after reading the justification, you are compelled to accept that it is the right way. I have taken that acceptance to what I know about Freemasonry. Some things should not be changed because they work perfectly as is.

No one knows what the future holds for Freemasonry; women may become members and sit side by side with their partners in the temples. I have no desire to be that woman, I want to be the one who openly praises her partner for the good work that he does as a Freemason. I want to be the woman who witnesses her partner become a better speaker, a respected member of a respectable society, a friend to many people who are pillars of their communities.

I also want to be the woman who informs other women on the educational, spiritual and personal advantages and enrichments their partners will gain by becoming Freemasons.

Freemasonry started off being a thorn in my life; it took away my husband and left me feeling like a single mother. I spoke harshly about it for years and turned my boys against it. The new family friendly Freemasonry is now a rose in my life; it has given me lifelong friendships and an opportunity to share with my husband a passion to learn and lead by example.

My ideas are respected and acted upon. In the Cedars' Lodge I am as much in the chair as Garry is, and I have never been closer to him. My sons respect the Craft and all that it stands for.

I may not be a Freemason but I am a valued member of Freemasonry.

– *Noha Sayed*

CHAPTER TWO

Masonic ceremonies

Ceremonies play an important part in all our lives. Coming of age, marriage, the naming of children, birthdays and the passing of loved ones are all marked by some form of ceremony. Indeed, psychologists say that ceremonies, and the rituals they use, are essential characteristics of the structure of our societies. They also help us to maintain our mental and emotional health.

In Freemasonry ceremonies are important too, so I'm pleased to have had the assistance of R.W. Bro. Doug Grigg, Grand Director of Ceremonies, United Grand Lodge of NSW & ACT.

Bro. Grigg contributed a great deal of the material in this chapter but I have added some from other sources, so if there are errors, they will be mine.

Freemasonry teaches men to live useful and fulfilling lives by following lessons in moral and civil behaviour. Chapter Seven of this book explains how symbols are used to illustrate these behaviours. Freemasons use ceremonies to emphasise the importance of these teachings and to help Masons remember them.

Four hundred years ago, in the beginnings of Freemasonry as it is now practised, much of the population was illiterate. Ceremonies were used as learning tools. Through repetition of these ceremonies Freemasons were able to learn elements of the Craft, in much the same way as children today learn the national anthem or other school songs.

Masonic Origins

The Masonic ceremonial seen in public has much of its origins in the royal courts of Europe, going back to medieval times.

The mayor of your city, municipality or shire probably wears a chain and robe at formal functions. Freemasons also use these symbols of authority with the Master of a Lodge and his Officers wearing ceremonial collars and 'jewels' to indicate their office and rank.

The Grand Ceremonial Officers retain original medieval titles. There is a Sword Bearer whose job it was to provide close protection and a Standard Bearer to make sure the ruler could be seen in the narrow streets of the towns. The king or prince was accompanied by a number of official attendants. The organisation of food and drink for celebrations and the housing and management of the king's or prince's retinue was organised by one or more stewards. The director of ceremonies, or Marshall, made sure the event was orderly and the ceremony was well prepared and conducted.

The king had his court of officials, the wardens. They are now the Masonic Master's second and third in charge. Their title comes from the same source as the warden of the Tower of London and wardens of prisons.

Public Ceremonies

While much of the ceremonial performed by Masons is private, there is a long history of public ceremonial involving Masonic processions and ceremonies.

It was the custom in the first half of the last century for Freemasons to be actively involved in the opening of public buildings. Frequently this included laying the foundation stone. Newspaper records report an active Masonic presence at the laying of the foundation stone of Captain Piper's house in 1816, at what is now Point Piper. The corner stone of St Mary's Catholic Cathedral in Sydney was laid by Freemasons.

The first Court House in Melbourne began with a procession of two hundred people and with Freemasons ceremonially laying the stone in 1842. A report in a newspaper at the time describes the order of the procession along Collins Street, made up of the military, the police, judicial officers, the mayor and councillors and a large number of Freemasons in the regalia of their Orders.

This ceremony remains much the same today. Freemasons move in procession to the site in order of precedence. The Grand Chaplain offers prayers for the building and the people who will work in it. The Grand Master and his Wardens then test the stone for Square, Level and Plumb. They anoint it with wine, oil, corn and salt to represent cheerfulness, peace, plenty and friendship. A quick search of the internet will reveal that this ceremony was common when churches, halls, Council Chambers and all sorts of public buildings were opened.

During the late 1800s and the early 1900s the regular street parades to commemorate important events were usually led by, or contained a large body of, Freemasons in their regalia.

In most Australian country towns the local church, the town hall, the public school, the Masonic Lodge and a number of commercial buildings still bear witness to the involvement of Freemasons at public ceremonies in which they officiated.

Grand Installations

One of the most public of Masonic ceremonies is the installation of the new Grand Master which usually happens every two to three years and attracts a large number of people from all over the country.

In New South Wales the Grand Installations have been held at the Sydney Town Hall with the assembled spectators filling the magnificent building. The members of the visiting delegations enter in procession. There is a lot of colour and pomp because the Grand Officers wear the gold and blue regalia as shown on the cover of this book. The Official Party is preceded by a Sword Bearer and an escort of Grand Officers.

Delegations from other states and countries wear different colours and the members of some of the Masonic Orders that are allied to Craft Freemasonry wear regal robes, mitres, swords and carry ceremonial batons. The combined effect is of great pomp, as seen in the photograph of the 1992 Grand Installation in the colour section. Some of the Masonic and civil dignitaries are listed in the caption.

At a Grand Installation the outgoing or Past Grand Master ceremonially places the new Grand Master in his Chair of Office. Then the other Grand Officers are decorated or invested with their insignia of office and saluted a number of times in proportion to their importance. As with most Masonic Ceremonies, a banquet follows and a number of toasts are proposed and responses given.

Masonic Balls

In the past, every Masonic Lodge held an annual ball allowing Freemasons to join with the community in celebrating a formal occasion. Frequently they were debutante balls. While the custom has become less common, many Lodges still hold debutante balls at which young ladies are presented to the Grand Master or the Grand Officer sent to represent him.

The ceremony involves a formal procession into the ballroom and the representative wears his Masonic Regalia and is accompanied by a Grand Director of Ceremonies and sometimes a Sword Bearer. Often the official party and the debutantes enter between Freemasons who make an arch of ceremonial swords. The purpose is to make the event especially memorable.

Masonic Tributes

One of the most moving Masonic ceremonies open to the public is the delivery of a Masonic Tribute at the funeral of one of the brethren. The Tribute is performed in a place of worship such as a church, a crematorium or at the cemetery.

The Master of the Lodge or the Grand Master, if the deceased was a Grand Officer, conducts a short ceremony. During the ceremony a white lambskin apron, the symbol of purity and innocence, and a sprig of evergreen leaves, a symbol of immortality, are placed on the casket. Masonic brethren form a guard of honour at the end of the service as the casket and the mourners leave the building.

Private Masonic ceremonies

Why private? Some Masonic ceremonies are not open to the public and are intended for use at Lodge meetings only.

As we saw in Chapter One, the history of Freemasonry begins in Europe and takes its origins from the guilds of stonemasons who constructed the great cathedrals. Stone masons or operative masons needed a body to care for them and for their families and to ensure they were qualified. Lodges were formed to do this.

The term 'Lodge' comes from the temporary buildings Masons lived and ate in. So that other Masons could recognise qualified craftsmen who could be trusted to do good and honest work, they developed signs and ceremonies to identify them. This also discouraged unqualified persons from claiming expertise. Nowadays skilled tradespeople use certificates and diplomas and letters of recommendation. The ancient stonemasons, who were rarely able to read or write, used carefully guarded handshakes as these were both their safeguard and proof of good reputation.

When a Lodge of stonemasons finished a great building in one city or one country, they would move to another where a new cathedral was about to be built. Even though they might not have been able to speak the local language, all that the Master of the Lodge needed to do was to approach the foreman or architect at the new building site and shake his hand.

That simple act told the new employer two important things – that the men under the control of this Master were properly qualified and that they could be trusted.

Once that piece of history is understood by non-Masons, the reasons for preserving the Masonic handshake become clear and make good sense.

The custom among modern groups of having special greetings is similar to this. We have all seen sporting teams and groups of young people give a 'high five'. This is like the greeting ancient operative stonemasons gave each other.

Why ceremonies?

Ceremonies provide a framework for a gathering.

In church services, at business meetings, at gatherings such as those of Rotarians, Lions, Quota, and CWA, a certain structure is followed so people can fit in easily and so meetings can proceed smoothly.

Masonic ceremonies follow the same pattern. They have the added purpose of making the event memorable and fixing the message of the ritual in the minds of those involved. Rituals are performed as speeches delivered from memory, encouraging self discipline and self education. Masons learn a catechism of questions and answers to help them remember the important lessons of Freemasonry.

Masonic Foundations

The ceremonies performed in an Australian Craft Lodge are based on the Old Testament of the Bible and deal with the events and people involved in the building of King Solomon's Temple in Jerusalem. In particular the books of Ruth, Kings and Chronicles and some of the characters are significant, such as King Solomon himself and King Hiram of Tyre.

Some Masonic Orders use ceremonies based on stories from other episodes in biblical history, like the exile in Babylon and the rebuilding of the Temple by King Zerubbabel. Other Australian Orders also use stories from the New Testament.

These ceremonies were formalised between 1717 and 1840 and even though they vary from one Grand Lodge's

Jurisdiction or Constitution to another, there are similarities across the Masonic world. This means that Masons can visit Lodges overseas and still participate in the ceremonies. Indeed, one of the enjoyable aspects of membership is that a Freemason can visit any Lodge anywhere in the world and not only be welcomed to participate but often to be taken to the homes of his international brethren and be treated as a part of the family.

A tour of the Lodge room

Of course to reveal the details of Masonic ceremonies would mean they would lose some of their mystique, their emotional appeal and their impact on new candidates as they first experience the theatre of Freemasonry.

Mankind has always sought to understand the unknown, the mysterious. We enjoy solving puzzles. The mystique of Freemasonry has been a magnet through the ages. It's the same reason people have enjoyed Harry Potter and Dan Brown. And the desire of Freemasonry to preserve that element of mystery is also the innocent reason why there has been so much misunderstanding about Masonry causing it to be seen as a 'secret society'.

However, as we've already said, nowadays anyone can read as much as they like about Masonry – not only in books (see Chapter Eleven), but also on the internet. Visiting a Masonic Centre also gives you some indication of what goes on, but there is no doubt that the best way to learn about Freemasonry is to experience the ceremonies as a candidate.

Are they spooky? Skulls and coffins and so on? This is another area that has been distorted – simply because of its potential drama. Much of the Masonic ceremonial has a theatrical aspect, partly because of its history, but also because of the power of experience in learning. As any teacher knows, experience is the most powerful way for a student to absorb the meaning of specific knowledge. And that's what Masons do in their ceremonies – create a memorable experience. What needs to be emphasised, however, is that there is nothing to be frightened of in these experiences. All of the teachings of the Craft are about brotherhood and compassion and love and trust: none of these commitments to the good and the ethical is breached in Masonic ceremonies.

Here is an extract from the ritual of the First or Entered Apprentice Degree. The Master of the Lodge says to the candidate:

> *Mr................, it is my duty to inform you that Masonry is free and requires a perfect freedom of inclination and action from every candidate for its mysteries. It is founded on the purest principles of morality and virtue. It possesses many great and invaluable privileges; but in order to secure those privileges to worthy men, and, we trust, to worthy men alone, vows or obligations of fidelity are required. Let me assure you, however, that in such vows there will be found nothing incompatible with your moral, civil or religious duties.*

This is typical of the reassurances you receive as you experience the valuable lessons of Freemasonry.

Approaching the door of the Lodge, the first thing you probably notice is a knocker and if you are there while the Lodge is open you hear a series of knocks given. These are in a certain pattern and are given to indicate to Masons outside what is going on inside.

Once inside you see three raised platforms supporting pedestals with throne-like chairs behind them. These are the seats of the Master and his Wardens. Prominent on the floor of the Lodge is a mosaic pavement with black and white squares and tessellated or toothed edges. As with most cultures, black and white represents opposites or variations. The squares are to remind you that the journeys of life offer choices, and that these may lead to both light and dark episodes.

At one end of the pavement is an altar which holds a copy or copies of religious texts such as the Old and New Testaments of the Bible, or the Koran, which Masons refer to as Volumes of the Sacred Law. This gives an indication that Masons allow every candidate to rely on his own, individual, religious beliefs as a guide to moral truth. Many Australian Lodges have several sacred books which are used during ceremonies to accommodate whatever beliefs are followed by the candidates.

The walls are often decorated with certificates or Charters that mark the history of the Lodge and remind Masons of the long history of their organisation. Replicas of the stonemason's tools are also a feature of every Lodge room, the most important being the square, the level and the plumb rule. The square and compasses are a readily recognised emblem of Freemasonry and this appears on the outside of Masonic buildings. Freemasons apply these tools of the stonemasons symbolically, to teach the moral concepts and values of Freemasonry.

In the Lodge room during the ceremony, as can be seen in public ceremonies like the Grand Installation, Masons walk in a regular pattern of squares and right angles to reinforce the teachings of right behaviour. Some phrases we commonly use in Australia are derived from these same stonemasonry tools. When we speak of 'being on the level' or acting 'on the square' in our daily lives, we are using some of the classic moral values of Freemasonry.

Music plays an important role in Masonic ritual and a piano or organ can usually be found in a corner of the room. Some Lodge rooms even have a Musicians' Gallery. Most Lodge rooms also display the national flag. Masons are taught to give allegiance to the authorities and government of their land.

You will notice that Masonic Lodges are oriented east and west. The Master's chair is in the east. This recognises that the Sun rises in the east and that learning came from there. Light and learning are important parts of Masonic ceremony. As you continue around the Lodge room you will notice that the pedestals are decorated with columns. The capitals of these are in the classical Doric, Ionic and Corinthian style. Classical columns also adorn the outside of most Masonic centres. They are part of the use of architecture to teach lessons and symbolise wisdom, strength and beauty.

What happens inside?

The actual ceremonies are only known to brethren who have qualified for that level of knowledge. As a Mason grows in his knowledge of the Craft he is able to participate in more of the ritual ceremonies.

This custom goes back many thousands of years and finds equivalents in other modern organisations. In traditional churches you are not able to take communion until you are confirmed. A Jewish boy must learn the Scriptures before his Bar Mitzvah. Young Muslim men are progressively taught the Koran.

A young sportsperson must learn the basics before being allowed to take on the more complex tasks of captaincy and refereeing. Similarly in Freemasonry a new member must learn parts of the ceremony before progressing further.

Briefly, the new member or Candidate is taken through a number of short ceremonies or plays that sometimes re-enact parts of biblical stories or legends connected with them. Each re-enactment conveys a lesson. The Candidate is expected to be able to learn and recite the answers to questions. The Officers of the Lodge play parts, or recite from memory, speeches or 'Charges' which deliver a message or explain the purpose of the ceremony.

Sometimes the ceremonies are performed in darkness or limited light to enhance the mystery and to emphasise that knowledge is light and by learning the candidate is led from the darkness of ignorance to a better understanding of life and how to live it.

> *... let me beg you to observe that light was ever an object of attainment in all ancient mysteries. It was then, as it is now, the symbol of Truth and Knowledge, a fact of which we must never lose sight, when we consider the nature and significance of Masonic Light.*

This book's title proclaims that *It's No Secret* and aims to demystify the Fraternity and its ceremonies. It seeks to explain what Freemasonry is and does. It would be possible to go into greater detail of every ceremony, but readers who seek to know everything can find detailed accounts in books or on the internet. It's all there, including the handshakes and the words of the Degrees. But be warned … much of what you would find is very old and often inaccurate. And we say, those readers who would like to experience the teachings and benefits of the Craft will certainly appreciate the details more from direct experience than from a book or a computer screen.

Ask any Mason about the Masonic ceremonies and you will hear that they are extremely memorable and deeply moving; that the impact of the teachings has changed his mind or reinforced his appreciation of life. It is no accident that some of the greatest and wisest of scholars, musicians, world leaders and literally millions of less famous men have benefited from membership in a Lodge of Freemasons.

Out of the ordinary

Masonic Lodges in the 1700s and 1800s frequently met in public houses and inns. In those less than peaceful times it was common for gentlemen to wear swords and for those acting as security outside a Lodge meeting to be armed. This custom is still followed symbolically as the Outer and Inner Guards have, as their insignia of office, a sword or dagger. Inside the Lodge, however, the members must be unarmed as befits a society of peaceful men.

There is a long history of military Lodges taking a travelling charter with them to places they were stationed. This was how Freemasonry came to Australia. Today there are Lodge meetings in Iraq and Afghanistan and these members have to be armed as they are in a battle zone. They meet in tents and huts and use temporary furniture. The Lodge is the people, not the building. The history of both the First and Second World Wars holds records of soldiers forming Lodges in POW camps and hiding their Lodge furniture and working tools from their captors.

The United Grand Lodge of NSW & ACT Museum of Freemasonry has on display implements made out of paper, old army mugs, wood and carved bone that were used by prisoners in the notorious Changi Prison. These wartime displays include handwritten ritual books from Japanese and Nazi prison camps. The brethren in these cases were using Freemasonry to cement the bonds between the prisoners and to give them hope in desperate circumstances.

In Australia, meetings are held in unusual places such as the Cathedral Cave at Jenolan Caves in central NSW; in wool sheds and shearing sheds in the far West; on mountains and in historic buildings. The historic village at Sovereign Hill in Ballarat, Victoria has a Lodge room from the period of the gold rushes that visitors can enter during the day, and is used for Lodge meetings at other times.

This is a brief overview of some aspects of Masonic ceremonial. For those interested in more information the websites of the Grand Lodges throughout the world are a good source. The magazine *Freemasonry Today* on the Grand Lodge of England's site is excellent and informative. The Grand Lodge of NSW and ACT website, www.uglnsw. freemasonry.org.au has a Library page that welcomes visitors and contains articles, lectures and newsletters of Masonic interest. And in Chapter Eleven of this book Bro. Bob James reviews many excellent books about Freemasonry.

THE CATHOLIC CHURCH AND THE FREEMASONS

Yes, over the past few centuries there have been tensions between the Catholic Church and Freemasonry. Early Papal decrees prohibited members of the Catholic faith from joining Freemasonry, but were later countermanded. The historic tension no longer exists but nevertheless, there are writers and websites who disagree and continue to promote misunderstandings.

Many reasons for discord between the Church and Freemasonry have been put forward and you can find them all elsewhere. I don't intend to go into detail, to argue or to give the conspiracy theorists any credit here. There have also been myths and theories about preferment in various government departments in years gone by. It was said that members of the NSW Police Force and the Fire Brigade needed to be of the Catholic faith – or a Freemason – in order to make progress in their careers.

In the NSW Police, the gossip went, the top job alternated between men of the faith and men of the fraternity. It was said that if you wanted to work at Fire Brigade HQ, you had to be a member of Lodge Fire Brigades. And there's more …

One theory had it that the reason the Church regarded Freemasonry with disfavour was because the secrecy of the Masons was at odds with the requirement for Catholics to reveal all to their confessors.

Suffice it to say that these and many other theories are no longer relevant.

- *The 2009 Catholic Bishops Conference was held in the Grand Lodge Convention Centre*
- *The Catholic Education Commission holds its Client Staff Training Centre at Freemasonry's HQ*
- *Many Freemasons are of the Catholic faith, including MW Past Grand Master Noel Dunn.*

The real point is that the Craft welcomes all races, all religions and treats all men as equal. It enables members to follow their own religious beliefs while meeting together in harmony and peace to reflect on the moral principles which unite us all. It's about being happy and conferring happiness.

From the working tools of the Second or Fellow Craft Degree:

The Level, which is an emblem of Equality, teaches us that, in the sight of God, all men are equal – that He makes His glorious Sun to shine as brightly upon the humble dwelling of the poor as upon the rich man's mansion, or the monarch's palace; and that, with Him, there is no respect of persons, save in regard to those who forget their duty and neglect or disobey His precepts. It also demonstrates that we are all sprung from the same stock, are partakers of the same Nature and sharers of the same hope ...

'SECRET MEN'S BUSINESS' AND (DARE I SAY IT?) CHANGE!

When Masons reflect on the traditional history of the Craft we think about the stonemasons of antiquity and the building of King Solomon's Temple. We think of the need for the stonemasons to protect their livelihood. They took pains to ensure that none but trusted and qualified brethren, members of the guild, would be employed to carry out the highly skilled work of constructing the great buildings of their day.

The stonemasons required apprentices to take vows not to reveal the handshakes and words which served as their passport to work, to payment, food and shelter.

Times have changed ... and they will continue to change. Exponentially! Change is the only constant, as Heraclitus of Ephesus said about 500 years BCE.

During the 25 centuries since, the world has indeed changed dramatically. We have benefited from new knowledge, new philosophies. We have sought to find all the answers to all the mysteries of the ages. We have revealed untold numbers of secrets. And we have learned to share that information more and faster than any other civilisation since time began. Indeed, today it is almost impossible to have secrets.

While there is still much that we don't know, there are very few secrets in the digital age. We carry our IDs with us. From our credit cards to our DNA, we are 'an open book'. Our diplomas spell out what we have achieved or what education we have undertaken. Our references describe our work history. Computers can instantly establish whether we have transgressed.

Now, the new acquaintance you just met can Google your name and read anything of importance you ever said and did.

Against the electronic background of 'total disclosure' and 'information access', we still take great care to guard some very valuable information – such as the formula for Coca-Cola, hidden and protected somewhere in a vault in Atlanta. The 'eleven secret herbs and spices' of Kentucky Fried Chicken remain mysterious, and so are some other very valuable formulae of modern life called 'commercial in confidence'.

Then there are more worldly matters that remain the stuff of romance. No doubt, most families have some dark facts and beliefs guarded as 'better kept inside the family' and away from the eyes of a curious or undeserving world. We distinguish on a daily basis between 'need to know' and 'no need to know'. And all the while, 'the times they are a-changing'.

In Freemasonry, the times are a-changing too ... but very slowly.

In particular, the older brethren tend to cling to the Craft's traditions of secrecy and they resent suggestions of change. I can almost see some of my brethren getting agitated as I write these words. I think I can even hear some of them ...

'I don't want anything to change.'

'If people today don't want to discover the good in Freemasonry, that's their bad luck.'

'So what if our numbers are declining, I'd rather have quality than quantity.'

'I'm over 70, the Craft will probably be around until I die, why change it?'

'What? You want to change words in the ritual so the young men can understand it? Over my dead body!'

'Go to Lodge in a lounge suit? I bought my dinner suit and black tie to see me out.'

'You want to invite non-Masons to have a look at our Lodge rooms! What? And show them our "secrets"?'

'I was taught to be cautious ... haven't even talked about it to my wife and family.'

... and lots more along these lines.

Of course, it is all totally understandable. Masons have taken vows to maintain the secrets. We refer to them at the end of every Lodge meeting and we remind the brethren present to 'keep the secrets of this night's proceedings' safe and sacred.

We are not all quite sure, however, of what are the secrets and what aspects of our meetings can be discussed. The view from the top is that Freemasons should re-think what is secret. Now, when there are 'no more secrets', when even the handshakes and words are available to anyone who can use a library or the internet, we need to reinterpret our view of secrecy. And if we want to share the wisdom and the beauty of the Craft, we need to be better at talking about it.

The trouble is that now, after all those decades when we kept quiet, we are gravely misunderstood. In my communication work, a client sometimes tells me that his business is 'gravely misunderstood'. I ask him how he communicates: how do you tell people about your business ... and about yourself?

It is an established principle of professional communication that if I am not being understood by others, that is not their fault but my own.

If 'my wife doesn't understand me' I have not communicated with her. And if I have kept secrets from her! Oh, please, let's not go there!

Throughout the ages people have hated secrecy. Today we clamour for transparency. And as we have always done, we suspect those who have secrets ... no matter how moral, valuable or innocent their secrets may be.

Freemasonry has lost the confidence of much of our community through secrecy. The Craft has become suspect because of our misguided caution. So tongue-tied have we become, that when you ask ten brethren to tell you why they are Freemasons and what it has done for them, you get ten answers, eight of them not at all satisfying.

Over the centuries, Freemasonry has refrained from marketing its benefits, from selling itself to the world. Masons have been required to avoid 'improper solicitation' of potential candidates for admission. That has been interpreted to mean Masons can't talk about Masonry – can't even ask non-Masons whether they might be interested.

Sons of Masons have watched their fathers go off to Lodge and have never been invited along or asked whether they might like to know where Dad was going, or why. Naturally these sons assumed that their father didn't think highly enough of them to invite them to join, and have had to be prompted by their mothers to ask about Freemasonry.

As Grand Master Greg Levenston puts it 'If you can have "improper solicitation" there must also be "proper solicitation"'. *Surely it is proper to invite your son – or your friend – to consider benefiting from the friendship, brotherly love and moral values of the Craft.*

In the age of unprecedented communication, the Craft needs to rethink what is secret and what is not. It needs a new understanding and a new approach to communication.

IN FREEMASONRY ALL MEN ARE EQUAL ...
BUT ARE SOME MORE EQUAL THAN OTHERS?

Freemasons from all walks of life have at least two things in common ... they want to make a contribution to their community and they tend not to make a lot of noise about it.

In gathering material for *It's No Secret ... Real Men Wear Aprons*, I kept thinking of the thousands of brethren who work quietly in the background to achieve valuable relationships with family and friends and help in small unnoticed ways to build community.

These brethren don't seek to advertise themselves. And they certainly outnumber the great and famous members of the Craft. But even the recognised leaders who stand out above the crowd are frequently quiet and unassuming.

In these pages I have gathered some 50 stories from the lives of outstanding Masons. These stories record the successes of our explorers, political leaders, war heroes, famous sportsmen, inventors.

Rather than put all the sportsmen in a chapter, or lump the politicians together (not a happy thought) – and in order to emphasise that, as Freemasons, they are all equal – they appear at intervals through the book and in alphabetical order.

I feel sure that the list is incomplete: readers may search for a worthy Mason of whom I was unaware or who may have been forgotten.

Certainly there are dozens of sportsmen who qualified and I apologise for any omissions. I invite readers to let me know in case there should be another edition at some time in the future.

The stories of these great Australians are as diverse and interesting as they are enjoyable: so enjoy.

Adolphus Appleroth
(1886–1952)

'I like Aeroplane Jelly ... Aeroplane Jelly for me ...'

Just about every Australian knows and loves the Aeroplane Jelly jingle. Although the company was sold to an American multi-national in 1994, we still claim the product – developed in our own backyard (actually bathroom) – by Adolphus Herbert Frederick Norman Appleroth, thankfully better known as 'Bert'.

Bert was born in Melbourne in 1886. His family moved to Sydney in 1892. His first job was as a messenger boy at Lipton's Tea. Later, as a tram conductor, Bert began experimenting with mixtures of gelatine and sugar in the bath at his parents' Paddington home.

Success in selling his jelly crystals door-to-door encouraged him to leave the tramways in 1917 and begin full time production of his De-Luxe brand jelly.

Always an aviation enthusiast, Bert renamed his product, Aeroplane Jelly. He ran big promotional campaigns, chartering Tiger Moth planes with Aeroplane Jelly splashed on their sides. The planes towed Aeroplane Jelly banners over Sydney beaches, dropping packets of jelly crystals to surfers.

The famous jingle, written in 1930 by Bert's business partner, pianist Lee Woods, is one of the longest-running advertising jingles in history. Played 100 times daily on radio in the '40s, just about everybody was singing:

'I like Aeroplane Jelly,
Aeroplane Jelly for me,
I like it for dinner, I like it for tea,
A little each day is a good recipe ...'

(I bet you're singing it now ...)

In 1981 Bert's grandson, Bert III, organised a stunt in which 35 people jumped into a swimming pool filled with 35,000 litres of watermelon jelly – earning Aeroplane Jelly a place in the *Guinness Book of World Records*.

Bert Appleroth was initiated into Freemasonry at Lodge Vaucluse on March 15, 1928.

Joseph Banks
(1743–1820)

The first Freemason to land in Australia, Joseph Banks was one of the fathers of modern botany and strongly influenced the continuing exploration of New Holland. He began his career working under Carl von Linnaeus, founder of modern botanical science, and was later responsible for introducing the Linnaeus system and the Latin naming system still in use today. Explorer, botanist and friend of royalty, Banks was an adviser to King George III, encouraging him to support new voyages of discovery.

Well before he was appointed to join the *Endeavour* on its expedition south, Banks was much better known than the ship's commander, James Cook. The aristocracy and the scientific community saw Joseph Banks as the star of the voyage.

The Endeavour made a great voyage of discovery, charting much of New Zealand before arriving on the East Coast of New Holland, where Cook became the first visitor to plant a flag and claim the land as a colony – New South Wales.

Joseph Banks and his team collected and recorded so much rich botanical material, that they named the place of their arrival, 'Botany Bay'.

Banks returned to England in 1771. Captain Cook then made two further voyages of discovery, primarily in search of the Northwest Passage.

Cook chose William Bligh to be his sailing master for the final voyage. After failing to confirm the existence of the passage, Cook and his ships landed on Hawaii in January, 1779. Cook was killed there, due to a cultural misunderstanding and a skirmish over a missing boat.

Bligh and the remaining crew returned to Britain with news of Cook's death, at a time when Joseph Banks was recommending Botany Bay as suitable for a convict settlement. Later Banks recommended William Bligh as Governor. Banks was knighted in 1781.

It is not known when Joseph Banks was initiated into Freemasonry but it is placed between 1764 and 1767. By the time he arrived in Australia he was already a member of the Old Horne Lodge, also referred to as the 'original No. 4 Lodge'.

Edmund Barton
(1849–1920)

Edmund Barton was born at Glebe in Sydney. As a boy at Fort Street Model School and Sydney Grammar School, he was said to be very intelligent, with a great love for music, literature and art. He graduated from the University of Sydney with first class honours and became a barrister.

In 1883, he became the Speaker of the NSW Legislative Assembly – and a tireless supporter of Federation and the Constitution. Although it was intended that Barton would become the first Australian Prime Minister, the new Governor-General, Lord Hopetoun, selected William Lyne instead. Australia's first federal Cabinet refused to work under Lyne, so Barton was elected.

Barton, a calm man with a rich voice, a lively sense of humour and a love of good food and wine, took office as Prime Minister at a grand ceremony – attended by a crowd of 200,000 – in the new Centennial Park on New Year's Day, 1901. The Prime Minister and his eight ministers were a new government with no parliament, no public service and no offices, so he borrowed a room in Sydney's Parliament House while his secretary sat in a hallway. In 1902 the government moved to Victoria's Parliament House, where it stayed 26 years before moving to Canberra. Barton was knighted that year.

The feminist movement was very active. In 1889 Louisa Lawson, speaking at the first meeting of the Dawn Club, said:

A woman's opinions are useless to her, she may suffer unjustly, she may be wronged, but she has no power to weightily petition against man's laws, no representatives to urge her views. Her only method to produce release, redress, or change is to ceaselessly agitate.

Barton's government granted women the vote in time for the elections of 1903.

Edmund Barton was initiated into Freemasonry at Australian Lodge of Harmony No. 556 English Constitution on 13 March 1878.

John Bisdee
(1869–1930)

Trooper John Hutton Bisdee was the first Australian-born soldier to be awarded the Victoria Cross. The eighth child of a Tasmanian pastoralist, he worked on his father's property before enlisting in the 1st Tasmanian Imperial Bushmen's Contingent and sailing for service in the Boer War in 1900.

On September 1, 1900, Trooper Bisdee was with a scouting party ambushed by Boers near Warmbaths in the Transvaal. Six of the eight soldiers were wounded, including two officers, one of whom was on foot as his horse had broken away and bolted. Dismounting from his own horse, Bisdee put the wounded officer in the saddle and ran alongside the animal until he was badly wounded himself. Then he mounted behind the wounded officer and successfully withdrew under heavy fire. This feat earned him the Victoria Cross.

Invalided home, he returned to South Africa in 1901 as a lieutenant and served until the end of the war. After some years farming in Tasmania, Lieutenant Bisdee again enlisted in 1906, this time in the 12th Australian Light Horse Regiment, Tasmanian Mounted Infantry. During World War I he served in Egypt as a Captain in the 12th Light Horse until a leg wound retired him from active duty. He was discharged from the Australian Imperial Force in 1920.

A Major in the Australian Military Forces from 1915, he retired in 1929 with the honorary rank of Lieutenant-Colonel. In January, 1930, he and his sister died of unrelated causes within a day of each other, and were buried in the same grave in Jericho, Tasmania.

John Bisdee was initiated into Freemasonry at Lodge Bulwer No. 1068 England on January 6, 1917.

Arthur Blackburn
(1892–1960)

A legal practitioner, South Australian born Arthur Seaforth Blackburn enlisted as a private in the 10th Battalion, landing at Gallipoli on April 25, 1915. He became a Lieutenant in August of the same year and served throughout the Gallipoli campaign as well as in France.

On July 23, 1916, at Pozières, Lieutenant Blackburn commanded a party of 50 men who, in the face of fierce opposition, destroyed an enemy strong point and captured over 350 metres of trench. This was the same section of trench where, only hours earlier, another Australian, John Leak, won his Victoria Cross. Blackburn personally led four successive bombing parties and was awarded a VC for 'most conspicuous bravery'.

Invalided home in 1917, and shortly afterwards discharged on medical grounds, Blackburn returned to practising law. From 1918 to 1921 he was Nationalist member for Sturt in the House of Assembly.

Arthur Blackburn fought again during World War II, leading the 2nd/3rd Australian Machine Gun Battalion in Syria, where as senior Allied officer he accepted the surrender of Damascus on June 21, 1941. In February 1942, Blackburn was appointed a temporary Brigadier and he and his battalion were hastily landed in Java to assist the Dutch against the rapid Japanese advance. Three weeks later the Allied forces surrendered. He was captured, and remained a prisoner of war until September 1945. In 1946 he received a Military Order of the British Empire for distinguished service in Java.

Arthur Blackburn was initiated into Freemasonry at Peter's Collegiate Lodge No. 58 SA on December 9, 1918.

CHAPTER THREE

Debunking the myths: perception and reality

FREEMASONS

We all know perception and reality are different. Every magic trick and many of the effects we see on television, in films, or on the stage turn out to be illusion. But it's not all about deliberate deception: perception and reality can be about how we see things and how we choose to see them. Whether your glass is half full or half empty has to do with how you view your life and how you lead it. Whether clean tap water in every house is ordinary or amazing depends upon where you were born.

In our own culture, urban myths abound. They're the sorts of things you hear in the office, at school, in pubs and clubs. Because they are usually 'tall stories' people hear them, wonder about their weirdness, then repeat them to their friends. We all know about the wet cat in the microwave, or the dirty one in the washing machine. Then of course, there's Elvis Presley and Adolf Hitler ... often still 'seen' somewhere around the world.

Through a long career in communication I have had to deal with plenty of these. They include all sorts of urban myths, deliberate stunts to attract attention, claims that proved to be false, stories about Freemasonry. Many of these urban myths have been related to friends with the prefix 'Would you believe?' That phrase is a common one in conversations between mates. It was also the title of the ABC television program that I had the fun of hosting for five years in the mid 1970's.

The panellists included some of Australia's best yarn-spinners: Frank Hardy, Cyril Pearl, Len Evans – sadly all gone to the great story-telling place in the sky – and fortunately still among the living, the actors Noeline Brown and Jacki Weaver, and the retired journalist, politician, close friend from school and long-time Freemason, Michael Baume. Those six people were on the panel show, would you believe, because they could spin a great yarn.

Of all the stories they told on TV, only one in three was true. The panellists and the audience had to select the true stories from the false. It was usually the most unbelievable stories that turned out to be true.

That's often how it is with perception and reality.

Perceptions of Freemasonry have done the Craft a great disservice. Freemasonry's desire to maintain silence about what it is and does has caused non-Masons to wonder what the Masons do. What is happening behind those closed doors? If it's secret, surely it has to be bad? Or at least suspect.

My experience in communication over more than 50 years has shown me that there are many rumours spread under the heading of 'would you believe ...?' My all-time favourite is called Kentucky Fried Rabbit.

'Kentucky Fried Rabbit'

As a young man I had the pleasure of publicising the arrival of Kentucky Fried Chicken (KFC) in Australia. The first store was at Villawood in New South Wales, a place which in the 1960s was further than any Sydney resident 'would go for their annual holidays'. Today Villawood is nearly at the centre of Australia's largest metropolis.

A few years later and maybe in response to a recommendation from me, the company arranged for 'the Colonel' to visit Australia. I led the team that conducted and publicised the visit of Colonel Harlan F. Sanders.

Yes – there really was a Colonel Sanders! – though the public perception was that he could not possibly be real. Many thought (possibly still think) that the Colonel is just a picture on a sign and on packaging for the company's products.

Believe me: he was real – and thereby hang other tales, that don't belong in this book.

The chief executive of KFC was Warren Boyd, a justly famous Australian Olympic swimmer who competed for us at the London Games of 1948. One day Warren called me with a problem. In a most conspiratorial whisper he said:

'Peter, we've got a problem. We need your help.'

'Sure, what's the problem?'

'Er … I don't want to say it out loud! Can you come to see me immediately?'

'OK … but can you give me a hint …?'

And in an even quieter voice Warren said:

'Would you believe, Kentucky Fried Rabbit?'

I hurried to his office.

Turns out that customers from several towns in the Central West of New South Wales had come to the view that KFC was made from rabbits, not chicken! So convinced were some that they sent the bones from their buckets with the famous 'eleven herbs and spices' to the Government analyst for identification!

Of course it was perception not reality. The sort of thing you simply had to tell your wife, or your friend as you passed a KFC store … 'Hey, would you believe this one … did you know … etc.'

Word of mouth moves like wildfire.

Warren wanted to put out a media release denying the story. It took me three days to convince him that this was a bad idea. It seemed to me that only the smallest number of people had yet heard the rumour and most would have been sensible enough to disregard it. Deny it in the media and instead of 1% of the public having heard this, 90% would hear the rumour … and of course, many would believe it.

At that time the rabbit problem which had plagued our farmers for many years had been greatly reduced by a comprehensive government eradication campaign (the myxomatosis program). Rabbits were in short supply and were much more expensive than chickens.

A denial would only have increased the public perception that 'Kentucky Fried Rabbit' could actually be real. A campaign of silence was clearly the right way to go. But I'll bet there are still people out there in the Parkes-Dubbo-Forbes area who will tell you that KFC used rabbits.

Where Freemasonry is concerned it is clear that the perceptions of non-Masons are often a long way from the truth. It is also likely that even a book such as this one, will only go part of the way to change those perceptions.

The objectives of Freemasonry are to help others, to build a society of trust, to develop good men into even better men, to be charitable and to embrace all races and religions in one family – one brotherhood in the sight of whatever supreme power you believe in – and all these things are good.

There are no ugly secrets. Anything you want to know can be discovered in books and on websites, but – would you believe? – the best way to find out is to experience Freemasonry for yourself.

Having said that, it is quite likely that even after the publication of this book, there will be many who still subscribe to the Masonic myths. So here's the truth.

'Riding the goat'

Freemasons do not ride goats when at Lodge or anywhere else. It's a joke, but a joke sometimes perpetrated by Masons themselves on nervous initiates.

Since the Middle Ages, the goat has been a symbol of the devil. Stories were told of witches calling Satan, who came riding into town on a goat to take part in their black rites. When Freemasons began to gain in popularity their detractors accused them of witchcraft, adding the notion that initiates rode a goat!

Some early Masonic texts referred to the Supreme Being as being 'God Of All Things' – which didn't help as it was abbreviated to GOAT. It was quickly changed, and the Supreme Being is now referred to by Masons as the Grand Architect Of The Universe.

There are other stories, too: some say the company that supplied sheets of parchment to early Lodges for their official records carried a goat (or was it a unicorn?) as a watermark, giving rise to a mistaken association of the goat with Freemasonry. Others say there was confusion about the lambskin aprons used for formal ceremonies ... that they may have been goatskin. (They weren't.)

Catalogues from the late 1800s actually offered mechanical goats for use by detractors to lampoon the Masons. In the golden age of fraternalism, hundreds of different groups appeared in competition with the Masons, with some clearly less serious than others. But the use of mail order goats in mock rites served to perpetuate the myth that some fraternities required a goat-ride ritual for their initiations. Freemasonry never has.

There is no Lodge goat. The Degrees of Masonry are serious business to Freemasons, and there is no horseplay (or goatplay)!

One of the more humorous aspects of this urban myth arose in Australia at North Sydney a couple of decades ago. The North Sydney Masonic Centre was a lovely old building fronting the Pacific Highway. It was sold some years ago and became a rug emporium. But in the days when it was still in use by the local Lodges, it had a typical backyard with a patch of lawn which tended to become rather untidy.

Would you believe, the committee responsible for maintaining the Lodge building decided it would be cheaper and more efficient to enclose the backyard and buy a goat to keep the grass down! This led to much hilarity among local Masons but also 'proved beyond any doubt' that Masons did ride goats!

'Drinking wine from human skulls'

The opening scene of Dan Brown's novel, *The Lost Symbol*, has a Candidate for a Masonic Degree drinking red wine from a human skull. It's a novel touch ...

The truth is that Masons do not drink red wine out of a human skull in any ceremony, or even after any ceremony, or even worse – at home alone. This myth began in the 1890s when a notorious French anti-Mason – working under the pen name of Leo Taxil – wrote lurid exposés of what he claimed to be Masonic rites.

Masons are, however, most congenial, and almost always offer guests – as well as enjoying for themselves – a glass of red or white wine at their Lodge suppers, known as the South. They also laugh and chat and speak among themselves as men and women tend to do anywhere good company is to be found. Wine out of skulls? Just think of the OH&S issue!

'Death rituals and mock murders'

Dan Brown also said that there are death rituals in which mock murders are performed. This is getting closer to the truth. At one point in the Third or Master Mason Degree, the candidate represents a character who would rather face death than betray the trust which has been reposed in him.

The story is that Hiram Abiff, architect of the Temple of King Solomon, allowed himself to be murdered rather than divulge the architectural secrets entrusted to him, and the rite uses the drama of this story to remind the candidate that morality, integrity and loyalty are essential virtues in a well-ordered community.

Nothing delivers the message more powerfully than a dramatic experience. Here's how one young initiate described his own emotions as he took his Entered Apprentice Degree:

> I was welcomed rather warmly and found that I would not be the only person getting initiated that evening. We both looked at one another, puzzled, mystified and excited. Every guy in

the Lodge came up to us and wished us well.

A series of loud knocks on the doors were made. We were told to change out of our suits into some weird garments. 'Weird!' I exclaimed to the other candidate.

As we approached the door to the Lodge room, the 'Tyler', pulled out two blindfolds. 'No chance I'm wearing that' I remember thinking to myself. A life of heart ache, broken promises and shattered dreams can make anyone not trust the world. My mind shifted to the thought of my dad. He would never let me be a part of something that would place me in harm's way.

'Come on: you can do this' I challenged myself. 'Trust them, what's the worst they can do.' I surrendered myself and went through the ceremony. I was guided through by a firm hand.

The moment the blindfolds were removed was out of this world. I opened my eyes and was full of emotion …

'Freemasonry is a religion'

Freemasonry is not a religion, nor a substitute for a religion. It accepts good men of all religions, and asks candidates only to declare their belief in a Supreme Being of some kind. After that, it discourages any further discussion of religion (or politics) at Lodge.

As Dan Brown points out in his latest book, Freemasonry fails the ABC test – Assure, Believe, Convert. 'Religions *assure* salvation; religions *believe* in a precise theology; and religions *convert* nonbelievers,' the hero, Professor Robert Langdon, explains to his class. 'Masons make no promises of salvation; they have no specific theology, and they do not seek to convert you.'

Freemasonry is all about taking responsibility for your actions now. It makes good men better by encouraging them to live more ethical, compassionate and cheerful lives. It encourages individuals to act 'on the square' and treat others fairly.

Its aims are secular and useful. Freemasonry helps candidates who start, metaphorically, as rough stones, to lose their rough edges – making them more useful as building blocks in the construction of a fairer, more compassionate society.

'The Masonic Bible'

Masons have been accused of having and using their own Bible in their ceremonies. And yes, many people will have seen Masonic Bibles for sale on eBay and elsewhere, suggesting that the Bibles used by Masons are somehow different. This is a myth in two parts that should focus on the Bibles Masons have as individuals, and the books of Sacred Law used in Lodges.

Masonic Lodges in predominantly Christian communities do often present new Master Masons with a commemorative Bible. In the United States, this is most commonly the 1611 translation of the King James version, published specifically for Masonic Lodges by Heirloom Bible Publishers of Wichita, Kansas.

These Bibles have a 'special dates' section in the front allowing the recipient to commemorate important dates in his Masonic progress. They also have a 94-page glossary of biblical references relating to Masonic ceremonies, along with Masonic essays and some common questions and answers. But the Bible itself is the entire King James version of the Old and New Testament – just like the Bibles available in any bookstore.

The second part of this myth has to do with the use of Bibles, and other sacred books such as the Koran, as Volumes of Sacred Law in Masonic Lodges.

Every recognised Masonic Lodge has a book, or books, considered sacred by its members, open on the Lodge altar during meetings. Depending on where the Lodge is located, and the religious beliefs of its members, this sacred book may be the Bible, the Hebrew Tanach, the Muslim Koran, the Hindu Veda, the Zoroastrian Zend-Avesta, or the Proverbs of Confucius. And if the Lodge members are of more than one belief, as is often the case in Australia, the altar may carry two or more of the above to meet the needs of all its members.

In Lodges that operate within the Grand Orient of France, atheists are also allowed to join. The Grand Orient believes that a man's religious beliefs – or lack of them – are his own business and that it is improper for their Lodges to require them to believe in anything. Furthermore, instead of filling up their altars with many sacred books to satisfy members of many faiths, their Lodges are allowed to substitute a book with blank pages as their Volume of Sacred Law, so as not to force any religious beliefs on any of their members. But note that The Grand Orient of France is 'irregular' – that is, not recognised by mainstream Grand Lodges around the world, including those in Australia. Even so, a blank book is no Masonic Bible either.

'The All-Seeing Eye and the US $1 bill'

The back of the US $1 bill is said to include Masonic imagery in the form of the All-Seeing Eye, which appears suspended over a pyramid. But is it a Masonic symbol?

Well, not really. The eye and the pyramid were actually included in the design of the Great Seal of the United States in 1776, and only later used on the $1 bill starting in 1935. Since then there has indeed been an All-Seeing Eye, floating over the unfinished pyramid, along with the words *annuit coeptis* (Latin meaning: 'He [God] has favored our undertakings'). Beneath this are the words, *novus ordo seclorum*, which translate as 'A new order of the ages.'

A committee of four men, with Benjamin Franklin as the only Mason, designed the Great Seal of the United States in 1776. The image of the eye within a triangle to represent God was suggested by the only artist among them, Pierre du Simitiere – who was not a Freemason. Two other committees tinkered with the design before it was approved. The unfinished pyramid was suggested by Francis Hopkinson (another non-Mason), and none of the final designers was a Mason.

The eye within a triangle to represent God appears throughout the Renaissance, long before modern Freemasonry began. The triangle, being three-sided, represents the Christian belief in the Holy Trinity – Father, Son, and Holy Spirit. The symbol does not appear in Freemasonry until 1797 – 21 years after the Great Seal was designed. So instead of being a Masonic symbol that was secretly applied to the $1 bill, it is actually a symbol from the Great Seal later adopted by some Masonic Lodges.

As for the unfinished pyramid, it represents the strong, new nation of the United States, destined to stand for centuries just as the famous pyramids have stood in Egypt. There are 13 rows of stones, representing the 13 original colonies, with the image of God watching over them.

Many Masonic Lodges, especially in Europe, also display the All-Seeing Eye just as it is used on the $1 bill – as a non-denominational representation of God. There is nothing sinister about it, and there are numerous instances of it appearing in Christian art from the 1600s onward.

More recently, Peter Sellers' last film *Being There* featured many philosophic statements which could be related to Masonic ideas and one scene shows the pyramid and the All-Seeing Eye. Peter Sellers was, of course, a Mason.

The Founding Fathers of the USA 'were Masons'

Allen E. Robert – who has written widely on Freemasonry – has made a special study of the myths surrounding the Founding Fathers in the United States of America. His studies have researched the following myths and facts.

Myth: George Washington was a Grand Master
Fact: George Washington was a Freemason. He was once suggested for the office of Grand Master of a National Grand Lodge. But the National Grand Lodge was never formed, and Washington was only ever Master of Alexandria Lodge 22 in Virginia.

Myth: Thomas Jefferson and Patrick Henry were Freemasons.
Fact: Neither Thomas Jefferson nor Patrick Henry were members of the Craft. An exhaustive search of Masonic records in Virginia, and elsewhere, offers no evidence suggesting they were Freemasons.

Myth: All, or almost all, Signers of the Articles of Confederation, Signers of the Declaration of Independence, and Signers of the Constitution were Freemasons.
Fact: Ten of the 48 signers of the Articles, nine of the 56 signers of the Declaration, and thirteen of the 38 signers of the Constitution – and only this number – were, or would become, Freemasons.

Myth: Washington was built by masons.
Fact: This is true, but not by Freemasons.

Myth: Freemasons are trying for a world takeover.
Fact: Freemasons are forbidden to discuss politics (or religion) in the Lodge – which would make it very difficult to plot a world takeover.

Regular Freemasonry does not now aspire, nor has it ever aspired, to be a world-dominating empire. It is a fraternal organisation that simply seeks to improve men so that they may, in turn, improve society around them. It makes good men better. But it does not tell them how to do it, nor does it give them political, commercial or religious instructions.

Donald George Bradman
(1908–2001)

When considering the stature of an athlete or for that matter any person, I set great store in certain qualities which I believe to be essential in addition to skill. They are that the person conducts his or her life with dignity, with integrity, courage, and perhaps most of all, with modesty. These virtues are totally compatible with pride, ambition, and competitiveness.

– Sir Donald Bradman, Freemason

Donald George Bradman – 'The Don' – was called 'Braddles' by his cricketing contemporaries. Born at Cootamundra, NSW in 1908, he is acknowledged as Australia's greatest cricketer. When he was two, his family moved to Bowral, NSW and 'the boy from Bowral' has been an inspiration to young cricketers around the world.

The young Bradman practised alone, using a cricket stump to hit a golf ball against a water tank in the backyard. It clearly worked, as his batting statistics are far ahead of any other cricketer.

Don Bradman scored 6,996 runs in 52 Test matches with an unbelievable average of 99.94. He hit 618 fours in Test cricket and if you like trivia topics, only a miserable six sixes – five v. England and one v. India. Guess he didn't want to risk getting caught …

One history describes him as a complex, highly driven man who hated the constant adulation of the huge crowds that followed him. After retiring from the field, he continued as a cricket administrator, selector and writer for three decades.

Bradman married in 1932. In his business life he became a company director serving on 16 boards, but left these for health reasons and to concentrate on cricket administration.

In 1949 he was knighted. A great deal of other recognition was also bestowed on him, including a Cricket Museum at Bowral, a Bradman Foundation, and commemorative stamps and coins.

While ever cricket continues to be enjoyed, his legacy will live on. But he was only one of many who also chose to be Freemasons.

A team of Australian Freemasons would include many of our very best. Grahame H. Cumming, the researcher and writer on all things Freemasonry, has put a team together in his authoritative booklet on the subject: *Freemasonry and Australian Cricket*.

The selectors could choose from 34 players who have worn the baggy green, including:

Thomas Andrews, Alexander Bannerman, Warren Bardsley, Donald Bradman, William Brown, Allan Connolly, Albert (Tibby) Cotter, Ian Craig, Alan Davidson, Geoffrey Dymock, Sydney Emery, Arthur (Wally) Grout, William Hunt, Barrington Jarman, Charles Kelleway, Alan Kippax, Bill Lawry, Hampden Love, C. G. Maccartney, Leonard Maddox, Arthur Mailey, John Martin, Arthur Morris, William Murdoch, M. A. Noble, Geoffrey Noblet, William (Bert) Oldfield, William Ponsford, Ronald Saggers, Robert Simpson, Hedley Taber, Donald Tallon, John Taylor, Francis Walters.

Drawn from these, The Freemasons XI would be likely to include:

Ponsford, W. H.

Lawry, W. M.

Bradman, D. G.

Simpson, R. B.

Maccartney, C. G.

Noble, M. A.

Davidson, A. K.

Cotter, A.

Dymock, G.

Mailey A. A.

Morris A. R

Oldfield W. A.(12th)

The Umpires would be:

Borwick, G. E.

French, R. A.

Commentator:

McGilvray A. D.

It's a team that could take on any other in the world.

Don Bradman was initiated into Freemasonry at Lodge Tarbolton No. 12, United Grand Lodge of New South Wales, on November 26, 1929.

Walter Brown
(1885–1942)

Regarded by those who served with him as 'a born soldier, quiet, friendly and loyal beyond measure', Walter Ernest Brown enlisted as an infantryman in 1915. He soon transferred to the Light Horse and embarked for Egypt, where he joined the Imperial Camel Corps.

In July, 1916, determined to reach the infantry in France, he contrived a transfer to the 20th Battalion with reinforcements, finally joining it at St Omer in July, 1917. A few months later he was awarded the Distinguished Conduct Medal for attending wounded under heavy fire at Passchendaele, and for other actions giving 'a fine example of courage and leadership'.

Wounded in November 1917, he was promoted to Corporal the following year. In July, Corporal Brown was with an advance party which took over some newly captured trenches near Accroche Wood. Learning that a German sniper post was in operation close by, he picked up two Mills bombs and ran towards it under fire. On reaching the post, he punched one German to the ground and threatened the others with his remaining grenade. The group surrendered and Corporal Brown captured 13 men, including an officer, ordering them back to the Australian lines and winning a Victoria Cross for his bravery.

In June, 1940, Brown enlisted again by giving his age as 40 instead of 54. Although his lie was soon discovered, he was allowed to continue his service for the Royal Australian Artillery and was posted to Malaya in August, 1941. Brown was last seen on February 14, 1942, the night before the Allied surrender of Singapore. Picking up some grenades, he told his comrades 'No surrender for me', before heading towards the enemy lines.

Walter Brown was initiated into Freemasonry at Lodge Gogeldrie No. 558 on April 7, 1931.

Stanley Bruce
(1883–1967)

Stanley Melbourne Bruce was born in St Kilda. His parents made the city of his birth his middle name, though the family divided its time between Australia and England, where he studied at Cambridge before living in London.

As a prep school boy in Australia he was remembered as delightful, serious, earnest, very good-looking, always 'a little gentleman' and very self-reliant. He went to Melbourne Church of England Grammar School in 1896, where he captained football, cricket and rowing, was a cadet-lieutenant and, in 1901, school captain.

During World War I, Stanley Bruce served as a captain in the British army in Egypt, where he was awarded the Military Medal, and at Gallipoli, where he received the French Croix de Guerre. In 1915 he was wounded at Gallipoli and invalided to London.

Captain Bruce returned to Australia as a war hero in 1917. A year later he secured National Party endorsement in the by-election for Flinders. From 1921 he served as Treasurer and became Prime Minister in 1923 when he led the first all-Australian-born Cabinet.

Voted out of office in 1929, Bruce regained his seat in 1931 before resigning two years later to become Australia's High Commissioner in London – a post he held until 1945.

During World War II he also served on the British War Cabinet and in 1947 became the only Australian Prime Minister to become a British peer – as Viscount Bruce of Melbourne.

From 1946–51 he chaired the Preparatory Commission and the World Food Council of the UN Food and Agriculture Organisation, and in 1951 became foundation Chancellor of the Australian National University.

After his death in London, it was learned that Bruce had willed that his ashes be scattered over Canberra – a city he helped to create. To this day, he is the only Prime Minister whose remains rest in Canberra.

Stanley Bruce was initiated into Freemasonry at Old Melburnians Lodge No. 317 Victorian Constitution on June 12, 1925.

George Cartwright
(1894–1978)

London-born George Cartwright was a quiet and unassuming man who migrated alone to Australia in 1912. He was working as a labourer in New South Wales when he enlisted in 1915, becoming one of the original members of the 33rd Battalion, part of the new 3rd Division. Wounded in action at Messines, Belgium, in June, 1917, Cartwright remained on duty but was hospitalised a year later when he and 270 others were gassed at Villers-Bretonneux, France.

Cartwright returned to duty. At Road Wood, overlooking Péronne, in France, his battalion was ordered to attack around sunrise on August 31, 1918. The troops lacked adequate artillery support and were halted by machine-gun fire. Undaunted, Private Cartwright stood firing his rifle from his shoulder and, walking towards the gun emplacement, shot several of the enemy. He then threw a bomb at the post, rushed forward and captured the gun and nine German soldiers. This action spurred the Australians to cheer loudly as they renewed their advance.

George Cartwright, who was awarded the Victoria Cross for his valour, was again wounded in the head and left arm the following month, during the attack on the Hindenburg line. Evacuated to England, he received his Victoria Cross from King George before returning to Australia and being discharged from the AIF in 1919. For some time, he lived in Sydney, working as a motor mechanic. Serving in the militia from 1932, he was mobilised for full service in March, 1940, and promoted to Captain in 1942. During World War II he performed training duties within Australia.

George Cartwright was initiated into Freemasonry at Lodge Merrylands No. 479 on November 1, 1923.

Edward Charlton
(1929–2004)

Billiards and snooker were always said to be the sign of a misspent youth, but the British television series *Pot Black* changed all that. Suddenly the public saw that snooker was a game that required great skill and patience.

A number of Australians have excelled at the game of snooker, but none more so than Edward Francis Charlton. 'Steady Eddie', as he became known, began playing billiards in his grandfather's club in the New South Wales town of Swansea.

Eddie was also a senior grade footballer, a champion surfer, a good cricketer and boxer. One of his proudest moments was when he carried the Olympic torch on part of its journey to the 1956 Games in Melbourne.

He soon turned to snooker, winning four amateur titles before turning professional in 1960. In 1964 he won the Australian Professional Snooker Championship on the first of many occasions. In 1968 he won the World Open Snooker Championship and when *Pot Black* appeared, he won that competition three times.

A quiet, unassuming man, Eddie Charlton died in 2004. He was married and had four sons and a daughter.

Edward Charlton was initiated into Freemasonry at Lodge Swansea, No. 755, UGL of NSW and ACT on July 14, 1961.

Joseph Cook
(1860–1947)

A coalminer and a man of great determination, Joseph Cook was born in England and started work in the mines as a pit boy at the age of nine. His father died when he was 12, leaving him to support the family. To make up for his lack of education he read and studied all he could. On Christmas Eve, 1885, Cook emigrated to Australia, later bringing his wife, Mary, to Lithgow in

New South Wales, where both he and his brother-in-law worked in the mines.

Cook was elected Secretary and President of the Miners' Association and entered the NSW Parliament as the Member for Hartley and one of the founding members of the NSW Labor Party.

In 1893 he was elected as the Parliamentary Labor Party's leader but feeling constrained by Labor's strict caucus rules, he joined George Reid's Free Trade Group. Following Federation, he was elected to the Federal Parliament as the Member for Parramatta, and 12 years later he became Prime Minister, replacing Alfred Deakin as the Liberal leader.

Cook's government lasted 15 months and ended in the first double dissolution in the Parliament's 13 year history. Britain's declaration of war against Germany in 1914 put Australia at war and a new Nationalist coalition was formed with Cook as Deputy Prime Minister, then Minister for the Navy (1917-20) and Treasurer (1920).

Joseph Cook represented Australia at the Imperial War Conference in 1918 and the Versailles Peace Conference of 1919. He became a Knight Grand Cross of the Order of Saint Michael and Saint George (GCMG) in 1920, and he resigned from Parliament in November, 1921.

Joseph Cook was initiated into Freemasonry at Lodge Independent No. 8 United Grand Lodge of New South Wales on February 12, 1892.

CHAPTER FOUR

Leading by example: explorers and settlers, innovators and entrepreneurs

From the earliest days of the Australian colonies, the fraternity of Freemasonry has attracted thousands of Australian men. Perhaps it is not surprising that so many of them were successful in various fields of endeavour. It's interesting to wonder whether the learning and the psychological security that the brotherhood provides encouraged them to stretch a little further, go the extra mile, do something a little different.

Some of these men were explorers of the physical world, in the days when that meant risking life and limb on sailing ships and finding ways across previously uncharted deserts and mountain ranges. No handy GPS system for guidance, or radio to summon help, these men opened up the interior of the country, sailed around the coast and drew new maps to stimulate the growth and success of the new nation.

Others were explorers in the world of the mind – doctors and scientists. Still more pushed the boundaries of the business world, creating new products and services to meet the needs of their communities.

Some of the most enduring icons of 20th century Australia were invented or developed by members of the Craft. Some are now working on creating the enduring icons of the 21st century.

The explorers

Joseph Banks brought the science of botany to this land, using the Linnean system of classification and Latin names for plants to catalogue everything he found here. We still use the Linnean system today.

Matthew Flinders sailed with Captain Bligh to complete the mission interrupted by the mutiny on the *Bounty*, then explored New Holland in a tiny boat called *Tom Thumb*. He used a bigger vessel to circumnavigate Tasmania, and got himself arrested on Mauritius on his way home. Banks bailed him out and Flinders named the new continent, Australia.

William Wentworth was a giant of a man. Best known for carving a path across the Blue Mountains with Lawson and Blaxland, he was more important for the introduction of democratic institutions in New South Wales. Wentworth owned the first independent newspaper. He successfully campaigned for self government in the colony and for trial by jury. He also introduced the first primary education system and wrote a new Constitution for the state in 1853. Wentworth was one of the visionaries who transformed New South Wales from a prison camp under military rule into a democratic colony.

These men, and others like Oxley and Hume, helped shape the place we live in now and they had one thing in common. They were all Freemasons: disciplined, dedicated to public service, and above all else enduring.

The inventors and entrepreneurs

Would life in Australia be the same without the small things we enjoy? Would Marmite be as good as Vegemite? Would milk be just as good to drink without Milo? If Aeroplane Jelly had never been invented, whose jelly would we sing about?

Could we live without little chocolate frogs called Freddo, or without Peters Ice Cream?

And what about excitement and recreation? Australians like Sir Charles Kingsford Smith and Sir James (Jim) Hardy are the very stuff of national heroes. And where would we be without the movie-making magic of Ken Hall, the father of Australia's film industry – and television too.

On the whole, Freemasons are ordinary men. Some make no public impact at all – preferring the peace and quiet of their own homes. Others, like Sir Charles Kingsford Smith, strode out around the world … well, he flew actually. And somewhere in between, there are those with relatively small ambitions that capture our imaginations in a big way, because they help to build our national psyche.

Edward Hallstrom is not a name that immediately springs to the minds of many. The Silent Knight refrigerators he developed, on the other hand, were very well known: they made everyday life easier for thousands of Australian families from 1940 onwards.

In Sydney, John Gowing is better known. His famous catchline 'Walk through – no one asked to buy!' was a masterpiece of early marketing finesse, while most Australians adopted the phrase 'Gone to Gowings'.

Soul Pattinson Chemists – 'for every body and soul' – are named for their founder, Caleb Soul. Ernest Fisk was a legend of radio, and Cecil Gregory helped us find our way around with his popular street directories.

In addition to their skills as inventors and as entrepreneurs, the men responsible for all these icons of Australian achievement were, one and all, Freemasons. Their stories, like those of our Masonic heroes and national leaders, are woven through this book to showcase the kind of men who choose to be Masons.

Leading the nation

The Commonwealth of Australia has had 25 Prime Ministers since Federation. Of these, 10 have been Freemasons. Does this mean that Freemasonry generates leaders? Or are strong men simply attracted to the discipline and principles of Freemasonry?

In addition to Australian leaders there have been a number of US political leaders, and many other notable individuals who have become Freemasons.

As we have seen, George Washington was a Freemason. So were many of the Founding Fathers, along with US Presidents Warren G. Harding, Andrew Johnson, James Monroe, Franklin Delano Roosevelt, Theodore Roosevelt, Harry S Truman and Gerald Ford.

Jesse Jackson, the US civil rights leader and politician is a Mason. So was Simon Bolivar, the South American independence leader, as well as the socialist president of Chile, Salvador Allende.

Sir Winston Churchill was a Mason, as was his adversary and Turkish national hero, Mustafa Kemal Attaturk – who fought the British and the ANZACs at Gallipoli. King Edward VII and King Edward VIII were both Masons. The latter's brother and successor, King George VI was a Mason. Prince Philip, the Duke of Edinburgh, is a Mason.

And those are just some of the ones we know about!

Lord Carrington was one of the first and most influential leaders in Australia. Educated at Eton and Trinity College Cambridge, he became the Liberal Member for High Wycombe in 1865. He was sworn into the Privy Council in 1881, then made a Knight Grand Cross (GCMG) and Governor of New South Wales – both in 1885.

When Carrington arrived in New South Wales, the colony was on the brink of drought and was struggling economically. He quickly proved an able Governor and his friendship with the Premier, Sir Henry Parkes, led both men to promote Federation.

Lord Carrington had strong ties with the governors of Victoria and South Australia too. These ties became important in setting the groundwork for the Federation Conference of 1890 – the conference at which delegates agreed that the time for Federation had arrived.

Lord Carrington was married to Cecilia Margaret, first daughter of Charles Harbord. The Carringtons were well-to-do and soon established Government House as the centre of Sydney's social circle. There were celebrations to mark Queen Victoria's Jubilee in 1887 and Lady Carrington established the Jubilee Fund for distressed women. A year later at the Centennial celebrations Lord Carrington, continuing to encourage Federation, officiated at the opening of Centennial Park in Sydney, and laid the foundation stone for Trades Hall.

Lord Carrington was an active Freemason and in addition to encouraging Federation he played a vital part in unifying the existing Grand Lodges in New South Wales – becoming the first Grand Master of the United Grand Lodge of New South Wales. He and Lady Carrington were very well liked and thousands lined the streets to farewell the couple when they left Australia.

Freemasons continued the drive towards Federation. Like Australia's first prime minister, Edmund Barton, Sir Samuel Griffith – the 'father of the Australian Constitution' – was a Mason.

In 1903 when the High Court of Australia was established, Griffith and Barton were two of the first Chief Justices of the High Court of Australia. Griffith played a vital role in Australia's move towards Federation as one of the principal authors of the Constitution of Australia. He was admitted to the bar in 1867 and served as Attorney-General and Premier for the Queensland Parliament before serving as Queensland's Chief Justice from 1893 until 1903, when he became Chief Justice of Australia.

According to Grahame H. Cumming in *Freemasonry and Federation*, Griffith was initiated into Freemasonry at the Victoria Lodge No. 1186, English Constitution (now No. 10 Queensland) and became a Master Mason in 1871.

The Australian Parliament sat for the first time on May 9, 1901 in Melbourne. It consisted of a Senate made up of 36 members (six from each state). Of the 36 members 14 were Freemasons: Albert Gould, Edward Millen, John

Neild, John Barrett, Robert Best, Simon Fraser, James Styles, David Charleston, Thomas Playford, Norman Ewing, George Pearce, John Ferguson, William Higgs and James Stewart.

Freemasonry also featured strongly in the House of Representatives: 30 of its 75 members were Freemasons. They included the future Prime Ministers, George Reid, Edmund Barton and Joseph Cook. Several of the electorates in the first Parliament were also named after Freemasons. These included Bland, Cowper, Dalley, Hume, Macquarie, Robertson and Wentworth in New South Wales, Flinders, Moira, Moreton and Oxley in Victoria, Grey in South Australia.

Freemasonry teaches that every member should seek ways to share in building a better world. Australia's Masonic Prime Ministers fully embraced this principle, transforming it from an aspiration into a way of life. Whatever their political directions and differences ... and no matter how history might judge their achievements ... such leaders become lasting role models for future generations.

Australia's first Masons

This chapter began with the statement that Joseph Banks was the first Freemason to set foot on Australian soil. When the Royal Society persuaded the British Admiralty that James Cook should command an expedition to observe the transit of Venus, it also urged that Joseph Banks, 'a gentleman of large fortune well versed in natural history' should join the party 'with his Suite'. His Suite amounted to a staff of eight, all of whom were aboard H.M.S. *Endeavour* when she sailed from England in 1768, some 50 years after the formation of the Grand Lodge of England marked the beginning of the modern Freemasonry movement.

After taking specimens and making astral observations at Rio de Janeiro, Tierra del Fuego, Tahiti and New Zealand, the expedition landed at Botany Bay on the east coast of Australia two years later. Banks named Botany Bay for the abundance of new plant species he found there, after which the expedition continued its voyage of discovery along the east coast of the land mass then known as New Holland.

The Dutch had visited New Holland in 1606 – 164 years before Cook's visit – but it was Cook who claimed the land for England on August 22, 1770, naming eastern Australia 'New South Wales'.

Despite claiming the land, the British did not consider occupying New South Wales until the loss of its American colonies in 1785. The First Fleet left Portsmouth a year later bound for Botany Bay with just over 1,000 souls, most of them convicts, in two naval vessels, six convict transports and three stores ships under the command of Captain Arthur Phillip.

Some of those aboard must have been Freemasons, for within three years three privates in the New South Wales Corps petitioned the Grand Lodge of Ireland for permission to establish a Masonic Lodge in New South Wales. The Grand Lodge of Ireland deferred a decision and nothing more was heard of the matter.

There are records of Masonic meetings being held on board H.M.S. *Glatton* and *Buffalo* while at anchor in Sydney Harbour in 1802, with some of the colony's settlers paying frequent visits to the ships.

The oldest Masonic document issued in Australia also dates from 1802, when a French exploration fleet was at anchor in Port Jackson. At a meeting held on board one of the French ships, Captain Anthony Fenn Kemp, a member of the New South Wales Corps who had been in France for part of the Revolution, was issued a certificate which, translated from French, read:

> *We, Knights of the Rose Croix, Master Masons and Companions of the same order, certify having received in Lodge not regularly constituted but properly assembled, and presided over by Sovereign Prince of Rose Croix J. St Criq* [a lieutenant on one of the French ships] *member of the Metropolitan Chapter of Paris, the dear brother Anthony Fenn Kemp, Captain of the New South Wales Regiment, stationed*

at Port Jackson, into the grade of Ancient Masonry. In faith of which we pray the Masons of both hemispheres to recognise and aid him in this capacity.

Like many early Australian Freemasons, Captain Kemp led a distinguished life. In 1804 he was one of the party that established the first settlement at Launceston in Van Diemen's Land (now Tasmania). In 1807 he joined the headquarters of his regiment in Sydney and took part in the rebellion against Governor Bligh, and was ordered to England to give evidence at the subsequent trial. Leaving the army in 1815, he returned to Van Diemen's Land where he selected land. Here, he gained the name 'Father of the People' for his strenuous fight against the despotism of Governor Arthur. Following his death in 1868 at the age of 95, the Tasmanian township of Kempton was named after him.

In 1803, a year after the Masonic meetings on the French and British ships, Sir Henry Browne Hayes – knight, man of wealth and convict – attempted to form a Masonic Lodge in Sydney Town. In Ireland, Sir Henry had been sheriff of Cork and a captain in the South Cork Militia. In April, 1801, he was found guilty of abducting a young heiress and forcing her into a mock marriage. He was sentenced to death, the sentence being commuted to transportation for life to NSW. Despite the severity of his sentence, it appears that his vast wealth, status and influence bought him a comfortable life in NSW. Yet when he petitioned to form a Masonic Lodge, he was sharply reminded by the Judge Advocate that he was still a convict. In a letter describing his attempt to form a Lodge, Sir Henry wrote he had been warned that:

The Judge Advocate will send for H.B. Hayes and inform him that if he is not sensible of the indulgence allowed him it is the Governor's duty to remind him of it and instead of being President of a Freemason's Lodge at Sydney, he will be put under a President at Castle Hill or Norfolk Island at hard labour.

Despite these warnings, Hayes proceeded with his Masonic plans, arranging for a Sergeant Thomas Whittle of the New South Wales Corps to write to his commanding officer asking for leave to give a party at his cottage on May 14, 1803. This party proved to be a meeting of Masonic brethren attended by Sir Henry and some sailors and settlers.

When Governor King, whose residence was nearby, found out about the meeting he sent a detachment of troops to arrest those who had assembled in defiance of his order. When nothing of a seditious nature could be found all those held, except Sir Henry, were released. An extract from an article in the *Sydney Gazette* of May 22, 1803, also warned:

> *It is to be clearly understood by all and every one of His Majesty's subjects resident or stationed in this Colony that any similar meetings without the express approbation of the Governor will be punished to the utmost rigour of the law.*

Hayes was sentenced to hard labour in Van Diemen's Land, but the sentence was never carried out. In a letter to Under-Secretary Sullivan, Governor King wrote: 'Every soldier and other person would have been made a Freemason, had not the most decided means been taken to prevent it.'

In 1803, the same year as his sentence, Sir Henry purchased land near Sydney's South Head on which he built Vaucluse House. This mansion was later occupied by two fellow Masons – military officer, public servant and landowner, Captain John Piper and statesman, explorer, barrister, land and newspaper owner, William Charles Wentworth. Governor Lachlan Macquarie, another famous Mason, later granted Sir Henry a full pardon and he returned to Ireland in 1812.

The next mention of Freemasonry appeared in the obituary of settler Charles Wood in the *Sydney Gazette* of September 9, 1804. This read, in part: 'Being of the masonic order, his funeral was one of the most respectful that has been witnessed for a length of time, being followed by a numerous procession of the fraternity.'

According to Masonic historian, Philip Crossle, the foundation of regular Freemasonry in Australia was *absolutely and essentially Irish in its origin and was due, in the first place, to an Irish Military Lodge in which young settlers were initiated, and granted dispensation by the military brethren to form a Lodge ... under a regular warrant granted by the Grand Lodge of Ireland.*

The first of these Irish Military Lodges was the Lodge of Social and Military Virtues attached to the 46th Regiment which arrived in the colony in 1814. On November 2, 1816, this Lodge held the first public Masonic ceremony in Australia – laying the foundation stone for Captain John Piper's home at Eliza Point. Thirty two Masons participated in the ceremony, including explorer and Surveyor General, John Oxley, who established the first penal settlement at Moreton Bay in Queensland.

The first Lodge meetings to be held in a specifically designated building were hosted by the 48th Regiment, which welcomed local inhabitants and 'young settlers' alike.

After some false starts and thirty-two years of colonial life, Freemasonry began to put down some firm roots. Its evolution makes an interesting case study of the growth and development of many kinds of community-based networks. For those interested in history – or sociology or the study of living systems – more details of its expansion throughout the country are set out in Appendix A.

The tyranny of distance

One of Australian Freemasonry's greatest problems was the painfully slow correspondence between Australia and Grand Lodges in Britain.

An example of the delays and frustrations involved in being beholden to overseas Grand Lodges, was the case of the original warrant authorising the formation of Lodge Burrangong St John in Young, NSW. The warrant was lost at sea when the ship *London* sank in the Bay of Biscay. The tragedy also took the life of Freemason Rev. John Woolley, Professor of Classics and Logic, and Principal of the University of Sydney. Later, the second warrant for the

Lodge was also lost at sea, and the third was not received until 1872 – 10 years after the original petition.

In another instance, in September, 1845 The South Australian Lodge of Friendship was informed that Henry Mildred had been appointed Provincial Grand Master for South Australia under the English Constitution. However his patent of office, the official certificate, took three years and four months in transmission and he was not installed until March 29, 1848.

'SALUTE THE PAST, CELEBRATE THE PRESENT, INSPIRE THE FUTURE'

Leon Carter, Town Clerk of Sydney from 1974 to 1993, is a long-time Freemason. Here he shares some of his recollections of the past and some sound recommendations for the future (see Chapter Twelve).

'An outstanding and lasting memory of being Sydney Town Clerk for 19 years was attending the splendid ceremonies when the Masons installed a new Grand Master in the magnificent surroundings of the city's famous Town Hall,' he told us.

The Town Hall and the Queen Victoria Building are possibly the only non-religious city buildings to retain their original 19th century function and interiors. The Town Hall includes the City Council Chamber, reception rooms, the Centennial Hall and offices for the Lord Mayor and councillors.

Leon Carter describes the annual installation of the Grand Master of the United Grand Lodge of NSW and the ACT as an awe-inspiring spectacle. Fifteen hundred Masons, wives and friends fill the Sydney Town Hall on two levels. The Grand Organist provides inspiring music for the event on the famous Town Hall organ, which was built in England and has a base note pipe 60 feet long. 'Playing it makes the building vibrate', Leon says.

The Sydney Town Hall is a splendid setting for Grand Installations. Grand Lodge Officers in full regalia and with near-military precision perform the traditional rituals, the Grand Heralds provide stirring trumpet voluntaries and the Grand Choir leads the 1500 assembled voices in singing the anthem and the odes.

His time as Town Clerk from 1974 to 1993 enabled him to serve some of Sydney's most interesting Lords Mayor including Sir Nicholas Shehadie, Leo Port, Sir Emmett McDermott, Nelson Meers, Douglas Sutherland, Jeremy Bingham and Frank Sartor as well as Commissioners Sir Eric Neal and Norman Oakes.

Together with Alderman Sutherland and Alderman Bingham, Leon Carter negotiated the restoration of the Queen Victoria Building, the main Centennial Hall and the Capitol Theatre, which has become one of the best acoustic spaces in the country. He also recommended that the City Council should acquire all the property opposite the Town Hall, from George Street to Pitt Street along the Park Street frontage to enable the creation of a public square for the future, and negotiated this outcome at almost no cost to the ratepayers.

According to Sydney Town Hall: A Social History, *by Margo Beasley, 'in 1906 a rifle range was built in the basement in the "interests of national defence"'*:

It was a time when civil defence training was in vogue and small shooting ranges were set up across the city as tensions in Europe gradually took the world towards two world wars.

When the conflicts were over, the shooting gallery … was used by payroll staff to hone their skills to foil attempted robberies.

'These days they might say "just give them the money", but they were a lot less likely to do that in those days,' said Leon Carter, the town clerk from 1974 to 1993.

'Mr Carter was partial to a bit of target practice,' a council officer recalls. 'He had two things in his top drawer – a black gun and a black book,' said the officer, who asked to remain anonymous.

The black book to which he referred was probably a book of Masonic ritual as Leon Carter has been a dedicated Freemason for the past 50 years. A great advocate for the Craft, he served as a Past District Grand Inspector of Workings and more recently as Grand Chaplain. He has also been awarded an OBE for his services to the community. In particular he believes in the role of Freemasonry to influence and raise the level of citizenship and public interest in the process of government.

In a speech delivered to senior Freemasons at Parliament House recently, Leon Carter said:

We are aware that the ethos of Freemasonry prohibits the discussion of theological and political questions. And so, before proceeding, I should like to make it perfectly clear that my comments today have nothing to do with politics, but are strictly for reflection on the actual process and objectives of governments, anywhere and everywhere. There is a direct relationship between Masonry, Citizenship and Government to which our Craft should awaken, if it is to fulfil its highest mission.

Whilst we believe democracy is the best system of government known to man, it is not, however, a perfect system in that it does not remove the distinctions of inequality. That is not possible. But, it does much to compensate for such inequalities. A growing number of people in the western world are now looking for more visionary government policies to give their countries and their lives more meaning and purpose.

If governments everywhere are to effectively resonate, they must react to the conscience of their people and understand that gross national product does not allow for the health of our children, the quality of their education, nor the joy of their play.

It does not include the beauty of our poetry, the strength of our marriages, the intelligence of our public debate nor the integrity of our public officials. It measures neither our wit nor our courage, neither our wisdom nor our learning, neither our compassion nor our devotion to our country.

The Prime Minister of Bhutan, when questioned recently in relation to the gross national product, was heard to respond, 'our principal concern is gross national *happiness.*'

It is not a sufficient discharge of our responsibilities as citizens to simply obey the law and pay our taxes. The Commissioner for Police will ensure the first and the Commissioner for Taxation will take care of the second!

The soul of democracy is – 'by the people' – not just – 'for the people.' One measure of good government is the level of public involvement. Freemasonry is a moral academy which prepares its members in the godly requirements of life. It has associated itself with human sympathies and charitable institutions and possesses many entitlements to respect.

It is well qualified to arouse the higher minded youth of our country, to raise the importance of greater participation in the process of government. This will slowly dispel ignorance and greed – which are fundamental causes of human suffering.

It was the custom in ancient Athens to hold a public ceremony every year, at which all young men who had attained their 18th year were formally admitted to citizenship. Each young man took the solemn oath of good citizenship, known as 'the Athenian Oath,' the principal theme being 'that he would respect and defend age, attainment and legal authority and leave his country not less, but better.'

Upon reaching a similar age, young men of good report can become Freemasons. The initial instructions to a young Mason are beyond the work of the Craft. They fit him to face his duty to the world, to spread the light of his example and the force of our Masonic precepts and teachings and help him to become a better citizen and a stronger part of civic life.

Our challenge today as Masons is to create a new spirit, blended of ancient tradition and modern endeavour, a real and vital power for good in the world, a rising to duty, not circumscribed by tiled doors or words, or signs, an open service to be known by all men for the good that it renders.

Leon Carter believes that while ever Freemasonry is seen to be secretive it will not reach its maximum potential to influence for good the communities in which and for which it exists.

Criticism and some negative perceptions of Freemasonry are to some extent our own fault. For example, when hearing Freemasonry referred to as a 'secret society', many Masons (including myself in the past), have responded, 'Not so, Freemasonry is a society with secrets.'

I now believe this response is frequently interpreted as slick, evasive, and even bordering on dishonest. The reaction to this response is predictably negative. We must understand we are living today in an age of great transparency. When we hear Freemasonry referred to as a 'secret society', we should respond:

- Freemasonry is a wonderful journey
- It welcomes men of good standing of any race, religion and creed
- It is without dogma and doctrine and is neither a religion, nor a substitute religion
- It gives substantial financial support to a wide range of charitable works
- It embraces and teaches ethical standards of morality, integrity, loyalty and universal tolerance.

Should any further explanation be required, the public library, the city library, the web or the Masonic Museum will tell anyone anything they wish to know about Freemasonry, our so-called 'secret society.'

We should stand tall, and profess our faith in our organisation. We should salute the past, celebrate the present and inspire the future.

THE GRAND MASTER WEARS EARRINGS
by John Tuffin

Tony Lauer, formerly Commissioner of Police in New South Wales and a past Grand Master of the United Grand Lodge of NSW and the ACT, wears an earring, or could that just be two – one in each ear?

This is not something that Masons often do. By and large the Masons are conservative. Or at the very least correct. They may – when in full regalia – be seen wearing Masonic jewels. But earrings?

We are midway through our conversation at Grand Lodge before this affectation gets a mention.

I see you wear earrings.

Yes I do, he says.

Did you wear them to the Grand Master's Proclamation?

No, he says. I wore diamond studs for that!

Tony Lauer took to wearing earrings fairly recently. And it must be said that he looks good in them. Lean and tanned, with silver hair and bright blue eyes he looks exactly as a past Grand Master, or a former Police Commissioner should. Reliable, likeable and retired. The sort of man whose reputation will allow him to wear earrings if he wants to. But that's not why he wears them.

The floor of a Masonic Lodge always features black and white squares like a chessboard. The first Lodge meetings in Australia were mainly military affairs, and because they couldn't bring the floors with them, the early Masons here would place a smaller carpet of black and white squares into the centre of the room they were using – often on board ship.

The black and white squares have an allegorical purpose, serving to remind those present of the fact that life is a journey full of choices and contrasts: good and bad bits, easy days and hard days. Tony Lauer has had both.

Tony was born in Newcastle north of Sydney. His father was a butcher – later a Master Butcher with a number of shops, and Tony was the oldest of five brothers.

'My father was a Catholic,' he said, 'and he showed a keen interest in aspects of the church before the war.'

'When he joined the Air Force we moved to the Blue Mountains and stayed there – but my father changed. I don't know what he saw during the war, but he once told me that he was no longer afraid of death.

'It sounds a bit Masonic, and it seemed to allow him greater freedom of thought. But he wasn't a Mason. There were no connections in our family and it wasn't until much later that I first became a Mason.'

Tony Lauer spent his childhood in the mountains and went to school in Penrith – quitting after Year 10 to join his father, who by then was back in the butcher's business. A loyal man, Tony married his childhood sweetheart, Joy, and they've been married now for more than 50 years.

'I left the butchering business at 19 and joined the police force. There were only two policemen in the town but I had grown to admire them and so I joined. In those days all the training was at Redfern and, in a couple of weeks, they let you go to learn the rest out on the street.'

Tony Lauer served with the police for more than 40 years, progressing from his first position as a uniformed officer to Chief Superintendent of the Criminal Investigation Branch and ultimately Commissioner of Police after John Avery in 1991.

'In the early days, I think it is true to say the police force was divided on religious lines. Catholics one side, Protestants the other. But even that divide was only social, it was never operational.

'Your religion was recorded on the service register, but even after that was stopped, you didn't have be a genius to work out who went off to Mass on Sundays and who took every third Monday off to go to Lodge.

'I became a Mason because the police I observed, that I admired in some way, I knew to be Masons. It was the way they behaved, the way they conducted themselves that caused me to make enquiries. I was initiated in 1960, at Lodge Nepean, number 29 – which shows it was a very early Lodge.'

Tony Lauer points out that there were four Masonic groups in the early days: the English, Scottish, Irish and the Grand Lodge of New South Wales ... They were brought together as the United Grand Lodge of New South Wales by Lord Carrington, who *afterwards remarked that in all the discussions to bring about the United Grand Lodge, not one word was said, by any party, that was later regretted.*

'That was quite a remarkable endeavour.

'When I joined Lodge Nepean I was 25 years old. It was a very strong Lodge with many prominent business people and policemen. I found the ritual side of it overwhelming and difficult to understand. But the social side was a very strong feature that drew everyone together.'

Later, with his police career approaching senior levels, Tony Lauer took a clearance from Lodge Nepean, and stayed away until after his retirement from the Force. 'The decision was deliberate,' *he says.* 'I wanted it to be clear that there would be no favouritism based on affiliations such as Freemasonry.'

Tony Lauer retired from the position of Commissioner and from the police force in 1996. Called back to appear at a secret hearing of the Wood Royal Commission some time later, he was shown an article from a recently published newspaper by Counsel Assisting, who asked him if he'd read it. No, he had not, he said. Counsel seemed surprised:

'So I told him I cancelled my subscriptions to the newspapers the day after I retired – and now felt better informed for having done so!'

So why does the former Commissioner and Grand Master wear the earrings?

'Some time before my retirement I learned my youngest daughter had a drug problem and that led – after my retirement – to my wife and me taking care of her three young children.

'On one occasion I drove the eldest to a skating rink, where all his mates were, and when he came home he said: 'Joy, will you drive me to skating in future?' When she said 'Why' he replied 'Because you look younger than Pa'.'

'I took up wearing earrings to mellow my age,' *says Tony Lauer* with a smile, 'to look a little more like the other kids' dads when they were still at primary school. I'm not sure that it helped ...'

Tony Lauer returned to Lodge Nepean after his retirement and in 2000 he was elected Grand Master of the United Grand Lodge of NSW and the ACT, a position he retained for the next four years.

During his time as Grand Master he began the process of engagement with the public as the first Grand Master to appear before the National Press Club in Canberra.

'It was April 2004 – and I was pretty sure that most Masons would be spinning at the idea. So the first question is offered, and a journalist asks: 'Is it true that they place a noose around your neck at your initiation into Freemasonry?'

'So I thought, in fact I had decided, that there's no point going public if you're not prepared to tell the truth so I answered: 'That is true, but it's not a noose, it's a cable tow – which was used for climbing and as a measure by operative stone masons in earlier times ..."

There have been those for and those against engaging with the public. Tony Lauer may well have been one of the first to support it.

So what has he, personally, gained from being a Freemason?

'Freemasonry is a source of education directed at moral issues. Its principles dealing with equality and charity are important.

'In my trophy case at home I have a penny. And when non-Masons ask me why it is significant I tell them that for my initiation I had to leave all my money outside the Lodge room. Later, during the ceremony, I was invited to contribute to a charitable cause but having no money I could not do so. And it was pointed out to me then that I should remember this: that there was once a time when I stood poor and penniless – when I couldn't help others. So I keep the penny to remind me of my obligation to help others.'

In addition to having been Commissioner, Tony Lauer has also served as President of the Police Association of NSW and was made a Life Member of the Association in 1983. He has also served as a member of the Police Board of NSW, the Operation Review Committee of the Independent Commission Against Corruption, the Management Committee of the State Crime Commission and as a Councillor of the Royal Humane Society of NSW.

He is currently a Director and Deputy Chairman of the Police Department Employees' Credit Union Limited, as well as being Chairman of Credit Unions' Credit Committee, and a member of the Risk Management and Compliance Committee. He also serves as a Legator with Police Legacy and as a member of the RSL's Anzac of the Year Award Committee.

Tony Lauer underwent training in the Australian Army with the 19th National Service Training Battalion, Holsworthy, in 1957.

He was named a Paul Harris Fellow by the Rotary Foundation of Rotary International in 1994 and has been awarded the Australian Police Medal, the Queen Elizabeth II Jubilee Medal, the National Medal, the Australian Defence Medal, the Police Long Service and Good Conduct Medal, the National Service Medal, and the New South Wales Police Diligence and Ethical Service Medal.

William Currey
(1895–1948)

William Matthew Currey's working class origins and war experiences influenced him to enter politics later in life. He was the first VC winner in the NSW Parliament.

The son of a miner at Wallsend, NSW, Currey moved to Sydney and became a wire worker. Though too young, he twice tried to enlist for WWI before being accepted. In 1917-18 he served with the 53rd Battalion, fighting at Polygon Wood, the Somme and Péronne, where he won the VC.

Early on September 1, Private Currey's battalion was taking heavy casualties, under attack from a 77mm field gun at very close range. Rushing forward under machine-gun fire, Currey killed the whole crew, capturing the gun.

The same afternoon he attacked an enemy strongpoint, firing a Lewis gun, rushing the post and thus allowing the battalion attack to proceed.

Early next morning one company became isolated. Private Currey volunteered to warn the men to withdraw. At 3 a.m., he stood in the middle of no-man's-land and called to the company, an action that attracted a barrage of enemy fire. After three attempts, during which his respirator was punctured, he was gassed – but his warnings allowed the company to return safely.

From 1930-32 he served with the 45th Battalion, citizen forces, rising to Warrant Officer and in 1940-41 with the Australian Instructional Corps. While working with NSW railways, Currey became active in the Australian Labor Party. In 1941 he won the seat of Kogarah and was twice re-elected. He made the interests of ex-servicemen his particular concern. He collapsed suddenly in Parliament House in 1948 and died on April 30. His funeral service was attended by four VC winners.

William Currey was initiated into Lodge Carlton No. 382 on March 11, 1930.

John Edmondson
(1914–1941)

An only child, John Hurst Edmondson was born into a farming family that moved to Liverpool, New South Wales during his childhood. He was a champion rifle marksman, and joined the militia in 1939. Enlisting the following year, he was posted to the 2nd/17th Battalion and was a corporal when his battalion sailed to the Middle East for training in Palestine.

In March 1941, the 2nd/17th moved to Libya, reaching Marsa Brega before an Axis counter-attack forced them back to Tobruk, where the siege began on April 11. Two days later the Germans probed the perimeter of the area, targeting a strongpoint section of the line garrisoned by the Battalion's No.16 platoon in which Edmondson was a section leader. The enemy plan was to clear the post so it could become a bridgehead for an armoured assault on Tobruk. During the night, 30 Germans with machine-guns, mortars and two light field guns infiltrated the barbed wire defences. When the commander of No. 16 Platoon, Lieutenant F. A. Mackell, led Edmondson's five-man section in an attempt to repel the enemy, they were spotted and came under heavy machine-gun fire.

Unknown to his comrades, Corporal Edmondson was hit in the neck and stomach but he continued to charge, bayoneting one German and saving Mackell by killing a further two of the enemy who were attacking him. Although Edmondson was treated for his wounds, he died before dawn on April 14, 1941, and was buried in Tobruk war cemetery. The Germans' armoured attack that morning was thwarted, partly as a result of the success of Edmondson's section. His Victoria Cross was the first awarded to a member of Australia's armed forces during World War II. At Liverpool, a public clock celebrates this young VC winner, as do the clubrooms used by the sub-branch of the Returned Services League of Australia.

John Edmondson was initiated into Freemasonry at Lodge Liverpool No. 197 on April 3, 1935.

Arthur Fadden
(1894–1973)

An amiable accountant from Queensland, Sir Arthur 'Artie' Fadden spent a total of 40 days as Prime Minister in 1941 although, through his long political career, he was acting PM for periods totalling nearly two years.

Having served a single term in the Queensland Legislative Assembly, Fadden joined the House of Representatives as a member of the Country Party in 1936. Entering the government of Robert Menzies as a junior minister, he was promoted to Treasurer after the October 1940 general election. When Robert Menzies resigned as Prime Minister in August 1941, Fadden replaced him until the Independents, who provided his government's majority, crossed the floor to support the John Curtin-led Labor Party on October 7. This brought about a change of government.

Remaining as Country Party leader, Fadden again became Deputy Prime Minister and Treasurer when the Menzies Liberal-Country Party government returned to power at the end of 1949. He held both posts until his retirement in 1958. During his years as Treasurer, Fadden was instrumental in establishing the Reserve Bank of Australia. In all, Fadden was a member of the House of Representatives for 22 years (1936–1958) and leader of the Country Party for 17 years

Arthur Fadden was initiated into Freemasonry at Caledonia Lodge No. 737 Scottish Constitution in Queensland on July 20, 1915.

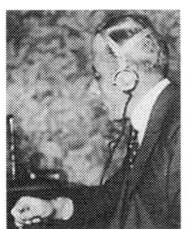

Ernest Fisk
(1886–1965)

Ernest Thomas Fisk made a vital contribution to the development of radio communications in Australia. Marconi commercialised wireless telegraphy making it accessible all over the world but Ernest Fisk was responsible for the first 'broadcast' in Australia in August 1919.

Born in England in 1886, Fisk's career in radio began when he joined the British Post Office as a wireless telegraphist. He joined the Marconi training school, learned Morse Code and wireless telegraphy at Liverpool and Chelmsford and qualified as a radio engineer and operator. From 1909 he worked for American Marconi and then at its London headquarters.

The company sent Fisk to Australia to demonstrate Marconi's apparatus for the Orient Steam Navigation Company in 1910. He convinced ship owners to fit Marconi equipment, then installed and trained telegraphists to operate it.

Following a dispute between the English Marconi Company and the Australian Government over patents, Amalgamated Wireless (Australasia), or AWA, was formed in 1913, with Fisk as Foundation Director, General and Technical Manager.

On September 22, 1918 Fisk made Australian radio history when he picked up the first Morse Code wireless transmission from Great Britain to Australia. Fisk was a member of the Royal Society of New South Wales and in 1919 achieved the first radio broadcast by transmitting the national anthem from one room to another.

In 1920 he demonstrated radio broadcasting in Federal Parliament House, Melbourne and then established the first wireless newspapers on British ships operating in the Pacific and Indian Ocean – an event roughly equivalent to the arrival of digital communication later in the 20th century.

In 1924 he made history again by using radio to speak with Marconi in England – the first ever voice contact between the two countries.

Fisk joined the New South Wales branch of the Royal Empire Society in 1934 and was President in 1941 and 1944. He was awarded the King George V Silver Jubilee Medal in 1935 and was knighted in the Coronation honours, 1937.

Ernest Fisk was initiated into Freemasonry at St John Lodge, Newfoundland No. 579, English Constitution on April 28, 1910.

Matthew Flinders (1774–1814)

Born in Lincolnshire, England, Flinders joined the Royal Navy at the age of 15 and two years later sailed with the famous Captain Bligh.

Bligh was between the mutiny on the *Bounty* and the Governorship of New South Wales when Flinders accompanied him on a two-year voyage to Tahiti – with Flinders tending the chronometers and helping to compile the charts on HMS *Providence*.

Flinders was an extremely ambitious man with a fierce determination that lasted all his life. Early in his career he noted enviously of Captain Cook: 'He reaped the harvest of discovery, but the gleanings of the field remain to be gathered.' And this is what he set out to accomplish.

Flinders' next major opportunity came at the age of 21 when he accompanied Governor Hunter on board the *Reliance* bound for New South Wales. George Bass was also on board as the ship's surgeon and this journey was the first of a number of significant adventures shared by the pair. Flinders and Bass unravelled many of the mysteries of the east coast of the Australian mainland. The exploits of the two daring young men included exploring Botany Bay and Georges River in the small boat *Tom Thumb*. They later circumnavigated Van Diemen's Land on board *Norfolk*, discovering Bass Strait and proving Van Diemen's Land to be an island.

In 1799 Flinders was recalled to duty in England, where his charts were published by Joseph Banks.

Banks persuaded the Admiralty of the importance of charting the coastline of Australia and Flinders set off in January 1801 on his journey aboard the *Investigator*, believing that: 'There will be no need for other men to follow after me.'

Flinders explored islands, bays, straits and gulfs around the Australian coastline, but these uncharted territories eventually took their toll on the man and the ship. Months at the masthead left Flinders almost a cripple and with the

Investigator's hull rotting right through, the ship was deemed unseaworthy.

Surviving shipwreck, Flinders made his way back to England in 1802. Oblivious to the war between England and France, he stopped at the French Colony of Ile de France (Mauritius) for provisions. He was treated as a spy and imprisoned. Banks campaigned for his release, which eventually occurred in 1810.

Flinders is credited with being the first person to use the name Australia, which appears in a letter to his brother written in August 1804. He will always be remembered for naming Australia, though this was not officially recognised until after his death in 1814.

At the time of his imprisonment on Ile de France, Freemasonry was very much in vogue and Flinders was attracted to it and its lifestyle. It is thought that he was initiated in Friendly Cultivator Lodge, which met at Plaines Wilhems where he lived on the island. In his Journal in July 1807 he refers to celebrating 'the fete of St John at the Freemason's Lodge established here'.

CHAPTER FIVE

Principles in practice

Freemasons believe in – and act out – the well established principles of faith, hope and charity. For this reason, the fraternity has created and still operates several charity organisations in Australia.

It is important to make it clear that Freemasons help needy and disadvantaged people whether or not they are associated with the Craft. As with membership, the test has nothing to do with who or what you are; the test is about whether help is needed and how Masons can help.

From the ceremony of the First Degree of Freemasonry:

Your duty to your neighbour demands that you should act towards him on the square, render him every kind office that Justice or Mercy may require, relieve his necessities, soothe his afflictions, and do to him as you would that he, in similar circumstances, should do unto you.

Freemasons are also credited with the founding of great organisations outside the Craft, which believe in and foster these ancient principles. Not least among these are the Salvation Army, the Mormon Church and The Smith Family. All owe their commencement, at least in part, to Masonic brethren.

The value of a man should be seen in what he gives and not in what he is able to receive. Albert Einstein

If you have much, give of your wealth; if you have little, give of your heart.   Arabian Proverb

and from the ceremony of the Third Degree of Freemasonry:

Universal charity and benevolence you are both to inculcate and to practise; and by the regularity of your own deportment, afford the best example for the conduct of others.

Every Mason is aware of the important duty of helping less fortunate members of the community. Masons cheerfully embrace the opportunity to contribute to charity whether financially or by volunteering. A proportion of annual membership subscriptions is allocated to charity and other opportunities to help are also encouraged through every Lodge in the country.

Since the Craft has existed in Australia, Masons have created and operated special funds for widows and orphans, supported needy people in our local communities, run hospitals, schools and retirement villages, operated a fund for youth welfare and contributed to disaster relief such as bushfire appeals and many other causes.

Masonic not-for-profit organisations are active in aged care in all Australian states. At the time of publication, there were nearly 10,000 senior citizens receiving care from Masonic aged care facilities.

Royal Freemasons' Benevolent Institution

One of the oldest charities in Australia – a benevolent fund established in NSW – is the Royal Freemasons' Benevolent Institution (RFBI), founded in 1880.

For 129 years it has focused on helping people in need, and many individuals and families have received annuities and grants. Any needy person can receive help from the RFBI, whether or not they are Masons, whatever their origins or religious beliefs.

As social security funding by governments has become more widespread, the RFBI – while continuing to assist needy people with annuities in special cases – has turned its focus towards providing care for the ageing.

Today it owns and operates more than 20 retirement villages in New South Wales and the Australian Capital Territory.

The founders of the Royal Freemasons' Benevolent Institution expressed the RFBI's philosophy like this:

> *For the sake of the poor – of our own obligations – and of the credit of the Order, it is hoped that a generous and universal support will be accorded to an Institution whose function will be to provide succour in distress and relief in necessity.*

All RFBI villages are managed to meet very high professional standards. They are well regarded for their affordable, attractive accommodation and are staffed by friendly, qualified carers. All levels of care (villages, hostels, nursing homes) are fully accredited in every aspect of their operations by the Aged Care Standards and Accreditation Agency.

Village accommodation is designed to suit individual needs, providing self-care housing and apartments or units where aged persons who are still active can maintain their independence in a comfortable, secure lifestyle. In RFBI retirement villages, 'caring' means enhancing the residents' self esteem by further development of independence and individuality.

RFBI hostels provide for the daily needs of those who require some care but who may not need continuous nursing supervision. For people who, for reasons of infirmity, illness or disability require a higher level of nursing care, RFBI nursing homes provide clinical assistance under instructions from professional medical practitioners.

'Our 2,450 residents are encouraged to take advantage of the opportunities available in retirement,' says RFBI President, Ken Thompson. 'We help residents to adjust to the new social experience of living together in a community, as distinct from private housing, and we do everything possible to compensate for their declining ability to freely participate in their environment.

'That helps to reduce the fears commonly associated with ageing.'

The Royal Freemasons' Benevolent Institution is presently building new facilities in four locations where aged care is urgently needed.

We make a living by what we get, but we make a life by what we give.   Bro. Winston Churchill

What you are is God's gift to you. What you make of yourself is your gift to God   Anonymous

The Whiddon Group: Masonic Aged Care

The Whiddon Group, a sister ('brother'?) organisation to the RFBI, is also a not-for-profit charitable organisation which has been providing aged care services to NSW clients for over 60 years. Founded on core principles of growth, integrity, excellence, dignity and autonomy, it owns and operates more than 20 specialist residential care and independent living facilities that provide comfort and security to some 1900 residential clients.

It all began in 1923, when social welfare was practically non-existent. A small group of Freemasons formed The Aged and Distressed Brethren's Comfort Fund Committee, visiting sick and elderly Freemasons and their wives.

The Committee was founded by Bro. Herbert Cracknell, W. Bro. Fred Greening and W. Bro. Harold Wilkens and they pursued their aim, virtually as a private group, providing funds and facilities for their less fortunate brethren. Other brethren joined the Committee over time and a plan was formed to construct facilities for aged Masons and their wives.

In 1945 when M.W. Bro. Frank Whiddon became Grand Master, he gave the Committee permission to receive donations from Lodges, which enabled the provision of comforts and ultimately accommodation for less fortunate Masons.

The Whiddon Group points out that older people are generally happier, healthier and more connected to their communities when they continue to live in their own homes. It also understands that most people want to delay entry to a retirement village or nursing home for as long as possible. For that reason it has designed a Home Independence program to help clients to stay in their own homes by providing them with a variety of services ranging from domestic care to personal care. It also teaches skills to help clients maintain their independence.

Below are four comments from people who have received help from Masonic retirement services:

'We who live here reap the benefit of your effort. I feel so contented and cared for, each of you are very special people to me. Thank you for the hugs, the shoulders to cry on, the cups of tea and tissues, the understanding and privacy when it was needed. Please accept our deepest and sincere appreciation for the respect and dignity all the wonderful staff showed.'

'We really appreciated the wonderful care and love you provided beyond the call of duty.'

'Thank you for your support and compassion over the last few days. The care Pop has received has been outstanding. From all the family we send our sincere thanks.'

'The world's a better place because of people like you, who take the time to do nice things the way you always do. Thank you so much.'

All Masonic retirement facilities are fully compliant with health and safety requirements and accredited by the relevant government authorities. All of them operate on a not-for-profit basis and they have earned the respect and gratitude of the Australian people.

The carers in Masonic retirement facilities are very special people who also recognise the values and ethics by which the villages are operated and they appreciate that Freemasons do all they can to live by the principles of the fraternity. In particular the great Masonic aim to be happy and to confer happiness is reflected in the lives of residents and carers.

As a result, the villages are nearly always fully occupied and most have waiting lists for those seeking access for themselves or for family members.

Masonic Aged Care organisations exist around Australia. Readers seeking more information on aged care provided by organisations under the umbrella of Freemasonry, will find it at the following websites:

NSW & ACT:	www.royalfreemasons.com.au
	www.thewhiddongroup.com.au
VICTORIA:	www.freemasons.net.au
SOUTH AUSTRALIA:	www.masonichomes.com.au
QUEENSLAND:	www.masoniccareqld.org.au
WESTERN AUSTRALIA:	www.freemasonswa.com.au
TASMANIA:	www.fmhtas.com.au
	www.masonichome.com.au

The Orphans Society

The NSW Freemasons' Orphans Society assists orphans from infancy until they are able to care for themselves. Many children have benefited from the care they received and some have grown up into brilliant careers. Like other Masonic charities and activities, the Society has provided assistance for decades and has been reluctant to trumpet its achievements.

The Masonic Youth Welfare Fund

The Masonic Youth Welfare Fund was established in 1923 to help children whose fathers were killed in World War I. Since that time, many thousands of young Australians of primary, secondary and tertiary education age have been helped to achieve a start in life, regardless of race, colour or creed, through The Masonic Youth Welfare Fund's Compass Youth Education program.

Children from drought-affected country towns, for example, and disadvantaged young people living in metropolitan areas receive financial assistance which provides for school clothing and uniforms, stationery, textbooks, tuition fees, accommodation and computers as well as assistance with dental and optical expenses. They also receive advice, guidance and practical help and reassurance so their future can be as bright as that of other children.

The program has helped young people like 15-year-old

Simon, a bright young Sydney boy, who has been raised by his grandmother since his mother died when he was six.

Due to her limited superannuation savings, his grandmother needed help to provide adequately for Simon's education needs. With financial and moral support from the Compass Youth Education program – and a computer to assist with school assignments and projects – Simon has achieved outstanding academic results, won the highest award for his Grade 8 piano studies and excelled in his sporting endeavours. He is a well respected student and schoolmate at his local high school.

Simon's grandmother wrote: 'We thank you most sincerely and to all who work so hard to help the Simons of this world ...'

Mr and Mrs D have been 'doing it tough' for years, battling through floods then extensive and continuing drought on their country property.

Financial pressures meant they were placed in the position of having to take their two daughters out of boarding school in their vital schooling years ... and possibly even having to consider schooling from home. Through a friend, Mr D heard about the Masonic Youth Welfare Fund and its Compass Youth Education program. The program came to the rescue, helping with tuition fees, board and uniforms.

As a result, the girls have been able to stay at their school and go on to achieve great results. The older daughter won a highly respected award for her academic achievements.

Similar funds are operated by Freemasonry to help young people in most other Australian states.

There are Masonic funds to support a wide range of community charities and relief funds for emergencies such as natural disasters. Again these Masonic organisations exist around the country.

Not he who has much is rich ... but he who gives much.
                                                    Erich Fromm

If you haven't any charity in your heart, you have the worst kind of heart trouble.   Anonymous

The Grand Charity

Established in 1999, The Grand Charity was created by the United Grand Lodge of NSW as its official charitable arm. While there are other Masonic charities (detailed above) the Grand Charity is the only one which operates directly under the jurisdiction of Grand Lodge.

Its mission is to promote and uphold the Masonic principle of charity and heighten public awareness of Freemasonry's commitment to the community. It aims to:

- deliver a range of charitable activities designed to improve the lives of those needing help in our community,
- enrich an individual's experience in Freemasonry and
- publicly demonstrate 'Freemasons In Action'.

In 2001 the Grand Charity decided to adopt a new name and logo to reinvigorate its work. To find the new name, a competition was conducted and some 1400 Masons suggested what the new name might be.

The winning name, masoniCare, says exactly what a Freemason feels towards helping others who are less fortunate. By the time this book was published, masoniCare had already distributed $4m to a range of charities that support sick people, education, youth and families at risk. Its work has changed the lives of thousands of people. masoniCare aims to increase the amount of its invested funds significantly and also to grow its disaster relief fund.

An example of the assistance which masoniCare has provided to worthwhile community organisations is the support given to the Royal Flying Doctor Service. Established in 1928, the RFDS was developed on a national basis in the 1930s. It is a story of health care brought to the people who live, travel and work in the remote areas of Australia. Beginning with emergency services, the RFDS was soon providing wider ranging health care and community services. The late Sir Robert Menzies, former Prime Minister and a Freemason, credited the Flying Doctor Service with having made 'the greatest single contribution to the effective settlement of the far distant back country that we have witnessed in our time'.

The RFDS was the first comprehensive aerial medical organisation in the world and remains unique for the range of primary health care and emergency services it provides. It also prides itself on the huge area of sparse population and climatic extremes over which it operates every hour of every day of the year.

Another charity that receives assistance from masoniCare is a medical research facility in the area of cochlear implants to help people of all ages who suffer from hearing impairment. The Sydney Cochlear Implant Centre (SCIC) at Royal Prince Alfred Hospital provides services to adults and children covering a range of ages, from three months to a woman who is over 90. Professor Bill Gibson from the centre said 'This lady was a volunteer with Meals on Wheels and had had her licence to drive revoked because of deafness. She said she had to get her licence back so that she could deliver meals to the "old people"!'

With the knowledge gained from over 2,000 recipients and the combining of resources and expertise, the SCIC is one of the largest and most experienced cochlear implant programs in the world.

Masonic Schools and Hospitals

From the late 19th century and until quite recent times, Freemasonry conducted Masonic Schools and Masonic Hospitals to augment what was available to Australian people in need. These institutions provided a wonderful service at a time when government agencies had not yet fulfilled these community requirements.

From the ceremony of the First Degree of Freemasonry:

> ... exercise that virtue which may justly be denominated the distinguishing characteristic of a Freemason's heart ... I mean charity. I feel assured I need not here dilate upon its excellence, doubtless it has often been felt and practised by you. Suffice it to say it has the approbation of Heaven and Earth and like its sister Mercy, blesses him that gives as largely as him that receives.

THE NEXT GENERATION

A group of young Masons recently started up a Masonic sensation – the SydneyMasons user group – as a means of conversation amongst the Brethren outside of Lodge. A keen member reports on its version of charity ...

We had become well aware that although we were pretty tight as a unit within the Lodge room, no-one really got together outside of Lodge unless they accidentally bumped into each other at another meeting. This [user group] really tickled my fancy. I liked the idea of conversing with intelligent people throughout my busy day. The subjects on the forum began to flourish. There were jokes, stacks of banter, pub invites, Lodge news and so much more posted. I met so many guys over the net that I hadn't yet seen around Lodge.

As a result of this forum, we were able to organise three events which, in my mind, were very successful.

1. Movember 2008 – Team Name – Free'Mo'Sons

Our team of nine brethren grew their shocking Mo's and raised $5050 to assist Beyond Blue and the Prostate Cancer Foundation of Australia. This was a great team effort. Some Brothers auctioned off Masonic books, others went to their friends, some promised to never grow it again (for 11 months!)

2. The Relay for Life 2009

This event was organized by The Cancer Council. Our team, NSW Freemasons, raised $6350 with a team of 17 brethren. A big thumbs-up to a Brother who sold 'million dollar notes' for $5, with the catch phrase to all his mates 'Give it to your partner and say they look like a million bucks!'

The event is a 24 hour walkathon. Some Brothers stayed in Sydney Centennial Park through the night where temperatures dipped to 5 degrees Celsius. We all agreed that the 24 hours we went through is nothing compared to those who battle this terrible disease.

We were recognised with an award at the closing ceremony called the Best Caterers award, for our gruelling 18 hours cooking halal sausages at a discount rate, for all to consume. We raised just under $500 with our food.

3. Freemasons Association Charity Ball

This was such an amazing event – something different compared with the other Masonic events I have attended in the past. The main difference was a lack of speeches. More than 350 people attended. With silent and traditional auctions, raffle tickets and lucky door prizes, the event was fun-filled and a complete success.

The entertainment was magnificent. Latin dancers performed a number of pieces engaging with the crowd consistently, getting the hearts of every male and dare I say it, most females pumping with their wonderful costumes and insane dancing styles.

This worked a treat for the piano playing musical DJ who could sing in six languages. The dance floor was awash with people of all ages, nationalities and religions, sharing the fraternal affection that Freemasonry provides.

The night was capped off with the news that over $40,000 was raised for the Freemasons Disaster Relief Fund which would be used to assist those in need.

A PERSPECTIVE OF MY LIFE AS A MASON

by Major Douglas N James, RFD (Retd)

My introduction into Freemasonry started at my birth. Both grandfathers (NSW policemen) were Masons, as was my father. My maternal grandmother and mother were part of a Lodge women's auxiliary that supported the Lodge but was also instrumental in raising funds to support the charitable work of a Masonic charity, the Freemasons Benevolent Institution as it was then known.

This connection by no means ensured that I would become a Mason. A principle is that you have to ask to be a Mason. It was a demonstration of your desire to become a Mason and to be part of its ethos. Even though there was this family connection and my uncles (all four) were Masons, there was no family pressure to suggest that I should ask to join Freemasonry.

In growing up with this background I could observe the activities that surrounded Freemasonry. Apart from the Lodge meetings, of which I could not be part, there were balls, Christmas parties, barbecues, and social occasions at the homes of members of the Lodge. All fun times.

So I could see that Masonry was not all about going to Lodge in an evening to practise the ceremonial that is part of Freemasonry. There was a very wide circle of men who had similar ideals and practised charitable work for the needy, with which I could meet and socialise. Hence my decision to join Masonry at the allowable age of 18 years because of my Father being a Mason.

I can say that at that time and at present Masons did not perceive the need to trumpet the work for charity. However as the need for charity is increasing there is a perception that we should be more open in our good work.

In the mid 70s I was honoured and surprised to be selected as the Aide-de-Camp (ADC) to the Governor of New South Wales, His Excellency Sir Roden Cutler, VC, AC, KCMG, KCVO, CBE. I remained on his personal staff for four years even though the permanent ADC was usually appointed for one year.

It has dawned on me that the selection process would not be generally known. It consisted of a long interview process from Commanding Officer, Military Secretary, Divisional Commander

(Major-General rank), Military District Commander, being short listed to five, Official Secretary to the Governor and lastly the Governor himself. All these steps were intended to assess your character and suitability, all done on a need-to-know basis. I could not even tell my family. In fact I was totally unaware of the names of the other candidates, and to this day do not know all of the names.

I heard of my acceptance when I was told by my divisional head to report to the President. Access to his floor, let alone his office was limited to divisional heads and some personal staff. As I had maintained secrecy and had not told my employer of the events leading up to the interview with the Governor, I was having some very dark thoughts regarding my fate.

On entering the office the President stood, came around his desk saying 'Congratulations. I have just received a phone call from the Governor asking me to release you to take up the position of his ADC'.

Well that took me to a whole new lifestyle which I have been honoured to do. Naturally I could not ask the Governor 'Why me?' but over those years through the little personal chats on the way or coming back from functions, or while enjoying a cigar and cognac on the colonnade overlooking Sydney Harbour (yes there were some perks), I gleaned some of the answers.

His Excellency was aware of the nature of Freemasonry, having been improperly approached to join. He understood the principles and held those in high regard. He could see these in my character and my ethical approach to making the best of the responsibilities of the office. Perhaps these factors gave me an edge over the other applicants.

From the Masonic principles such as perseverance, fortitude, and fidelity I was able to apply myself to the requirements of the position which involved contact with persons from all walks of life – from royalty to citizens of the state.

On the first day at Government House fortitude was required. His Excellency has an Afghan hound named Khyber. He and the Alaskan husky would spend the day in the day sitting room. Khyber was a timid dog but had the bad habit of bouncing out behind a person walking past the door and barking.

Not long after His Excellency commenced his appointment, the Rector of St James Church King Street called on him. Khyber not only did his trick but bit the priest on the buttock. As all of the male personal staff had suffered a scare from Khyber it was decided to form an Order of Chivalry to be known as the Survivors of the Afghan War (not very PC these days). We adopted a tie with a Griffin motif (the Griffin was part of His Excellency's coat of arms) and a monocle. His Excellency's private secretary affected a monocle. When the personal staff had a private function we would all sit around wearing our ties and monocles. The Order was not discussed openly, but His Excellency eventually found out.

The personal staff gave an 80th birthday dinner for His Excellency and when we had been seated for drinks he produced his own monocle, saying he had a right to be a member of the Order. A wonderful touch.

Masonry teaches perseverance and that goes with an eye to detail. Also military training hones a detailed mind. This served me well at Government House in preparing briefs for His Excellency's attendance at functions. He had very high standards in this regard as every function was treated as if it was the only occasion of his attendance. The reasoning was that the host and those attending the function should feel important and happy that they had Vice Regal patronage for their function. Hence every single move would be planned and documented to ensure that all was well and smoothly executed. I have to say that I also received the pleasure that the planning and briefing meant a happy event. It was pleasing to see smiling and happy faces as you were leaving.

I mentioned at the beginning my family involvement in Freemasonry and in particular the charitable aspect. Both my grandfather and father were directors of the Freemasons Benevolent Institution, now the RFBI. I have been lucky to follow in their footsteps, now being the third generation on the Board of the RFBI. My understanding and perhaps teaching gained from them about charity prepared me well for this role.

So is Freemasonry a value in life? I believe that my story fully bears out this fact.

James Gordon
(1907–1986)

Born in Western Australia, James Hannah (Heather) Gordon was the son of William Beattie Gordon, a member of the Legislative Assembly, and the nephew of politician and judge, Sir John Hannah Gordon. By the time World War II began, Gordon was working on the goldfields, having previously tried his hand at droving, roustabouting and farming.

In 1940 he enlisted in the Australian Imperial Force, understating his age, and substituting Heather for his middle name of Hannah. He embarked for the Middle East, joining the 2/31st Battalion in early 1941. Later that year the unit was fighting in the Syrian campaign against the Vichy French.

On the night of July 9-10 Gordon's company, which had been ordered to seize high ground overlooking the villages of Amatour and Badarane, was being held up by an enemy machine-gun post. On his own initiative, Private Gordon crept forward through a hail of bullets and grenades and charged the machine-gun post, killing four crew and taking the rest prisoner. His courage inspired his comrades to attack. It also earned him the Victoria Cross.

James Gordon arrived back in Australia in 1942 with his unit and recovered from a bout of malaria prior to rejoining the 2/31st in Papua where they were fighting the Japanese around Gona. In 1943, now a sergeant, he led a charge against a machine-gun nest in the advance towards Lae, New Guinea, although no award followed this action. 'Just as well, too,' he said later. 'Imagine what my cobbers would have called me then.'

He returned to Australia in 1944 where he spent more time in hospital with malaria before being discharged in 1947. That same year he took up a brief civilian job before returning to army life. Gordon retired from the army in 1968 and became a groundsman at Campbell Barracks, Swanbourne, until 1975. Sir William Dargie's 1941 portrait of Gordon won the 1942 Archibald prize and is now held by the Australian War Memorial in Canberra.

James Gordon was initiated into Freemasonry at Lodge United Service No. 307 WA on April 2, 1956.

James Gorman
(1834–1882)

The Victoria Cross was created to recognise valour at the close of the Crimean War, and Seaman James Gorman was one of the original recipients. Born in England, he emigrated to Australia after the war and lived here for the remainder of his life.

At the age of 19, Gorman volunteered for the Royal Naval Brigade and sailed on HMS *Albion*. He was recognised for deeds of conspicuous bravery at the battles of Balaclava and Inkerman. He saved the life of Captain Lushington (later Admiral Sir Stephen Lushington) after the captain had fallen from his horse and was surrounded by the enemy.

In 1854 Gorman's Naval Brigade took part in a soldiers' battle in dense fog and light rain. The 8,000 British troops fought hand-to-hand against nearly 50,000 Russians until 6,000 French soldiers reinforced the British and helped to defeat the enemy. Gorman risked his life to protect wounded soldiers and sailors at the Lankester Battery. With four comrades, he defied an order to retire and stood at the battery until reinforcements arrived and the strategic position was saved. It was for this that James Gorman received the Victoria Cross.

The decoration brought with it an annual gratuity of £10.

When he arrived in Australia, James Gorman served for 15 years as an officer on the training ship *Vernon*. Later he was appointed to take charge of the gunpowder magazine on Spectacle Island in the Parramatta River. He died on the island in 1882 and was buried with military honours at Balmain. A large number of Grand Lodge Officers attended at the graveside.

James Gorman was initiated into Freemasonry in The Leinster Marine Lodge of Australia in 1878.

John Gorton
(1911–2002)

Friendly and relaxed, with a larrikin streak, John Grey Gorton had some very famous schoolmates: film star Errol Flynn at Sydney's Shore and painter Russell Drysdale at Melbourne's Geelong Grammar. Gorton went on to Oxford University and in World War II enlisted in the Royal Australian Air Force.

Posted to Singapore, Gorton was forced to crash-land his Hurricane in Sumatra on January 21, 1942, when his face was seriously injured. Eventually rescued, he left Singapore on an ammunition ship that was torpedoed by a Japanese submarine. He spent 24 hours on a crowded life raft before HMAS *Ballarat* rescued the survivors.

When he had recovered, Gorton joined No. 77 Squadron and was posted to Darwin. Here a mistake nearly cost him his life but he executed an 'extremely successful' crash-landing on a beach after inadvertently cutting the fuel supply. In February the squadron was sent to Milne Bay in New Guinea to assist with mopping-up operations as US forces pushed the Japanese from the islands they had occupied for a year. There Gorton had a third flying accident – he miraculously escaped when his Kittyhawk stalled and flipped over at take-off. Even plastic surgery could not fully repair his facial injuries.

In 1949 he was elected to the Senate. He entered the Menzies ministry in 1958 as Minister for the Navy, a position he held until 1963. Other ministries followed in the governments of Menzies and Harold Holt. When Holt disappeared while swimming in December 1967 Gorton, being a Senator, did not appear a likely candidate for Prime Minister. However Country Party leader, John McEwen, refused to work with the most likely contender, Billy McMahon. Gorton was elected, making him the only PM sworn in while still a member of the Senate.

When Gorton and William McMahon drew even in a party room ballot in 1971, Gorton used his casting vote to vote himself out of office and McMahon replaced him as Prime Minister.

He became a Knight Grand Cross of the Order of St Michael and St George in 1977.

John Gorton was initiated into Freemasonry at Kerrange Lodge No. 100 Victorian Constitution on February 5, 1948.

John Gowing
(1835–1908)

The famous advertising slogan 'Gone to Gowings' has become synonymous with the history of the retail industry in Australia. Established in 1868, Gowings still holds the record as Sydney's longest running family-owned retail store – and in these days of constant change the company's 138 years of operation are unlikely to be topped.

John Ellis Gowing arrived in Australia on Christmas morning 1857 as an enthusiastic 22-year-old. After struggling as a farmer in England, he came to Australia with £400 – a lot of money in those days – and stepped ashore at Sydney Cove with the hope of making his fortune in the goldfields.

Sadly that was not a success so he took a job in a waterfront warehouse. Next, he joined the live-in staff at the already well-known David Jones store, where he soon became manager of the Mercery Department.

In 1863 he set up his own drapery business in Crown Street, Sydney. It quickly became one of Australia's leading department stores for men, retailing casual clothing, camping gear, and knick-knacks until it closed its doors in 2006.

Five years later he went into partnership with his brother, Preston Robert Gowing, renamed the business Gowing Bros and moved to a new site at 344 George Street. A second store opened soon afterwards at 498 George Street and Gowings became a household name.

During the 1890s Depression, Gowing Bros became known as a great supporter of local manufacturers and appealed to rising nationalist sentiments with one of their early slogans: 'Australian wool for Australian people'.

Preston died in 1900 and John died in 1908 but the business remained in the family. The famous slogan 'Gone to Gowings' was developed by John's grandson, Ted Gowing. It was so well known that when the notorious criminal, Darcy Dugan, escaped from custody he graffitied the prison wall with 'Gone to Gowings'. In response, the Gowings staff were told 'if you see Darcy Dugan, give him a suit'.

John Ellis Gowing was initiated into Freemasonry on March 4, 1867.

Lord Gowrie
(1872–1955)

Sir Alexander Gore Arkwright Hore-Ruthven, First Earl of Gowrie, is Freemasonry's honorary Australian hero. Born at Windsor, England, he was the second son of the 8th Baron Ruthven and his wife, Lady Caroline Annesley. Lord Gowrie's Scottish family referred to him as 'Sandie'.

A Victoria Cross winner while in the British militia, he was later Australia's longest serving Governor-General.

In 1898, as a Captain at Gedarif, he saw an Egyptian officer lying wounded some distance away in front of the charging enemy, the Dervishes. He raced forward, picked up the man and carried him towards the 16th Egyptian Battalion – a daring rescue made more hazardous by having to put down the officer several times to fire at the enemy and check their advance. He saved the officer's life and received the first Victoria Cross ever awarded to a militia officer.

In 1899 he was mentioned in dispatches three times. In 1908 he married Zara Eileen Pollok, against her family's wishes. Hore-Ruthven later wrote that his wife's family considered him *'the impecunious son of an impoverished family, with indifferent prospects'*.

In 1908 he served as military secretary to Lord Dudley, the newly appointed Australian Governor-General. When war was declared in 1914 he became Arabic interpreter to the Meerut Division in France, later serving in the Welsh Guards at Gallipoli where he was severely wounded.

In 1918 he was appointed Brigadier-General, 7th Army Corps. Shortly afterwards, he was mentioned in five despatches and awarded the DSO with Bar.

Retiring from the army in 1928, Lord Gowrie became Governor of South Australia and was appointed a KCMG. In 1935 he became Governor of New South Wales, was created Baron Gowrie of Canberra and Dirleton and received a GCMG. The following year he became Governor-General of Australia, remaining through six years of WWII.

A portrait of Lord Gowrie by Charles Wheeler hangs in Parliament House, Canberra.

Lord Gowrie was initiated into Freemasonry at Lodge St Andrews Military No. 668 on March 15, 1893.

CHAPTER SIX

Masons at war

Freemasonry provides a blueprint for responsible, ethical behaviour, for harmony and peaceful coexistence with all of humanity. It is also about loyalty and service, courage and fortitude. In this chapter we salute the courage of Freemasons who have served in times of war.

The fellowship that exists between Freemasons from all religious groups and from all walks of life, is deeply anchored in personal trust and personal accountability. Trust, service and accountability form part of the way Masons approach their everyday life. And while these qualities are highly sought in times of peace, they are tested to the limits in times of war; essential to the survival of the individual and the enterprise itself. And in battle, when trust in each other and integrity in action are still not enough, there are the few, the very few, who offer themselves to turn the tide, to help a mate, to make a difference.

Indeed, the concept of mateship – like trust – was forged in the furnace of war long before we began to celebrate the watered-down civilian equivalent on summer afternoons around the BBQ. In war, mateship is everything, and those who go far 'above and beyond' the call of duty may be recognised for something wonderful, and rare, and sad and often heartbreaking: For Valour.

The Victoria Cross is the highest award for acts of bravery

111

in wartime. Conceived by Prince Albert, Queen Victoria's consort, as a way to recognise the conspicuous bravery of British troops in the Crimean War, the medal was first presented by Queen Victoria to 62 sailors and soldiers from that conflict.

Now, as then, every Victoria Cross is hand made from the gunmetal of artillery pieces captured in the Crimean War. Suspended from a plain red ribbon, the medal itself takes the form of a Maltese Cross adorned by a crown surmounted by a crowned lion, the emblem of the British royal family, with a scroll bearing the inscription, *'For Valour'*. The date of the action is inscribed on the reverse, and the name and regiment of the holder are inscribed on the back of the suspension bar.

Ninety-eight Australians have been awarded the Victoria Cross for actions in the Boer War (6), Crimean War (1), World War I (65), the Russian campaign (2), World War II (20), the Vietnam War (4) and Afghanistan (1).

Australia's most recent VC hero – and the first to receive the award in 40 years – was Special Air Service soldier Mark Donaldson, 29, from Newcastle, New South Wales.

Governor-General Quentin Bryce presented the award to Donaldson for his rescue of a wounded Afghani interpreter who was under heavy fire, in September 2008. Donaldson ran 80 metres across exposed ground to attend to the interpreter, carrying him to a vehicle and performing first aid before returning to the conflict.

Australia's first-ever VC winner, James Gorman, was one of the original recipients of the award and one of 16 who were, or became Freemasons.

The Craft has always been a powerful influence on our servicemen, especially when they are at war. Lodges were held on board ships, in army huts and in tents while the men were between battles. Masonic Lodges were held in Changi Prison Camp – at great risk to participants – and in other military and prisoner of war camps. The sharing of difficult conditions and the ever present dangers of war no doubt added to the feeling of brotherhood in these makeshift Lodges.

After World War II, membership numbers in Australian Freemasonry reached their peak.

Throughout this book we have detailed the brave actions of our Masonic VC winners – yet, of all Australia's war heroes, none is remembered more proudly or more fondly than surgeon, soldier and prisoner of war, Sir Edward 'Weary' Dunlop – who was never awarded a VC. Surely no man has ever fulfilled more superbly the Masonic ritual's encouragement to 'live respected and die regretted'.

More than 10,000 people lined the streets of Melbourne to pay their respects at Weary Dunlop's funeral in July 1993. Many hundreds more crammed into St Paul's Cathedral, including the Prime Minister, Leader of the Opposition, former Governors-General and foreign dignitaries. But pride of place was reserved for Weary's 'old lags' – the former prisoners of war he had so diligently protected and cared for during World War II.

Chief among these was former British Army transport driver, Bill Griffiths, who flew in from England with his wife, Alice. Bill Griffiths lost his eyesight and both hands when he was forced by his Japanese captors to defuse a booby trap in Java, 51 years earlier. Weary's medical care saved him but the Japanese now saw Griffiths as a liability, unable to work. Moving between Griffiths and the bayonets of his captors, Weary said: 'You will need to put those bayonets through me first.' Such was the nature of the man.

In his eulogy at Weary's funeral, the former Governor-General and High Court Justice, Sir Ninian Stephen, said:

> Weary … attained a lone Australian eminence, perhaps shared only by Douglas Mawson, of sustained heroism and superb achievement; … he was a hero when Australia had a dearth of heroes and a saint who would have been surprised to have heard himself described as one.

The nickname 'Weary' was given Dunlop by his university student friends and was a play on words around Dunlop Tyres. Weary demonstrated through a career of unflagging enthusiasm and devotion that the nickname was undeserved.

Although not a VC winner, Weary Dunlop received numerous honours and awards during his life in recognition of his civic, sporting, educational, military and medical achievements. These included the Order of the British Empire (1947), Knight Bachelor (1969), Companion of the Order of Australia (1987), Knight Grand Cross, Order of St John of Jerusalem (1992), and Knight Grand Cross (1st Class) of the most Noble Order of the Royal Crown of Thailand (1993).

He was an Honorary Fellow of the Imperial College of London, an Honorary Fellow of the Royal College of Surgeons of Edinburgh, Honorary Life Member of the RSL and Life Governor of the Royal Women's Hospital and the Royal Victorian Eye and Ear Hospital. In 1977 he was named Australian of the Year and in 1988 one of 200 Great Australians.

Former prisoner of war, Don Stuart, made it clear that heroes are those who, by example, teach us how to live: 'When despair and death reached us, Weary Dunlop stood fast ... he was a lighthouse of sanity in a universe of madness and suffering.'

Freemasonry is extremely proud to be able to claim Sir Edward 'Weary' Dunlop as one of the finest of Australians, and one of the finest of its own.

Young Edward showed unusual stoicism from an early age on his family's farm in Victoria. His own self-invented hero was an American Indian brave he called 'Deerfoot', who endured pain, hunger and thirst without complaint. Emulating this imaginary friend, young Edward chose to walk barefoot over burning summer sands and frosty winter ground.

Edward's imagination and sense of service to his country were further fired by listening to his grandfather's military exploits while in India, and those of four family members who had served in World War I.

Since his mother, Alice, was a former governess, Edward and his older brother, Alan, were educated at home before they were old enough to ride their ponies to the district's single teacher school. As the second son, Edward was only expected to finish primary school before leaving to join his father on the family farm. However his teacher, Vera Hilliear, believed he had the ability to excel with further schooling and rode her bicycle over to the Dunlop house to persuade his parents to send him on to Benalla High School.

Edward breezed through his secondary studies, finishing high school a year early. He then began an apprenticeship with a Benalla chemist while studying pharmacy by correspondence. In 1927 he travelled to Melbourne where he graduated top of his pharmacy course, receiving the first H.T. Tompsitt Scholarship, the Gold Medal of the Pharmaceutical Society, the Silver Medal for Botany and Certificates of Honour in Chemistry and Materia Medica.

He went on to study medicine at the University of Melbourne, where he excelled both in his studies and at sport. Having grown to six feet four inches tall, he was selected to play in Australia's Rugby Union team, the Wallabies.

As a former school military cadet, he continued his part-time army service until 1929 when his studies took precedence. However he re-enlisted in 1935 and was commissioned a captain in the Australian Army Medical Corps.

In 1934 Dunlop received his medical degree, followed in 1937 by his Master of Surgery degree. In 1938 Weary Dunlop gained his passage to London as a ship's medical officer. There, he attended St Bartholomew's Medical School, later becoming a Fellow of the Royal College of Surgeons.

In 1939, Weary enlisted in the 6th Division Australian Army Medical Corps and was posted to Jerusalem. Promoted to major in May 1940, he was moved to a position covering Gaza and Alexandria, and by 1941 had served in Greece and Crete. Weary and the Casualty Clearing Station in which he served were transferred to Java, landing there only three weeks before the Dutch capitulation to the Japanese invaders. In that time, Weary and his crew turned a school into No. 1 Allied General Hospital, treating 1300 sick and wounded. When Java fell, Weary and his hospital patients became prisoners of war.

Although Weary might have escaped, he never considered leaving his patients. After the hospital was broken up by the Japanese he took command of the Bandung prison camp over higher ranking officers. Later, the Australian POWs on Java under Weary's command were transferred to Singapore.

Early in 1943 some, including Weary, were railed in crowded rice trucks to Thailand to work on the Burma-Thailand railway. More than 400 kilometres long, it became known as the 'Railway of Death' by the prisoners who built it. Weary, in his dual role of Commanding Officer and surgeon, had responsibility for over 1,000 men known as the 'Dunlop Force' or 'Dunlop's Thousand'.

Working to Tokyo time meant rising at 3 a.m. for a breakfast of one mug of rice and another of watery tea. Rice was the staple diet for lunch and dinner too, with an occasional egg added. Working from early morning to well into the night, the men were exhausted and slowly starving.

Many survived this nightmare only to succumb later to their injuries or tropical diseases. Yet the death toll would have been much higher if Weary and his dedicated team of medical officers had not fought on with outstanding courage and self-sacrifice in appalling conditions.

Often battling malaria, amoebic dysentery and tropical ulcers, Weary and his team used amazing ingenuity to overcome the lack of medicines and equipment. One group distilled surgical alcohol in old condensed milk tins using waste rice and a yeast found in the jungle. Dehydrated cholera patients had drips made from Japanese beer bottles, stethoscope tubes and blunted syringe needles. Prisoners also made needles and artificial limbs from bamboo. Such improvisation often meant the difference between survival and death.

Using his position as a doctor and Commanding Officer to protect his men, Weary endured many punishments on their behalf. Perhaps the hardest part of his impossible job was to decide which of his POWs were unfit to work. Such decisions were always made in favour of his men, often causing him to be in sharp disagreement with his captors.

On one occasion, as punishment for speaking out, he was made to kneel on gravel and hold up heavy stones for many hours while a bamboo shaft was placed behind his knees.

The depth of respect his men had for him is summarised in this statement from one of his 'old lags':

... thousands of us starved, scourged, racked with malaria, dysentery, beri beri, pellagra and the stinking tropical ulcers that ate a leg to the bone in a matter of days, and always Weary Dunlop and his fellow [medical officers] stood up for us, were beaten, scorned, derided, and beaten again.

His extraordinary qualities were so admired – even by many of his captors – that on his 38th birthday in 1945 he received 'extraordinary gestures of affection from all sides, an example of the impact he had on those around him'.

Following the end of World War II and liberation, Weary was appointed a lieutenant colonel. Returning to Australia in October 1945, he was demobilised early the next year, transferring to the reserve list of officers with the rank of honorary colonel. Three weeks after returning to Melbourne, Weary married his university sweetheart, Helen Ferguson, to whom he had been engaged since 1940.

While establishing a thriving private medical practice, Weary was also appointed to a number of honorary surgeon roles at Royal Melbourne Hospital. In 1948 he was made a Fellow of the Royal Australasian College of Surgeons. He also joined the staff of the Royal Victoria Eye and Ear Hospital and in 1956 was appointed Consultant Surgeon to the Peter MacCallum Clinic.

Over many years he was actively involved with Australian and international professional bodies, including the International Society of Surgeons. He served as Chairman of the Executive Committee of the Anti-Cancer Council of Victoria from 1974 to 1980 and as President of the Victorian Foundation on Alcoholism and Drug Dependence from 1970 to 1982.

Weary's friendship with Lord Casey also led to his involvement in the Colombo Plan. Weary taught and undertook surgical work in Thailand, Ceylon (now Sri Lanka) and India, encouraging and promoting Asian medical personnel to train in Australia. In 1969 he was also leader of the Australian Surgical Team to South Vietnam. His commitment to India was rewarded in 1972, when he became an Honorary Fellow of the Indian Association of Surgeons.

Throughout his career Weary continued to treat former POWs, maintaining his deep concern for their health and welfare and supporting men making pension claims. As Chairman of the Prisoners of War Trust Fund he stayed in touch with POWs and veterans' associations.

Shortly before his 86th birthday, Weary Dunlop died from pneumonia. Many of his papers are held within the Private Records collection at the Australian War Memorial's Research Centre, where they occupy 25 shelf metres of space. Among these are a number of folders relating specifically to his strong involvement with Freemasonry. While the information in these papers does not reveal whether or not Masonic meetings were held at the prisoner of war camps in Thailand, we know that Freemasonry was alive and well in Changi Prison Camp in Singapore.

Although he could have been a Masonic role model, Edward Dunlop didn't become a Mason until after the war. According to the website of the United Grand Lodge of NSW and ACT, he was initiated into Lodge Liberation No 674 Vic. Const. on 23rd April, 1954. This Lodge which was consecrated in 1949, was 'conceived in the minds of a number of brethren who had met together in Changi POW Camp.'

A booklet written by two of the prisoners who were Freemasons, entitled *Masonry in Changi POW Camp*, details how these wartime Lodges were held. Here are some extracts.

[The Japanese forces] drove us down the mainland of Malaya, across the causeway onto the island of Singapore and, after a very fierce, bloody battle which lasted for just seven days, the allied forces capitulated [and] we found ourselves prisoners of war.

The invading general – Yamashita – found himself embarrassed by upwards of 50,000 POWs and he was at a loss what to do with them. Our own commanders suggested that the white troops go out to Changi on the eastern tip of the island, about 16 miles from Singapore City.

Here were the quarters of the section of the British Army which was on tour of duty at the time. The barracks were quite large and sound – there was very little damage during the fighting. The sick and wounded were transported in ambulances and trucks; the rest of us walked.

The first thing we had to do after settling into our billets was to wire ourselves in. It was a huge area and the job took several weeks. Strangely enough, it was not until the wiring was finished, the gates on and the Japs had mounted their guards that the full impact of the loss of liberty struck the men. And it struck very hard indeed. A period of depression set in which lasted for weeks.

We lived as far as possible in our own units, in our own buildings and went out to work as occasion demanded by the Japs. The work was hard and the hours long. The boys went out at daybreak and came home at dusk. After the evening meal there was nothing to do in those early days but sit around and think and talk of home. It is easy to realise how this period of depression set in. But they were young and, at the time, healthy, and they soon began to adjust.

This ability to adjust was, in my opinion, due to several factors. [The members of the 8th Division band] got together again and organised some impromptu concerts. They had nothing to help them but their own enthusiasm, no props, no stage and very few musical instruments, but they stuck to it like heroes.

A few chaps who had been in World War I [also] banded together. In addition to doing whatever they could for their sick and wounded mates, they related the experiences of their various postings to the troops. It was not uncommon to see groups of up to sixty men sitting around on the grass in the dark listening to these chaps talking. They did a very fine job in lifting morale.

The Masons were not to be denied either. As early as April in our first year, regular meetings began to be held. The first of these were in the clock tower beside the Barrack Square. They were held on Sunday afternoons. Our average attendance was 28.

We soon found there were several other [Masonic] meetings going on. I belonged to another group meeting in a bombed out house. There were about eight or nine of us and one of them had brought to light J. Fort Newton's [Masonic] book, The Builders. This was a precious treasure and had to be jealously guarded.

Down in the hospital area, a place called Roberts Barracks on the eastern end of the camp, both the Australian and British hospital units had amalgamated. They were rich in Freemasons – and very keen – and held their meetings in the store room. They had the doubtful pleasure, with empty bellies, of sitting on cases of Marmite and bully beef – yet there was no record of anything being stolen. Our meetings went on until December in our first year [when] one of the chaps [reminded] us that the Japs had put a veto on meetings of Masons. Any prisoners found attending meetings of Masons would be severely punished.

It was decided it would not be fair to proceed with further meetings without the consent of the Group Commander, so a deputation of two was appointed to wait on Colonel Collins. They did this with a certain amount of trepidation [but the] Colonel said he was only too pleased to give his permission for the meetings to be held. He was proud, he said, to have men of integrity under his command – men in whom he could trust. He went a little further saying that should, by any chance, the meetings be discovered, he would do everything in his power to provide some sort of alibi for them. What a wonderful tribute to Freemasonry!

It was decided that the meetings should be held in the Command church – a lovely little chapel in a grove of trees set apart from the main buildings. There were no Masonic furnishings or implements so we made them. All the buildings [were] equipped with ceiling fans and the blades in our area were made from aluminium. These began to go missing. We knew where some of them went – Norman James pinched them, flattened them out, cut them to shape and etched them with a broken hacksaw blade. You wouldn't mistake what they were – the working tools of the three Degrees. (These can now be seen in the Masonic Museum of the United Grand Lodge of Victoria at 300 Albert Street, East Melbourne.)

Someone set to work and produced a pair of wands from the architraves around the doorways and some bright spark sawed fifteen inches off the hospital broom to serve as a baton. But our most prized possessions were our tracing boards. They were produced by one of our English brethren, evidently an artist. He would never reveal where his inks and colours came from but it was obvious that some of the colours were from the soil of the grounds on which we were imprisoned. They were so lovely that, after the war, they were taken home to the Grand Lodge of England.

'Nit-keepers' were posted at vantage points around the building to give timely warning of approaching danger by throwing rocks on the roof or by word of mouth. It was decided that should this warning come, a change would be made from a Masonic service to a church service [as the Japanese guards] didn't care how many church services we had but Masonry was out.

We had the keenest Freemason I have ever known. He was only a young chap, an Australian, who had been wounded during the fighting and had developed cancer of the spine from a shell splinter. He knew he would never come home and made one last effort to attend with the members of the Lodge. They carried him into the Lodge room strapped to a stretcher [and] stood him up against the wall alongside the Secretary's table. From there he witnessed his last meeting of Masons.

The Great Architect called him home the following week. He was so loved by his brethren that they decided to give him the

121

finest funeral it was possible to have. They scrounged around and obtained timber from all sorts of places and built a coffin. They made a square and compasses of aluminium from a fan blade with his name and number etched on them. He was carried to the AIF section of the cemetery and laid to rest in the presence of 92 Freemasons.

Our own Padre carried out the funeral service [and] also conducted the Masonic Funeral service and led the Masonic Grand Honours which followed, in the presence of at least six Japanese guards. They weren't in the least bit aware that anything Masonic was taking place.

There was nothing to eat. But when the time came for the first anniversary of our regular meetings someone suggested that we have a South (a Masonic supper normally taken after a Lodge meeting). Food was very scarce but it was decided that we'd give it a go. So they began to scrounge rice; they gave it to the brethren in the cookhouses to 'do something with to make it taste as if it isn't rice'. Now you can't do that! No matter what you do with rice, you can't disguise it. But they were helped in their endeavours by some of the richer members of the fraternity.

These chaps went to work in trucks to the railway sidings and wharves and never missed an opportunity for doing a bit of good for themselves. They generally managed to sell their ill-gotten gains to the Chinese or Indians in the district in return for dollars – hundreds of dollars. It was invasion money, of course, and not worth a cracker. You had to work for six weeks to get enough to buy a pound of salt. But they were able to get hold of a native sugar which was very sweet and sticky. They brought this home and handed it to the cooks who banged it in among the rice.

When the meeting night came they turned out a very reasonable feed. Word of the meeting had got around and about twice as many brethren as usual turned up, but it turned out there was plenty for all.

In order to make the occasion more Masonic, they decided to have coffee. We made our own: you get a pound or two of rice, put it on a sheet of iron, light a fire under it and reduce it to charcoal. Pour boiling water on it and you have coffee. Not a bad sort of coffee either – providing you haven't tasted the real thing for a long time!

Everyone went home that night feeling very happy that they had been to a fair dinkum Masonic meeting. Unfortunately it was the only South we ever had.

Our numbers had been sadly depleted by working parties going to other parts of the world – 2,000 up to Moulemein in Burma, half British, half Australian; 2,000 to Bangkok in Thailand – they were the poor devils who started the railway line. They were reinforced by two other batches of 2,000; 2,800 went across to Borneo and out of our 1,400 we had only six survivors. Thousands were taken off to Taiwan and to Mukden in China and to Japan itself.

The Japs decided they would close us up into a smaller area. When this was done, their patrols came through the camp much more often and their temper – which was never any good – began to get worse. It seemed they were taking out on us the defeats they were suffering in the south Pacific.

It was decided no further meetings of Masons should be held.

We hadn't been in this smaller area very long when they moved us again into the new Changi Jail which had been finished only about six months before the war. Built to hold 480-odd prisoners [it] was soon holding well over 5,000. The men spread from the cells to the catwalks, from the catwalks to the corridors and from the corridors to the exercise yard where conditions were appalling. Those who were billeted out there suffered all the privations of the monsoon season. Their only shelter was rotten tents and humpies built to keep off the rain.

When we first went into the jail, our commanders made overtures to the Japanese to allow us to build accommodation for these men outside the wall. We were able to build half a dozen huts, each 100 metres long, outside the wall, providing a bit more comfort than had been available before.

When the exercise yards were empty, the various padres resumed their Sunday evening church services. This included our own Padre Benjamin and we built him a little dais in one corner. There, on Sunday evenings, he would preach to his congregation which consisted mainly of Masons.

But on Sunday nights after the church services ten shadowy figures made their way into [a store room] and, when the last entered, the door was propped closed, the light shrouded and the meetings of Masons were held again.

[Following the POWs' liberation] when the Japs were behind the wire, a wonderful Masonic thanksgiving service was held outside the walls of the jail. Again, our beloved Padre was the speaker. That day he spoke to over 200 Masons drawn from 52 constitutions in all parts of the world. There were even Masons from Japan – Europeans who had belonged to Lodges [there]. I don't think there was a man who left that meeting that day without a deep sense of thanksgiving in his heart to the Great Architect of the Universe for having brought him safely through the ordeal.

It is obvious that many POWs valued their Freemasonry beliefs and principles so deeply that they were prepared to risk serious punishment in order to keep holding regular meetings. During their years in captivity, these meetings helped the POWs battle deprivation, illness, hunger and exhaustion, giving them a strong sense of brotherhood and purpose. Once liberated, the Freemason's philosophy of treating all people as equal regardless of race, religion or social standing also hastened their healing process.

Despite his wartime experiences, Weary Dunlop, like so many other Masons, was able to forgive his Japanese oppressors. He wrote the following account of an incident involving some wounded Japanese sent to Thailand from Burma along the infamous Burma-Thailand Railway – an incident that left him filled with compassion for his former enemies.

I paused before a man whose wretchedness equalled the plight of one of my own men – one leg had been hacked off at the mid-thigh and the bone stump projected through gangrenous flesh; his eyes were sunken pools of pain in a haggard, toxic face. With indomitable spirit he had hopped hundreds of suffering miles. Some bombs fell and [Japanese] soldiers desperately fought for a place on the moving train. I moved to help him when he was trampled under the rush, but his hand was limp and dead, and his tortured face was at peace. The memory dwelt with me as a lingering nightmare and I was deeply conscious of the Buddhist belief that all men are equal in the face of suffering and death.

It seems a travesty of justice that such a noble and compassionate man never received a Victoria Cross. Yet his was not a life marked by one brave deed covering a few minutes, hours or days. His was an endlessly courageous and inspiring life – a life where hero merged with saint and saint effortlessly became hero.

Cecil Albert Gregory (1894–1974)

Before 1930 Sydneysiders used public transport for long journeys and walked or rode bicycles for short trips. Maps were not needed. Following World War I, motor cars became affordable and people needed maps.

Wilson's Authentic Directory, published annually, provided only some suburban maps and street locations. Cecil Albert Gregory recognised an opportunity. In 1934 he produced the first edition of his famous street directory.

Born in Forbes, NSW in 1894, Gregory was educated there and became a journalist. In 1921 he joined the Daily Telegraph and produced its Guide to Sydney including coloured maps.

Gregory married Sylvia Dowling in September 1922. They had two daughters who grew with the business – taking on the task of double-checking street names. Margaret D'Arcy (Gregory's daughter) reminisced in a 1995 Sun Herald article by Rochelle Tubb: 'We lived in Stanmore and I remember the first publication because we sat around the table and put everything in alphabetical order. I was too young to read but I packed all the papers up and tied them in bundles.'

In 1925 Gregory joined the National Roads and Motorists' Association (NRMA) and edited its Open Road magazine from 1927 to 1932. He agreed to a low wage in return for the NRMA's distribution of his guidebooks.

He set up the Australian Guide Book Company in 1933 with cartographer, Clive Barrass. Sydney, now with over 1.3 million people, needed a comprehensive street guide.

In 1934 Gregory's Street Directory of Sydney and Suburbs was produced. Designed for the glove box, it had the edge over Wilson's Authentic Directory by including 300 suburbs and localities, 4,000 streets and the tramlines. Five thousand copies sold at four shillings and sixpence.

By the 1940s Gregory was producing a wide range of guide books. He sold the business in 1961 and died in August 1974. The new owners, Universal Press, continued to publish the guide

A modern Masonic Lodge Room at United Grand Lodge Centre in Sydney.
All Lodge rooms feature pavements with black and white squares, the letter
'G' suspended from the ceiling and other items of Lodge furniture which have
symbolic significance.

These two stone blocks represent the journey undertaken by Freemasons. The Rough Ashlar (at left) represents the mind in its uninformed state while the Perfect Ashlar shows the benefit of education – making Masons useful 'building blocks' in their society.

Every Australian Freemason's journey begins in the 'Blue Lodge'. These are the lambskin aprons with which Freemasons are invested as they complete the First, Second and Third Degrees. The Entered Apprentice wears the plain apron at left. The middle apron is for Fellow Craft Freemasons. Master Masons wear the apron at right.

The long history of Masonic Ceremonies is an example of the durability of Masonic thought and action. Compare the installation (above) of Sir John Northcott, KCMG, CB, MVO – who also served as Governor of New South Wales – as Grand Master of the United Grand Lodge of NSW in the Sydney Town Hall in 1952, with the installation of Noel Frederick Dunn as Grand Master in 1992 (below).

Portrait of the First Grand Master of the United Grand Lodge of NSW, His Excellency, the Rt Hon Baron Carrington, KG, PC, GCMG, Governor of New South Wales and Grand Master from 1888 to 1891. Lord Carrington united the Irish, Scottish and New South Wales Grand Lodges to create the United Grand Lodge of NSW.

Portrait of Grand Master William Thompson (1914 to 1924) founder of the
William Thompson Masonic School, which for many years provided an
education to orphan children of Freemasons. This portrait, one of the finest
in the Museum of Freemasonry's collection, was painted by George F. Harris,
father of Australian entertainer and painter, Rolf Harris CBE, AM.

This stained glass memorial window from the William Thompson Masonic School commemorates Rubert S. Cropley, Principal from 1922 to1949. The window is now in the collection of the Museum of Freemasonry at the Masonic Centre in Sydney.

Tracing boards can be found in every Lodge room in Australia. They show the symbols used to teach the lessons of Freemasonry to candidates. This is a picture of the First Degree Tracing Board created by Richard Reid in 1827 and held in the Museum of Freemasonry. See page 172 for a full description.

Reid's Second Tracing Board shows the Temple flanked by two columns representing the pillars of fire and smoke that accompanied the Israelites in their search for the Promised Land. At the top of each column is a sphere representing the terrestrial and celestial globes. See page 173 for a full description.

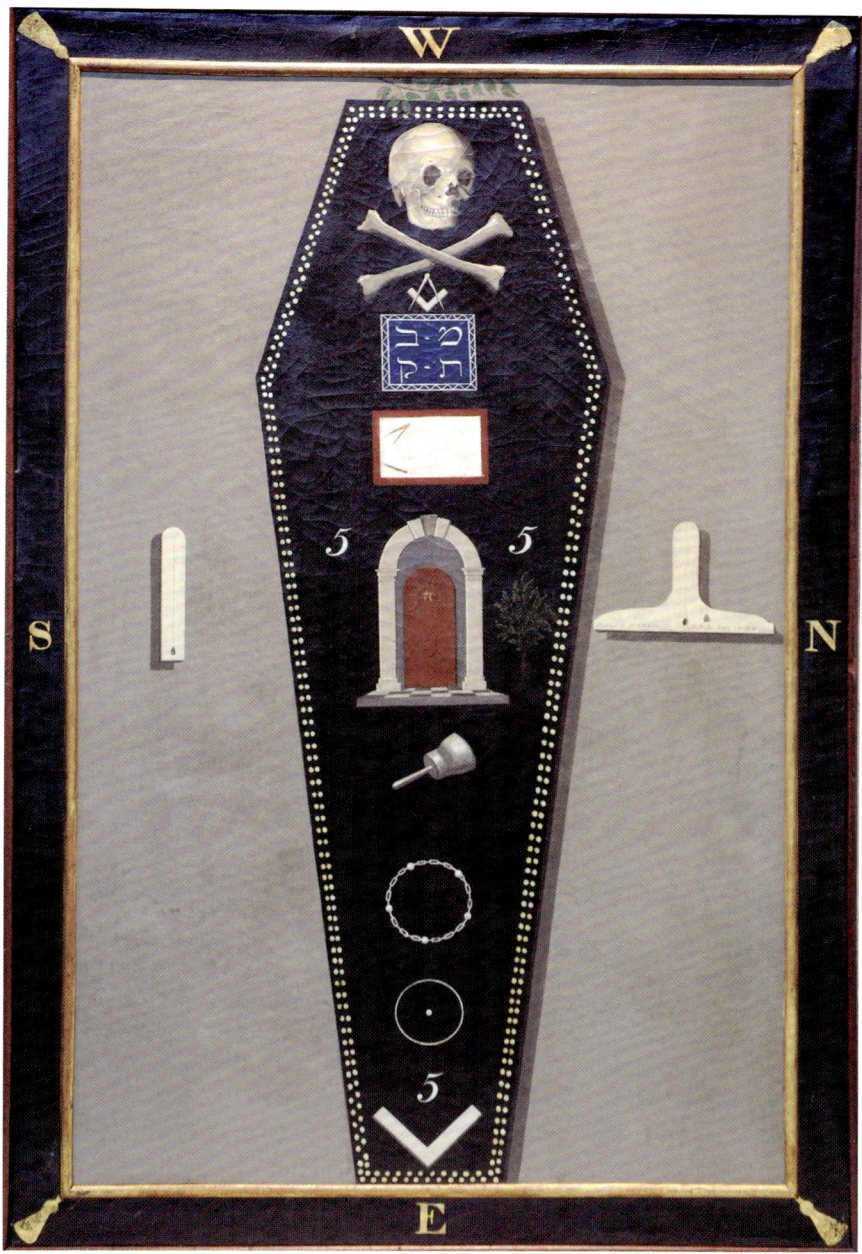

Reid's third board is starkly simple. The lesson of the Third Degree is how to die. The black coffin stresses that death is inevitable and that every man must achieve his life's work while he is alive. It teaches the Freemason that he who lives his life by the teachings of the Craft has no need to fear death. See page 174 for a full description.

Also in the Museum is a set of boards by John Harris, one of the most popular creators of tracing boards. This is the First Tracing Board of a set painted in 1845. The Sun represents the Great Architect of the Universe. Faith is represented by the chalice and hand, Hope by the anchor and Charity by the heart. See page 174 for a full description.

The second Harris board departs from the austerity of Reid's Georgian Temple. The curving staircase symbolises the journey of a man's life: as he makes his way up, the curve conceals what may lie ahead. Note the black and white squares of the pavement and the suspended letter 'G'. See page 175 for a full description.

Harris's Third Tracing Board is exuberantly coloured and ornamented. The backdrop to the coffin is a glowing orange. The acacia sprig on the coffin emphasises the continuity of the soul. These Masonic paintings are just one aspect of a rich arts tradition that includes architecture, music, literature, decorative and fine art.

under its original name and increased the range to include maps, guidebooks, atlases and automotive repair manuals.

Gregory's is still a household name, but street directories are now being challenged by internet maps and GPS technology.

Cecil Gregory was initiated into Freemasonry at Lodge Arcadia No.177 United Grand Lodge of New South Wales on May 12, 1922.

Ken Hall (1901–1994)

Ken G. Hall won Australia's first Oscar. Born in Sydney in 1901 he produced and directed 19 films in the 1930s – the 'golden era' of the Australian film industry.

Hall was educated at North Sydney Boys' High School. In 1916 he became a cadet for the *Sydney Evening News* before joining the publicity departments of Greater Union Theatres, Australasian Films and first National Pictures.

Hall and Stuart Doyle (head of Greater Union Theatres) created Cinesound Productions in 1931 – a Hollywood-style studio employing actors and technicians. The Cinesound Recording System was Australia's first successful sound-on-film recording process.

In 1932 Cinesound released *On Our Selection*, launching Hall's career. Hugely popular, it screened four times daily even in the Depression. Hall produced and directed another 16 films with Cinesound including *The Squatter's Daughter* (1933), *Strike Me Lucky* (1934), *Orphan of the Wilderness* (1936) and *Lovers and Luggers* (1937).

The most successful of all the Cinesound films were the *Dad 'n Dave* films starring Bert Bailey and Fred MacDonald. In 1938 Ken Hall persuaded Cecil Kellaway to return to Australia from Hollywood, for one of his best films, *Mr Chedworth Steps Out* (1939). The film starred Peter Finch in his first film role.

During WWII, Ken Hall turned his attention to newsreels and documentaries including *Kokoda Front Line* (1942) for which he won Australia's first Oscar and the worldwide success,

Smithy (1946), a film biography of Freemason, Sir Charles Kingsford Smith.

Hall left Cinesound in 1956, when Frank Packer invited him to head up Sydney's TCN Channel Nine, Australia's first regular television broadcaster.

He wrote two autobiographical books: *Directed by Ken G. Hall* (1977) and *Australian Film: The Inside Story* (1980). His contribution to the Australian film industry was recognised with a Raymond Longford Award for Lifetime Achievement in 1976.

Following his death in 1994, the National Film and Sound Archive developed the Ken G. Hall Film Preservation Award, encouraging individuals and corporations to support the preservation of film images.

Ken Hall was initiated into Freemasonry at Lodge Anima No. 421 on December 12, 1922.

Edward Hallstrom (1886–1970)

Sir Edward Hallstrom invented the Silent Knight refrigerator which ran on gas or electricity. A celebrated philanthropist, he helped many great causes – especially Taronga Park Zoo in Sydney.

Edward Hallstrom was born in 1886 near Coonamble, NSW. The family moved to Waterloo in Sydney when he was four. Here he met William McKell, later Australia's 12th Governor-General. The two differed politically, but were lifelong friends.

Hallstrom's parents separated while he was young and at age 10 he was working to help out. He left school at 13, continued to study, managed a furniture factory, then set up his own business manufacturing bedsteads.

In 1912 he married Margaret Jeffery, an artist who shared his love of animals. They lived in Dee Why on Sydney's northern beaches. In the backyard, Hallstrom experimented in refrigeration. He saw a market for kerosene-powered refrigerators for outback stations, which then relied on evaporative cooling.

In 1923 Hallstrom produced the Icy Ball, a kerosene-powered chest model and he 'went bush' to sell it. He continued experimenting and invented the Silent Knight upright refrigerator, which ran on gas or electricity.

Hallstrom moved the business to a factory in Willoughby, NSW. During WWII it produced munitions as well as refrigerators. After the war, his company was selling 1200 refrigerators a week. Imported refrigerators were expensive. The local Silent Knight competed on price, making Hallstrom extremely wealthy.

A life-long animal lover, Hallstrom donated generously to Taronga Park Zoo, helping to import many large exotic species including two rhinoceroses from Africa. In 1941 he became a trustee of the Zoo and then President (1951–1959).

Despite his philanthropy, Hallstrom encountered criticism from scientific circles because he lacked professional training. This upset him but he continued to support the Zoo and other charities, especially in medical research. He donated to Sydney Hospital for a cancer clinic and to Royal Prince Alfred Hospital (RPAH) for cardiac research.

When his wife died in 1968, Hallstrom gave his collection of birds and animals to Taronga. He also supported the Central Methodist Mission and established the Margaret Hallstrom Home for unmarried mothers at Leichhardt.

Hallstrom was knighted in 1952 and in 1957 became Australia's first Father of the Year. He died in 1970.

Edward Hallstrom was initiated into Freemasonry at Lodge Roseville No. 334 on August 24, 1922.

Lawrence Hargrave (1850–1915)

Lawrence Hargrave – engineer, explorer, astronomer, inventor and aviation pioneer – developed modern fuselage construction, curved wing surfaces, propellers and engines, all vital to the development of the modern aeroplane.

Born in England in 1850, Hargrave arrived in Sydney in 1866. His father, a prominent judge, wanted his son to study law, but Lawrence – more interested in engineering – joined the Australasian Steam Navigation Company as an apprentice.

From 1872 to 1877 he explored in Queensland and New Guinea. With the Italian, Luigi D'Albertis, he made an epic 800km journey along the Fly River.

Returning to Sydney, Hargrave was elected to the Royal Society of New South Wales and became Assistant Astronomical Observer at Sydney Observatory in 1878.

Twenty years before the Wright Brothers made their first flight, Hargrave studied the movements of birds, fish and reptiles, sea waves and air currents. He experimented with monoplane models of light wood and tissue paper, propelled with flapping wings or primitive airscrews.

To continue his research he moved the family to Stanwell Park, NSW, which offered excellent conditions for flying. In 1894, during one experiment, four box kites lifted him five metres from the ground in a 35 kph wind.

Hargrave's work on engines looked at many fuels – steam, carbonic acid, kerosene, petrol and gunpowder. In 1889 he developed a rotary engine used later as the prototype for French WWI airplanes.

Hargrave received little recognition in Australia and retiring in 1910, sold his models to Deutsches Museum, Munich. When war broke out in 1915 he was branded unpatriotic for this as 'the Germans then had superior air power'.

Hargrave's only son was killed in Gallipoli in 1915 and Lawrence himself died only nine weeks later.

Hargrave refused to patent his inventions because he hoped they would bring 'peace and goodwill to all'. His achievements went largely unrecognised in his lifetime, but his contribution to aviation is now acknowledged.

Hargrave featured with Kingsford-Smith on an Australian $20 banknote. In 1965 an Australian stamp commemorated the 50th anniversary of his death.

Lawrence Hargrave was initiated into Freemasonry on April 2, 1877 at United Service Lodge of New South Wales No. 937, English Constitution.

George Howell
(1893–1964)

Born in Sydney, George Julian Howell was working as a builder when he enlisted as a private in June 1915, and sailed for Egypt with the 7th Reinforcements for the 1st Battalion. He served at Gallipoli until the evacuation. In France, Howell was wounded at Pozières and evacuated to England, where he was promoted to Corporal.

In April, 1917, Corporal Howell received the Military Medal during the capture of Demicourt. A few weeks later, near Bullecourt, he climbed onto a parapet and realised that a large party of Germans was threatening to outflank his battalion. Despite heavy fire, he bombed the enemy back along the trench, supported by one lieutenant with a Lewis gun who fired bursts as he followed Howell along the trench. When he ran out of bombs, Howell jabbed down at the Germans with his bayonet until, severely wounded, he fell into the enemy trench.

Even before leaving his own trench, Howell sustained machine-gun wounds in both legs and had more than 20 injuries when he was rescued hours later. His citation stated that the 'prompt and gallant conduct of this non-commissioned officer in the face of superior numbers was witnessed by the whole battalion and greatly inspired them in the subsequent successful counter-attack'. He was awarded a Victoria Cross for his outstanding bravery.

Howell was hospitalised in England before returning to Australia in 1918. In World War II he served with the 2nd AIF but found this 'too unexciting' and joined the United States Army Sea Transport Service, taking part in the landing at Leyte during the invasion of the Philippines.

George Howell was initiated into Freemasonry at Lodge Coogee No. 322 on December 2, 1920.

CHAPTER SEVEN

Symbols of an ancient Craft

FREEMASONS

Teaching from symbols is an age-old practice. Freemasonry shares the use of symbols with many of today's organisations including the state, the churches, the armed forces and others – as well as companies with well-known trademarks and logos.

The Macquarie Dictionary says that a symbol is 'something used or regarded as something standing for or representing something else … a material object representing something immaterial, an emblem, token or sign'.

The working stonemason's symbols are the most important in Freemasonry. The best known of these are the square, the level, the plumb rule and the compasses – traditional tools still used by stonemasons and builders today.

In the ancient Craft guilds of stonemasons a man became an apprentice, learned to use the basic working tools and, once proficient, was allowed to pass to the next stage of his development. He was then known as a Craftsman or a 'Fellow Craft'. Further learning eventually enabled him to become a Master Mason.

Freemasonry applies similar stages of development to the progress of its members through the First, Second and Third Degrees – and uses the traditional working tools symbolically at each level of progress.

Like the early guilds, Freemasonry also teaches its members how to behave and how to act fairly and honestly towards others. This is one of the central objectives of Freemasonry. Words and phrases such as 'being on the level' and 'acting on the square' have come directly into the language from the principles of Freemasonry.

As you have taken the solemn obligation of an Entered Apprentice Freemason, I am permitted to inform you that there are several Degrees in Freemasonry, with peculiar secrets restricted to each. These are not communicated indiscriminately but are conferred upon candidates as they evince merit and proficiency.

I shall now proceed to entrust you with the secrets of this Degree, or those signs by which Masons are known to each other and distinguished from the uninstructed world who are not Freemasons. I must premise for your general information, that all squares, levels and perpendiculars are true and proper signs whereby to know a Mason. You will therefore stand perfectly erect ...

– from the ritual of the First or Entered Apprentice
Freemason's Degree

The traditional stonemason's tools can be seen in all Masonic Lodges in Australia and around the world. They are most often made of wood, and are used only as symbols to illustrate moral lessons.

Stonemasons use working tools to shape stone and prepare the finished blocks for placement into walls or buildings. Freemasons use the same tools to create moral lessons that help to make good men better and shape their thinking and actions to make them more useful to society.

The First Degree

Freemasons in the First Degree are known as Entered Apprentices. They take symbolic meaning from the gauge, the gavel, and the chisel.

The 24-Inch Gauge was used by stonemasons to measure and lay out their building work.

Freemasons use the gauge as a symbol for the planning necessary to make the most of the time available each day. Because the 'two-foot rule' is divided into 24 equal parts, it serves to remind Freemasons of the 24 hours of the day, and the need to apportion adequate time for reflection, family, work, and rest.

The Gavel, mallet, or hammer is an important physical instrument of labour, used by stone masons to shape the building blocks (often of many different sizes) that they need. From this, Freemasons learn that action has to follow planning – that

> *labour is the lot of man, for the heart may conceive, and the head devise in vain, if the hand is not prompt to execute the design. It represents to us the force of conscience, which should keep down all vain and unbecoming thoughts ... it teaches us to correct the errors and irregularities of our temper, to curb the aspirations of unbridled ambition, to moderate the ebullitions of wrath, to repress the malignity of envy and to encourage every good disposition.*

> – from the ritual of the First or
> Entered Apprentice Degree

The Chisel is used to carve the final designs into the stone or to carve shapes from the stone. Though small, chisels can be used to shape the largest stone, and play an essential role in the completion of the most impressive structures. Freemasons learn from the chisel that perseverance is a virtue which helps enlighten the mind, and purify the soul.

The Chisel represents the advantages of discipline and education. The mind, like the stone, is, in its natural state, rough and unshapen, but, as the Chisel in the hands of the sculptor transforms the shapeless mass into a thing of beauty, so education soon discovers the latent qualities of the mind, and, by cultivating the ideas and polishing rude thought, transforms the ignorant savage into the civilised and enlightened being, capable of appreciating and of performing his duty to God and man.

So in the First Degree, Freemasons learn that planning and preparation, hard work and perseverance will start them on the road to a better, more useful, sustainable and happier life – all of which will benefit not only themselves, but everyone around them.

Thus, from the Working Tools of an Entered Apprentice Freemason we deduce this moral: knowledge, grounded on accuracy, aided by labour and sustained by perseverance, will, in the end, overcome all difficulties, raise ignorance from despair and promote happiness in the paths of science.

The Second Degree

Freemasons in the Second Degree are known as Fellow Craft Freemasons. They add meaning taken from the square, the level, and the plumb-rule.

The Square is used by stonemasons to measure their progress – to check that building blocks, and the buildings they create are on the square. Freemasons use the square as a symbol to regulate their actions and their thoughts – to conform and synchronise their conduct with the purest principles of morality and virtue. The square is also worn by the Master of the Lodge as the emblem of his office.

The Square is an implement which enables the operative Mason to adjust with precision the faces and angles of his work and thus bring rude matter into due form … an emblem of Morality and Justice, [it] teaches us to regulate our lives by the unerring and unalterable law of God's Word, to live in charity

135

with all mankind and so to discipline our conduct as to render us acceptable to the Grand Geometrician of the Universe, from whom all goodness emanates.

– from the ritual of the Second or Fellow Craft Degree

The Plumb-Rule is used to check that vertical lines are 'true'. An emblem of integrity and uprightness, it teaches Freemasons to do things as well as they can be done, to be fair and truthful in their relationships with all people and to observe the balance between greed and abundance. The plumb rule is worn by the Junior Warden as an emblem of his office.

The Level is used to check that both the upright and flat surfaces are true and level in construction. In Freemasonry the level is used to demonstrate that all men are equal, and that although distinctions among men are to be found in society, no such differences should make us forget that we are all brethren. Within the Masonic fraternity, there are no distinctions of race or religion or of social standing. Members of any religion can join and participate in its teachings. The level is worn by the Senior Warden as an emblem of his office.

No eminence of station should lead us to forget that we are all Brethren and that he who has but placed his foot on the lowest step of Fortune's ladder is as fully entitled to our regard as he who has attained the summit; for a time will surely come, and the best and wisest of us know not how soon, when all distinctions, save those of goodness and virtue, shall cease and death that great leveller of human greatness shall reduce us all to the same state ...

As the operative Mason erects his temporal building with strict observance to the plumb-line, which will not permit him to deviate one hair's breadth to the right or to the left, so the Free and Accepted or Speculative Mason, guided by the unerring principles of right and truth, inculcated in the symbolical teachings of the same implement, is steadfast in the pursuit of truth, neither bending beneath the frowns of adversity nor yielding to the seductions of prosperity.

Thus, by the Grace of God, square conduct, level steps and upright intentions, we hope to ascend to those immortal mansions whence all goodness emanates.

In summary then, in the Second Degree, the square teaches morality, the level teaches equality, and the plumb-rule teaches uprightness for a Freemason's life and actions.

The Third Degree

Freemasons in the Third Degree are raised to the level of Master Mason. They add meaning taken from the skerrit, pencil, and compasses, tools used by the more experienced stonemasons.

The Skerrit is an instrument which acts on a centre pin, from which a line is drawn, chalked and struck onto the ground to mark out the foundation for the intended structure. For Freemasons the skerrit points out that a straight and undeviating line of conduct is laid down for our guidance and our actions in the Volume of the Sacred Law we use, whether the Bible, the Koran, or any other sacred text.

The Pencil enables the skilful architect or trained workman to mark out the building in a draft or plan for the instruction and guidance of the workmen. It teaches that a Freemason's words and actions are observed and recorded by the Great Architect of the Universe, to whom we must give an account of our conduct through life.

The Compasses allow the stonemason to calculate and describe the limits and proportions of the various parts of the job with accuracy and precision. They remind a Freemason of the unerring and impartial justice of the Great Architect of the Universe – who, having defined the limits of good and evil, will reward or punish us as we have obeyed or disregarded these limits.

Thus the working tools of the Third Degree ...

the tools of a Master Mason, teach us to bear in mind and act according to the laws of our Divine Creator, so that, when summoned from this sublunary and probationary abode, we may ascend to that Grand Lodge above, that House not made with hands, eternal in the heavens, where the World's Great Architect lives and reigns forever.

– from the ritual of the Third or Master Mason Degree

The Masonic Apron

The Masonic Apron is derived from the aprons worn by stonemasons in the Middle Ages. These were large enough to cover the wearer from chest to ankle, and were held by a leather thong which passed round the neck. Other thongs extending from the sides allowed the apron to be tied around the waist, with a bow and end-strings to the front.

The earliest freemasons' aprons were also large, but wearing the bib or 'flap up' soon fell into disfavour, with the flap later being cut off, or worn downwards as a fall.

From 1731 onwards the apron began to assume a more convenient shape, usually knee length. Leather gave way to softer fabrics, silk, satin, velvet, linen, and chamois-leather. The flap, when retained, was either cut to a triangle or in a semi-circular line.

These smaller aprons were often elaborately painted or embroidered according to the owner's design. Many of them were home-made, often artistically finished and adorned with symbolic designs. Printed and engraved aprons also appeared, many of them subsequently coloured by hand.

The most popular designs often incorporated the All-Seeing Eye, the Columns which allude to the columns at the entrance to King Solomon's Temple, and the Square and Compasses.

Little emphasis was placed on uniformity before 1784 when the apron was greatly reduced in size, and general uniformity was not ordered by the United Grand Lodge until 1814. In Australia, The Blue Lodge – to which most

Freemasons belong – now uses the apron illustrated in the colour section of this book.

Entered Apprentice

When an Entered Apprentice has been initiated, he is invested with a plain white lambskin apron.

> ... I invest you with the distinguishing badge of a Mason. It is more ancient than the Golden Fleece or Roman Eagle, more honourable than the Garter or any other Order in existence, being the badge of innocence and the bond of friendship. You will observe that this apron is made from the skin of a lamb and, as the lamb has been from time immemorial the universally acknowledged symbol of purity and innocence, you will thereby be reminded of that purity of mind and action which should ever distinguish a Freemason ... I trust you may live many years to wear that badge with pleasure to yourself, usefulness to the Craft and honour to the Lodge in which you have been initiated; and let me further exhort you never to disgrace that badge, for you may be assured that it will never disgrace you.

– from the ritual of the First or Entered
Apprentice Degree

Fellow Craft Freemason

After passing through the ceremony of the Second or Fellow Craft Degree, the candidate is invested with a plain white lambskin apron, similar to that of the Entered Apprentice, except it has two sky-blue rosettes at the bottom ...

> ... the distinguishing badge of a Fellow Craft Freemason ... not only to mark your progress in the Science, but is intended to point out to you that, as a Craftsman, you are expected to make the liberal arts and sciences your future study in order that you may be the better enabled to discharge your duty as a Mason and rightly estimate the wonderful works of the Almighty Creator

– from the ritual of the Second or Fellow Craft Degree

Master Mason

Next, of course, is the Third Degree, the Degree of Master Mason. Here the candidate is invested with an apron like the previous one, except it has sky-blue lining and an additional rosette on the fall or flap. No other colour or ornament is allowed except for officers and past officers of the Lodge, who may have the emblems of their offices in silver or white in the centre of the apron.

The tassels, in rudimentary form, must have appeared at a very early date as a natural development of the waist-strings being tied at the front and hanging down over the apron. When they were introduced is not known, but the Grand Lodges of Great Britain, Australia and Canada are the only jurisdictions to wear them.

> ... the badge with which you have just been invested, not only points out your rank as a Master Mason, but is likewise intended to remind you of those great duties you have this evening solemnly engaged yourself to perform. While it marks your own superiority, it calls on you to afford assistance and instruction to the Brethren in the inferior Degrees.

> – from the ritual of the Third or Master Mason Degree

Master and Past Master

There appears to be no official name for the squares or levels that decorate the apron of a Master or Past Master. The 1815 *Constitutions* described them as 'perpendicular lines upon horizontal lines, thereby forming three several sets of (two) right angles', and originally they were to be of inch-wide ribbon. Nowadays the emblems are usually of silver or white metal. They were designed only for purposes of distinction.

Neville Reginald Howse
(1863–1930)

Lieutenant Neville Howse was Australia's first Victoria Cross winner, and the only medical member of the Australian forces to be awarded this honour.

Born in England, he was the second surviving son of a surgeon and, together with all three of his brothers, followed his father into medicine. After completing his studies in London, Neville Howse emigrated to Australia in 1889. Early in 1900 he sailed for South Africa and the Boer War as a lieutenant in the New South Wales Medical Corps.

Lieutenant Howse earned his VC in a battle on July 24, 1900. His contingent encountered fierce fire from Boer troops in the Orange Free State near Vredefort. Among the first to fall was a young trumpeter who lay shot through the bladder and bleeding profusely. Despite heavy fire, Lieutenant Howse spurred his horse and charged towards the wounded man. He hadn't gone far before his horse was shot from under him. Ignoring the hail of bullets, Lieutenant Howse continued on foot. He reached the wounded man, dressed his wounds, lifted him onto his shoulders and carried him to safety. He was promoted to Captain, and in 1901 was awarded the Victoria Cross for his actions in saving the trumpeter.

The Victoria Cross was the first of the many awards and decorations won by Howse. Following a distinguished military and political career, he died suddenly in 1930 and was buried next to his father at London's Kensal Green cemetery.

Neville Howse was initiated into Freemasonry at Lodge Ophir on August 29, 1901.

Hamilton Hume
(1797–1873)

Hamilton Hume was the first great Australian explorer to be born here. His parents were free settlers who established themselves in

Parramatta. His father became Superintendent of Convicts. His mother provided Hamilton's education.

In 1814, when Hume was 17, he began exploring with his brother, John, then only 12, and with an aboriginal boy. They travelled as far as Berrima, discovering excellent grazing land, which Hume reported to Surveyor-General John Oxley, who established a sheep station there.

In 1816 Hume led an exploration with James Meehan and Charles Throsby to further investigate the Berrima area, discovering Lake Bathurst and the Goulburn Plains.

In 1819 he travelled with Oxley and Meehan from Liverpool to Jervis Bay and in 1821, with his brother and others, he discovered the Yass Plains. In 1822 he sailed down the east coast on the *Schnapper*, searching for rivers.

Hume's biggest adventure came in 1824 when he and former Royal Navy Captain, William Hovell, were commissioned by Governor Brisbane to journey to the Spencer Gulf to seek new grazing and establish where New South Wales' rivers flowed. Brisbane did not provide adequate funding so the men took on the journey using their own funds.

Hume and Hovell had different backgrounds and different skills, and their personalities clashed. Hume happily relied on his own ability, while Hovell doubted Hume's bushcraft. Five weeks of exploration and many disagreements later, they had discovered the Murray River, naming it the Hume. They also discovered the overland route between Sydney and Port Phillip, where Melbourne now stands.

In 1827 Hume won a government grant to discover a new road over the Blue Mountains. He succeeded, but his line of road was not adopted.

Hume and Sturt explored western New South Wales in 1828, discovering the Darling River. In 1860 Hume was elected a Fellow of the Royal Geographical Society.

Hume and Hovell featured on the Australian £1 banknote (1953–1966) and on a stamp (1976). Hume was one of Australia's greatest explorers and the Hume Highway – connecting Sydney and Melbourne – is named after him.

Hamilton Hume was initiated into Freemasonry at Leinster Marine Lodge of Australia No. 266, Irish Constitution on September 12, 1825.

William Donovan Joynt
(1889–1986)

After starting his adult life as a Melbourne office worker, William Joynt worked in North Queensland doing various bush and farm jobs. When World War I began he was dairying and digging potatoes on Flinders Island, off Tasmania. He enlisted in the Australian Imperial Force on May, 21 1915. Arriving in France in 1916, he joined the 8th Battalion.

William Joynt was wounded while fighting in the Ypres sector in Belgium, and evacuated to England. Commended in divisional orders, he was promoted to Lieutenant. Early in 1917 he rejoined his battalion, serving on the Western Front in the second battle of Bullecourt and at Menin Road and Broodseinde. On August 23, 1918, attacking troops from his battalion suffered heavy casualties and were pinned down near Herleville. Lieutenant Joynt rallied this attack by leading an advance that first cleared the wood's approaches, followed by a bayonet charge that captured it – and more than 50 prisoners.

At one stage Joynt had 20 enemy troops advancing towards him with their rifles ready. To counter this attack, the lieutenant covered their leader with a revolver and they surrendered. There were no Australian casualties and Joynt's 'most conspicuous bravery' won him the Victoria Cross.

Later that month he was seriously wounded and evacuated to England, and in October he was promoted to Captain. The following February he returned to Melbourne and became a soldier settler, as well as a pioneer of colour printing in Australia. He was also active in the militia, being promoted to Major in 1930.

Mobilised for World War II, he was camp staff officer and quartermaster at an Australian base camp. He was placed on the retired list as an honorary Lieutenant Colonel in 1944. Joynt wrote three autobiographical books – *To Russia and Back*

Through Communist Countries (1971), *Saving the Channel Ports, 1918* (1975) and *Breaking the Road for the Rest* (1979).

William Joynt was initiated into Freemasonry at the Old Melburnians Lodge No. 317 Victoria on October 12, 1923.

Charles Kingsford Smith (1897–1935)

In June 1928 'Smithy' and Charles Ulm made the first flight across the Pacific from America to Australia. On the final leg they fought a fierce storm, landing the Southern Cross at Brisbane and creating history.

Smithy enlisted to fly in World War I, was transferred to the Royal Flying Corps and nearly ended his career in a dogfight. 180 German bullets struck his aircraft but despite losing three toes, he managed to return. He was awarded the Military Cross.

In England after the war, Smithy flew joy-flights in surplus warplanes. In California, he joined a flying circus, graduating to Hollywood, as a stuntman crashing planes.

Back home In 1921, Smithy did more joy-flights, then with Western Australian Airlines flew the first airmail service between Geraldton and Derby.

Obsessed with flying the Pacific, Smithy, Charles Ulm and Keith Anderson sought sponsorship. After they flew around Australia in 10 days 5 hours – twice as fast as the record – the NSW government offered £9,000 towards the Pacific flight, but then withdrew.

Shipping magnate, Alan Hancock, funded the venture. *Southern Cross* left Oakland California on May 31, 1928 arriving in Brisbane on June 9. Smithy, and Ulm, now national heroes, were greeted in Sydney by the Governor-General and 300,000 people.

The team achieved numerous 'firsts' before establishing Australian National Airlines, an inter-state service.

Smithy was appointed Honorary Air Commodore of the RAAF, carried the first official air mail from Australia to England in 1931 and was knighted in 1932.

Smithy sold *Southern Cross* to the Commonwealth Government and continued flying his new *Lady Southern Cross*, making the first west-east crossing of the Pacific in 1933.

In 1935, flying from England to Australia, his aircraft disappeared. He was 38.

Smithy's portrait appears on Australian $20 banknotes; and on Australian stamps. Parks, streets and Sydney's airport are named for him. The *Southern Cross* is displayed at Brisbane airport.

His Master Mason apron is at the AIF Memorial Lodge, Queensland and is used as a tribute to fallen brethren each Anzac Day.

Charles Kingsford Smith was initiated into Freemasonry at Gascoyne Lodge on April 9, 1925.

John McEwen
(1900–1980)

Nicknamed 'Black Jack' by Robert Menzies for his swarthy looks and beetle brows, John McEwen enjoyed a 16-year coalition partnership with Menzies, setting a milestone for amicable relationships within Australian politics.

John McEwen was born in Chiltern, Victoria, in 1900. His early years were shadowed by his mother's death in 1901 followed by his father's in 1907. He grew up 'in frugal circumstances' with his grandmother, who at that time ran a boarding house.

His adult years were spent as a farmer and later as a clerk in the Crown Solicitor's Office, Melbourne. After becoming active in the Victorian Farmers' Union and the Victorian Country Party, he was elected to the House of Representatives in 1934. McEwen was promoted to the ministry in 1937 but lost his position when the Country Party dropped out of the governing coalition as Menzies became leader of the United Australia Party.

When the Country Party rejoined the Coalition under Arthur Fadden, McEwen held a number of ministerial portfolios. In opposition for most of the 1940s, he was again a Minister in the Menzies' government of 1949. In 1958 he succeeded

Fadden as both Country Party leader and Deputy Prime Minister – but it was only towards the end of his 37 year parliamentary career that McEwen became Prime Minister following the tragic disappearance of Prime Minister Harold Holt in wild surf on Victoria's Mornington Peninsula in 1967.

On January 10, 1968, Sir John McEwen stood down as Prime Minister in favour of the new Liberal Party leader, John Gorton. Although he was only Prime Minister for a matter of weeks, McEwen served as Deputy Prime Minister for a total of 12 years in the governments of Robert Menzies, Harold Holt and John Gorton.

John McEwen was initiated into Freemasonry at Lauderdale Lodge No. 361 Victorian Constitution on July 28, 1926.

William McMahon
(1908–1988)

After studying law at the University of Sydney, William 'Billy' McMahon practised as a solicitor before enlisting in the 2nd Australian Infantry Force in early 1940. He was discharged with the rank of Major in 1945, having served throughout in Australia.

McMahon entered Parliament in 1949, winning the Sydney seat of Lowe for the Liberals in the election that returned the Coalition to power for the next 23 years. He served on the back bench for only 18 months before being promoted to Minister for the Navy and Air, a position he held from 1951-54.

William McMahon served as Deputy Leader of the Liberal Party under Prime Ministers Harold Hold and John Gorton from 1966 until 1971 before challenging Gorton and becoming Prime Minister. He lost the 1972 general election but remained in parliament until 1982. He was appointed a member of the Privy Council in 1966, made a Companion of Honour in 1972 and knighted in 1977.

William McMahon was initiated into Freemasonry at Lodge University of Sydney No. 544 United Grand Lodge of New South Wales on March 22, 1974.

CHAPTER EIGHT

Architecture and Freemasonry: 'To Build the New Jerusalem'

by Dr Bob James

Coming from a labour history background, I was interested in temples long before I thought of becoming a Freemason.

I often used to say that when you 'understand' temples you can see them everywhere in our cities and towns. Many of our public buildings, and some of our more modest domestic ones, mimic the Greek or Roman temple form in which imposing columns hold up a triangular lintel over the front entrance.

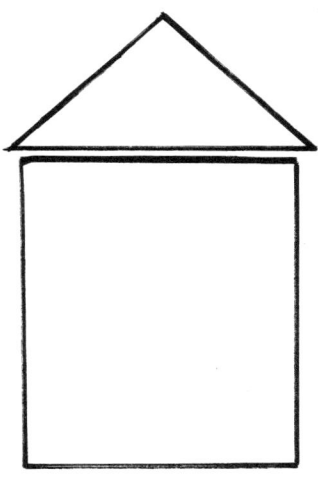

The form of this Graeco-Roman temple appears simple: it's a triangle on columns, and it seems to involve very straight-forward building practices.

But its construction is actually extremely complex, and it's the complexities of this and other building practice which lead directly into the different stories of how, where and why Speculative Freemasonry originated. Different kinds of columns, sacred attributes claimed for the various number and geometric shapes involved, numerous philosophical treatises written and argued about from the medieval to the modern period, and exotic byways such as the Knights Templar and Rosslyn Chapel: all these things add up to the rich and fertile soil from which Freemasonry, the organisation appears to have sprung.

Trade union banners once commonly displayed what I mistakenly thought were uniquely Masonic symbols. I have at least two large books of labour history with titles speaking of building 'a new Jerusalem' out of the old world. I was interested, not because of a background in the Australian Labor Party or in the trade union movement, but because of an interest in working people, their beliefs in their 'heart of hearts' and the ways in which they expressed those beliefs, such as in their processions. No trade unionist today speaks in these terms.

Neither will the many members of today's health funds talk of the same symbols in the certificates and honour boards of their organisations, which used to be known far and wide as 'friendly societies'. They know little if anything of the history and seem not to care. They don't appear to think anything, either, when they use such terms as 'all square', 'being on the level', 'pillar of the community' or experiencing 'the third Degree'.

Freemasonry has always gone further than mere mimicry. Every Freemason can tell you that the allegories, or stories, that veil Freemasonry and the symbols that illustrate them are drawn from architecture and building. In fact, Masonic practice is located right in amongst the arts and mysteries of the traditional building trades, and actually keeps alive the old tools, techniques and even the traditional 'heroes'.

Why is it then that only Freemasonry maintains connections with this history?

It has often been said that mere dusty artisans could not possibly have known, let alone worked with allegories and symbolic meaning, whereas in Speculative Freemasonry:

*The story of King Solomon's Temple runs, like a continuous thread, through all of the recognised and ancillary Degrees of Freemasonry. Yet, we here, are not operative stone-masons, but rather speculative thinkers concerned with the moral education and improvement of the individual and, for us, the Temple is not a problem in construction but **a symbol of the greatness of the moral law.** Wherever and whenever in our ceremonials you encounter the narrative of the Temple, whether it concerns the construction, the furnishings or the builders, whether it concerns Biblical fact or legendary occurrence, **you must always recognise the symbol and seek the symbolic meaning ...***

As we saw in Chapter Seven, in the First Degree of Freemasonry, what are called 'the working tools' are the twenty-four inch gauge, the gavel and the chisel; in the Second Degree, the square, the level and the plumb rule; and so on. Candidates are instructed by way of such moral tales as this:

Consider the Fellowcraft who, for his day's task is given the drawings and dimensions for a certain stone. He carefully prepares his tools, checks his gauge or rule, sharpens his chisel, and then proceeds to the quarry to collect a suitable rough ashlar for the job. But, despite his careful preparation, hardly has he set upon his task and given the stone a mere two or three strikes with his chisel, than the stone splits and is spoilt.

What moral lesson can we learn from this? Quite simply that the worthiest motive, the most careful plan, the greatest skill will all come to naught – if the quality of the material is lacking.

It is easily said that the many connections between Freemasonry and architecture exist because of the importance to Masonry of the Biblical stories about Solomon's Temple. But it's necessary to add immediately that, over time, simple connections have been overgrown with other layers of speculation and other events until one, simple explanation is no longer possible.

The masonry arch is a case in point. The particular form of the arch which is so important to Freemasons is sometimes called the true arch.

149

It involves a series of wedge-shaped stones held in place, not by mortar, but by a key-stone at the top and centre, the whole designed to spread the load and to last a very long time. But that simple, curved arch is not the style of arch you will most commonly find in Gothic cathedrals.

At its simplest, the story of Freemasonry begins with the operative stonemasons using a Lodge or 'site office' to store their tools, to meet together and for all the other activities that might arise on any medieval building site. Such a group of workers had Craft secrets which they jealously guarded but which they were also expected to pass on to suitable, younger men just starting out. Thus, there developed levels and grades of proficiency and rewards for achievement within the Lodge group, and barriers between 'the insiders' and 'the outsiders', or those who had been accepted as brothers and were 'in the know' and those who had not been so accepted. All of this is perfectly reasonable and understandable, and not unknown in other trades at the same time since all the medieval trades would have experienced similar pressures with regard to their livelihoods and working conditions.

The simplest version of the transmission of operative to speculative masonry involves 'gentlemen' non-artisans joining operative Lodges to learn the secrets supposedly contained therein. With these aids, these 'gentlemen' supposedly developed the Royal Academy, the scientific method and insights into 'the hidden mysteries of nature and science.' Initiated architects included people like Sir Christopher Wren, who designed St Paul's Cathedral and Inigo Jones, who designed the banqueting hall at Whitehall for James I, or so it is said.

Even this much suggests a more complicated account. It seems necessary to allow that 'the secrets' were more profound than how to find the centre of a circle, how to construct a right angle given only a point or how to develop a building elevation from a flat drawing. A Gothic cathedral was intended to celebrate God and to replicate divine perfection in its floor plan and elevation, was it not?

So, the first major complication enters with the question: were the various tests that distinguished levels of a mason's competence concerned only with practical skills and with solid objects, or were they also concerned with abstract notions, and with symbols, especially religious symbols? In other words: to what extent did the outside world, the Bible-based world centred on King Solomon's Temple, penetrate the Lodge world and determine the content of the lessons being taught and the tests being applied?

Would the operative stonemasons, and the artisans practising related crafts, have drawn on the Bible stories and used them to drive home a need for good and honest work, in the sight of God, or would they not?

The next complication enters with questions about the sacredness or otherwise of the tools being used by the artisans, the skills being taught and the ceremonial being developed to welcome operative brothers from one level of achievement to the next.

Obviously involved here are questions such as: who are the experts and therefore probably doing the teaching – religious personnel, such as monks, or the artisans themselves? How secretive was the Lodge brotherhood? How much, if any, of what they were doing was written down or recorded in some other way, and when?

As soon as possible records are mentioned, the relationship between numbers, used in counting and formula, and pictures, used in geometry, becomes of interest. Euclid's 47th Proposition is well-known to Freemasons whether or not they understand the mathematics involved. It is the statement of a theorem of Pythagoras which asserts that 'in any right-angled triangle the longest side, or hypotenuse,

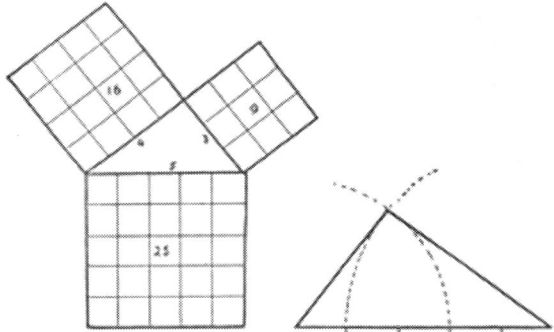

equals when squared the combined squares of the other two sides'.

The computations required to prove the theorem, or those involved in applying it, are of absolutely no concern to Freemasons. It is only the claimed connections between the mathematics and universal truths which are of interest.

God is sometimes in Freemasonry named as 'the Great Architect' and sometimes as 'the Grand Geometrician'. Speculative Freemasonry is sometimes said to be 'geometry' by another name, and sometimes said to be 'architecture' by another name. But in medieval times, and later, the connections between geometry, architecture and number systems were not straightforward, and they certainly could not be contained within practical, bricks and mortar-type thinking.

Many Masonic writers have assumed that the letter 'G' which takes a prominent position in Lodge rooms stands for 'Geometry'. A very early catechism printed in 1730 has the following exchange:

Q: Why were you made a Fellow-Craft?
A: For the sake of the letter 'G'.

Q: What does that 'G' denote?
A: Geometry or the Fifth Science.

This is a reference to a belief that Geometry was one, indeed the most important of the liberal arts and sciences, which have held all useful knowledge from the time civilisation emerged from the so-called 'Dark Ages'. In other Masonic texts architecture is named 'the supreme art'. The one cannot exist without the other. If you like, upright buildings cannot exist without the abstractions of straight lines, circles and squares. But the letter obviously also denotes 'God' and these two references together produce the sense of the 'Great Architect of the Universe' or 'the Grand Geometrician.'

What's become known as 'Sacred Geometry' throws up many issues for an enquiring Freemason. Simon Cox in his useful little book, *Cracking the Da Vinci Code* (Barnes & Noble), describes it as 'the art of passing on divine wisdom through the use of geometric forms as symbols' and points out that such a secret language has been used for thousands of years. It's hard to imagine that operative stonemasons were not at least aware of it, and not incorporating it into their Lodge practices.

Involved here are such abstract notions as the Fibonacci Sequence, the Golden Mean or Ratio and the Golden Rectangle. Not only were medieval cathedrals built in conformity with formulae deriving from these abstractions but innovative artists such as Leonardo da Vinci and Michelangelo created breath-takingly beautiful work based on them. The paintings of Mona Lisa and the Last Supper, and statues such as the famous David use these 'Golden' principles. More recently, Claude Debussy's music, Mondrian's 'modern art', and Le Corbusier's 1930s buildings can be shown to involve the same ideas.

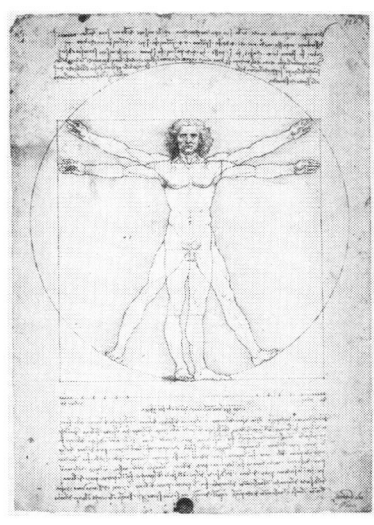

Perhaps the best known image created by Leonardo, and used as a major clue in *The Da Vinci Code* was that of Vitruvian Man.

Standing with his arms and legs outstretched, this figure has appeared in hundreds of applications. Vitruvius was a Roman engineer and architect of the first century BC and the early 1st century AD. His book,

De Architectura, has 10 chapters on town planning and the 'sciences' involved, but also discusses the proportions of the human body. The re-discovery of the man and his book led directly to much of the building and design in what is now called the Classical Period.

All of which takes us to the ground plans of cities and the creative work of fictional authors such as Dan Brown.

Parts of the city of Edinburgh are believed to have been 'Masonically inspired'. A group of buildings on North Castle Street in Edinburgh, for example, were the last houses built in Scotland in the late 18th-century by stonemasons, also Freemasons, who shortly afterwards left for America to help construct Washington DC. George Washington was a member of a Scottish Lodge in Fredericksburg and these travelling Scots Masons helped construct the building which has become known as the White House. It also just happens to be the case that the original planning for the Australian Federal Capital was done by a pair of architects influenced by similar notions.

All of the above also takes us to the many Masonic halls around the world being called 'temples' and designed to look like temples. For Australia, distinguished architects who were Masons, such as Edmund Blacket (1817–1883) and W.C. Vahland come to mind.

Best known for his designs for the University of Sydney, St Andrew's Cathedral in Sydney and St Saviour's Cathedral in Goulburn, Blacket pioneered the revival styles of architecture, in particular what's now called 'Victorian Gothic'. He was the most favoured architect of the Church of England in NSW for much of his career, and was for a time the official Colonial Architect for the State. Sometimes referred to as 'The Wren of Sydney', he also designed houses, government buildings, bridges, and business premises. His work is now understood to have been highly influential in the development of Australian architecture.

Wilhelm Vahland was another European immigrant who worked successfully in the architecture of his adopted country. At 27, not long after completing his studies, he emigrated to Australia, arriving in Melbourne in September 1854. For a while he built gold-washing cradles for the alluvial diggers on the gold fields, and then started his architectural career which lasted nearly 50 years. In partnership, he designed many churches, banks, schools, hotels, theatres and private homes in Bendigo and the surrounding area. Masonically, he is best remembered for the Bendigo Masonic Hall, described in 1873 as 'the finest in Australia'.

Inside such buildings Masons have been encouraged to reflect inwardly on the lessons they are given as they advance in proficiency and to build a temple in their hearts, sturdy and true, on sound principles. But the nature of that Temple has changed throughout history. Even during the 300 years in which Freemasonry, the organisation, has been in existence, the lessons that the wider world have seen reflected in the work of individual Masons have changed. Many books have been written, speculating about the thinking behind the creations.

Operative stonemasons, tramping from work site to work site in medieval times, no doubt imagined angels and demons influencing their natural world and no doubt that affected the stories they told and the carvings they made. But when their children or their children's children sought work in the sixteenth and seventeenth centuries, what was understood about the natural world, about society and about how such things might be expressed, had altered greatly.

During the period now known as the Enlightenment, the years when Freemasonry, the organisation, was establishing itself, a vast range of buildings, and outdoor spaces incorporating obelisks, mazes, tombs, monuments and sundials in gardens, parks and cemeteries across the western world were designed by enthusiastic Masons. Teaching within Lodge rooms at this time emphasised the inevitability of the journey of life ending in death despite our greater understanding of and dominance over nature:

> *In all initiations there is a symbolic death and a rebirth – a death to a past life, a raising to a future one. What more natural than that the young Mason should die to his apprenticeship and rise a master? What more appropriate to symbolise this than the legend of Hiram Abiff, King Solomon's architect?*

When those Scottish stonemasons shipped out for the USA in the eighteenth century, it has been suggested that uppermost in their minds and those of their co-workers were ideas about justice, equality and freedom, and that is why these secular ideals are found embodied in the layout of the North American capital. In 1792, the year that he laid the foundation stone for the White House, Washington identified Freemasonry as 'a Society whose liberal principles are founded in the immutable laws of truth and justice'. He finished his address on this occasion, '... and I sincerely pray that the Great Architect of the Universe may bless you here, and receive you hereafter in his immortal temple'.

And when the English-born Blacket, the German-trained Vahland, or the Burley-Griffins from Chicago began designing the Australian buildings which have made them famous, what were they thinking?

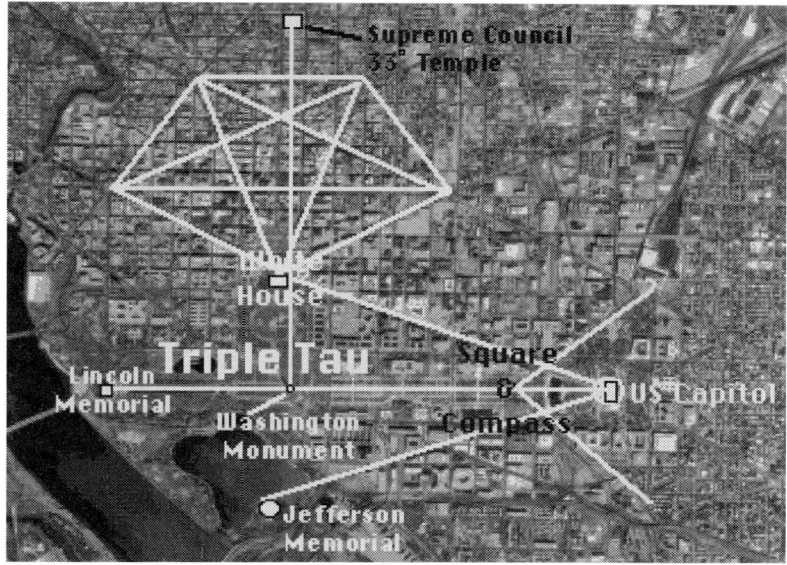

The truth is that we don't know, because this side of Masonic studies has been neglected. It would be useful, I think, for Freemasons to think about how their message has changed over time and how individual Freemasons have expressed their beliefs at different times and in different circumstances.

'Seeking the Light' as a basic virtue was an enormously powerful idea when it was given concrete form in those soaring Gothic windows. Medieval men and women must have been awe-struck when they moved from their dark and dingy cottages to their churches where the light, and God's message, streamed in through coloured glass story-pictures over their heads.

The highly-coloured trade union banners were often referred to as the workers' stained glass windows in the 19th century. Temples and the Eye of Providence and doves and cornucopias appeared then in Eight Hour Day marches, or in frames in miniature versions hanging on a kitchen wall. All memories of that time are just about gone now, of course.

History has always been badly taught in this country – too much timidity, too much conformity. Freemasonry doesn't make enough of what it has in its collective memory, either.

There is clearly plenty of stirring material. A red-blooded approach, involving imaginative use of that material could bring Freemasonry its own 'Ripping Yarns'.

Dr Bob James is a retired school teacher, hippy farmer and public servant. He completed his PhD in Australian History at the University of Newcastle in 2004 and entered Freemasonry in 2008. He is now Convenor of the (re-badged) Australian Centre for Secret Societies, Fraternalism and Mateship, details of which can be located on www.fraternalsecrets.org. He has recently been appointed to the (NSW) Grand Master's 'Masonic Light Committee'.

Note: Dr James thanks Bernard Jones, *Freemasons Guide & Compendium*, and Dr Radcliff's *Understanding the Lessons of the Craft Degrees*, for quotations used.

Thomas Mayne
(1901-1995)

When Thomas Mayne developed the delicious milk beverage, Milo, he knew he was on a winner. It was tasty, which kids would love. It was healthy, which would make parents happy. But he may not have imagined that people would still be enjoying his delicious drink 70 years later.

After graduating with a diploma in industrial chemistry and engineering from Sydney Technical College in 1933, Mayne became a laboratory assistant for Bacchus Marsh Concentrated Milk Company, eventually taken over by Nestlé in 1921. Mayne moved up the ranks in Nestlé and became the chief industrial chemist.

In the 1930s during the Great Depression, many children weren't getting the nutrients they needed. Mayne started experimenting with different products that would be both nutritious and delicious.

After 8,320 hours experimenting in a lab, he emerged with a product he called Milo. He had managed to create a healthy drink with a chocolate taste that also used up excess cocoa. Made from malted barley, it contained six vitamins and minerals and was high in protein. The milk gave children calcium.

Mayne named the drink after the Roman mythological character, Milon of Croton, a champion Roman athlete who won several Olympic and Pythian Games held in Greece in the 6th Century B.C.

In 1934 Mayne and Nestlé launched Milo at the Sydney Royal Easter Show. Originally sold in pharmacies as a 'tonic food drink', Milo became part of the Aussie troops' rations in World War II.

Mayne continued to work for Nestlé until 1966, then remained a consultant to the company. In the late 1950s and 60s he was involved in setting up the Maggi range of products in Australia.

Milo sponsors the Australian Institute of Sport and is now promoted as the 'ever popular energy food drink': 90,000 tons of Milo, worth $420 million, are sold each year in 30 countries.

Mayne died in 1995. His Milo was recognised in an obituary in *Time* magazine, which pointed out that the famous chocolate malt drink was by then a staple in Asian and Australian households.

Thomas Mayne was initiated into Freemasonry at Lodge King Edward, No. 189, Victorian Constitution.

Harry Melbourne
(1913–2007)

Freddo Frog has been loved by Australian children for over 70 years. Without Harry Melbourne, Freddo could have been a mouse.

Melbourne was born in Gainsborough, England in 1913. His family migrated to Australia when he was 16. Two years later he started working at MacRobertson's Chocolates in Fitzroy, Melbourne, unloading bags of cocoa from horse-drawn carts. The company soon moved him to chocolate-making.

MacRobertson's wanted a fresh, new idea for a chocolate to capture the imagination of Australian children. It was thinking of a chocolate mouse until Melbourne heard this and told his boss, Macpherson Robertson, 'It won't sell. Women and children are scared of mice'. Instead, he suggested a chocolate frog 'because kids love catching tadpoles and frogs'.

Melbourne thought he would lose his job for standing up to the boss, but instead, Robertson asked him to produce a mould and products for sampling in three days. Melbourne made the moulds and had four flavours on his desk inside the given time.

When it came to naming the frog, Melbourne declined suggestions from workmates to call it 'Harry'. Instead he named it after his friend at the factory, Fred. Freddo Frog was born.

Cadbury bought MacRobertson's in 1967. Rather than taking a senior role with Cadbury, Melbourne retired a few years later after 38 years on the job.

An ardent supporter of the Caulfield Football Club and Caulfield South Cricket Club, Melbourne took the job of keeper of Caulfield Town Hall, enabling him to work for his beloved club raising funds for a new pavilion.

Melbourne never received a cent for the Freddo Frog idea. This didn't bother him because, *'Freddo was made for the love of the company'*. When Melbourne died in 2007 (aged 94) his coffin was draped with a Freddo Frog flag.

One hundred million Freddo Frogs are produced in Australia every year. The cartoon frog has become an institution with its own website, entertaining children with games and puzzles on line. Harry Melbourne would be proud to see his little frog hopping into cyberspace.

Harry Melbourne was initiated into Freemasonry at Victoria Park Lodge No. 388 Victorian Constitution on April 24, 1944.

Robert Menzies
(1894–1978)

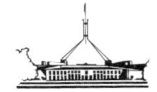

Of modest birth, Robert Gordon ('Bob') Menzies received a first-class education by winning a series of scholarships throughout his secondary and tertiary education. Best known as Australia's longest serving Prime Minister, Menzies held this office for a total of 18 years, five months and 10 days during two terms – from 1939-41 and again from 1949-66.

Menzies completed the plan of Canberra with the construction of Lake Burley Griffin. A prominent constitutional lawyer, he first entered politics in 1928, became Attorney-General in the Lyons-led United Australia Party (UAP) and deputy leader seven years later. Robert Menzies was elected leader of the UAP after Lyons' death in 1939 and shortly afterward became Prime Minister.

A period of dissension forced Menzies to resign in 1941 and he was replaced by Arthur Fadden. Three years later he was instrumental in forming the Liberal Party of Australia and in 1949, became Prime Minister for the second time. Menzies' win – considered one of the most extraordinary resurrections in Australian politics – led him to success in the next six general elections before he retired in 1966. In 1963 Sir Robert Menzies became the only Australian appointed Knight of the Thistle and was further honoured in 1965 by being appointed Constable of Dover Castle and Warden of the Cinque Ports.

Robert Menzies was initiated into Freemasonry at Austral Temple Lodge No. 110 Victorian Constitution on March 10, 1920.

Henry Messenger (1883–1959)

Henry 'Dally' Messenger was born in Balmain, Sydney. His father and grandfather were both champion scullers, and Dally himself was a cricketer, 18-footer sailor and champion canoeist.

He received his education at Double Bay Public School and then became a shipwright, working at his father's boatshed – but it was rugby that interested him most. He played Rugby Union for the Warrigal Club at the age of 17, then joined Eastern Suburbs and was captain of the winning Second Grade team.

The following year he played for New South Wales against Queensland and the New Zealand All Blacks – showing great tactical skill, and delighting the crowd by running with the ball hidden behind his back.

When Dally was 12, a new game was beginning far away in the north of England, where rugby players – tired of losing their work pay because of rugby injuries – formed a break-away code called the Northern Union, later to become rugby league.

Similar injuries, suffered without any form of compensation, were also causing dissent in Sydney. A meeting of rebellious players took place at Victor Trumper's sports store – and Australian Rugby League was born.

The first club was Newtown, which held its inaugural meeting in January 1908. Trumper knew that a personality like Dally Messenger would be crucial to the success of the new venture, and Messenger agreed to accept a fee of £150 for three matches – a fortune in those days. Messenger was duly expelled from Rugby Union and in 1908 went to England with the touring Kangaroos. In one match, against Hull, he kicked an 82 metre goal from the Australian quarter line.

Henry Messenger was initiated into Freemasonry at Lodge Thespian 265 in 1915.

Bert Oldfield
(1894–1976)

Named *Wisden Cricketer of the Year* in 1927, William Albert 'Bert' Stanley Oldfield was a classy wicketkeeper, and filled that position in the Australian team for most of the years between the World Wars.

Born in the Sydney suburb of Alexandria in 1894, Oldfield enlisted in World War I and played for the Services Cricket Team. In France, he narrowly escaped death at Polygon Wood; he was found, semi-conscious and partly buried, hours after a bombardment.

In World War II he was commissioned lieutenant in 1939, serving on the staff of Eastern Command Headquarters and rising to major in 1943.

His international cricket career began in 1920 when he was selected for the NSW Sheffield Shield Team and playing in three Tests (1920–21) for Australia.

In 1922 he opened a sporting goods retail store in George Street Sydney. He proved to be a good businessman and had a devoted clientele.

During his 15 years as a test wicketkeeper he made 130 dismissals including 52 stumpings – still a record as a proportion of stumpings to catches. He also proved a capable lower-order batsman, accumulating 1427 Test runs at an average of 22.65 and scoring six first-class centuries.

A short, dapper man, he was punctilious in his preparation. Before keeping he taped his finger joints, covered them with stalls and two pairs of chamois inner gloves. Neat and quiet, he was known as the 'gentleman in gloves'. His appeals were modest and were only made when he believed a batsman was out.

During the controversial 'bodyline series' of 1933, he was knocked unconscious by a Larwood fast ball and suffered a fractured skull. He disapproved of 'bodyline' bowling, but took the blame himself for 'ducking into a fair ball'.

Oldfield was married and had two daughters. He was a non-smoking teetotaller and published two books on cricket, *Behind the Wicket* and *The Rattle of the Stumps*.

He was made a Member of the British Empire in 1970. Bert Oldfield died in 1976.

Bert Oldfield was initiated into Freemasonry at Lodge Arcadia, No. 177, UGL of NSW, on June 11, 1920.

Hubert Opperman
(1904–1996)

Hubert Ferdinand Opperman was one of Australia's greatest sportsmen.

Born at Rochester, Victoria in 1904, he moved to Melbourne with his family soon afterwards. His first job was as a telegram messenger – delivering by bicycle.

In 1921 'Oppy' came third in his first race – an 80 mile road race. The prize was a racing bike by Malvern Star Cycles, Melbourne. The owners, Bruce and Frank Small, offered Oppy a cycling career riding for Malvern Star.

Opperman, at age 20, won the Australian road title in 1924 and again in 1926, 1927, and 1929. He captained the Australian team for the Tour de France in 1928 and 1931.

His popularity rose dramatically in France when he won the Bol d'Or, a 24-hour continuous event around Montrouge Velodrome. During the first hour his bike's chain snapped. Sabotage was suggested, but Bruce Small borrowed a heavy roadster for Oppy to complete the race. Seventeen laps behind, he caught up by the 11th hour. Thirteen hours later he won, breaking the race record. The French Magazine *L'Auto* praised 'his courage, his perfect loyalty and his eternal smile'.

Opperman broke more records in England and France. In 1937 he cycled from Fremantle to Sydney in 13 days, slashing five days off that record.

Oppy's cycling career ended with World War II. He served in the RAAF, then entered politics. He joined the Liberal Party and in 1949 was elected Federal Member for Corio, Victoria. He became Government Whip (1955), Minister for Shipping and Transport (1960-1963), then Minister for Immigration 1963–1966. He retired from Parliament in 1967, becoming Australia's First High Commissioner to Malta.

Opperman continued cycling until aged 90 when his wife, Mavys, concerned for his health, begged him to stop. He died in 1996 of a heart attack – yes, while riding an exercise bike.

Opperman was knighted in 1968 for his services to sport, also becoming a Knight of the Order of St John of Jerusalem.

Hubert Opperman was initiated into Stonnington Lodge No. 368 Victorian Constitution on 23 December 1925 and maintained a life-long association with Freemasonry.

CHAPTER NINE

Masonic art

FREEMASONS

Tracing boards are works of art that can be found in every Masonic Lodge around the world. Wikipedia defines these works as 'painted or printed illustrations depicting the various emblems and symbols of Freemasonry.' It continues: 'They can be used as teaching aids during the lectures that follow each of the three Masonic Degrees, when an experienced member explains the various concepts of Freemasonry to new members. They can also be used by experienced members as self-reminders of the concepts they learned as they went through their initiations.'

In fact, tracing boards represent a major art form that has yet to be widely studied. One day it will take its place in the narrative of western art history. Until now, however, there has been little opportunity for mainstream art experts to place these artworks within a wider context. They sit uneasily between sacred and secular art, occupying neither space comfortably: they do not celebrate a particular religion, but their content is definitely intended to be spiritual.

The tracing boards are stories illustrating stories. Their own story draws on the most ancient history of the Craft, but begins in earnest in the early days of modern Free-masonry, during the medieval period when 'free masons' moved around Europe building cathedrals and other major constructions.

In those days, members of the fraternity met in private rooms in taverns, or in private houses. Everything they used in their ceremonies and rituals had to be portable. Diagrams, used to illustrate lectures and talks, were often scratched into or chalked onto the floor of the room being used for the meeting.

The stories carried lessons, codes and symbols that were simplified over time, and a visual language developed that was loaded with obscure and mysterious references. Carefully preserved by the Craft over the centuries that followed, this visual language is still an integral part of contemporary Masonic iconography.

As the movement grew, the desire to create more permanent materials led to development of the floor cloth – the same stories transcribed onto cloths that could be taken from place to place.

These painted cloths are referred to in Lodge Minutes increasingly through the second half of the 18th century, according to a book called *Tracing Boards: Their Development and Their Designers*, by T.O. Haunch.

It notes that the Lodge of Union, No 129 (UK), holds a set of floor cloths dating from 1772 that 'clearly demonstrate the iconography of the Three Degrees', containing working tools and other symbols that form a basic part of the imagery of later works.

These illustrations on cloth allowed artists within the Craft to express themselves in a more permanent form. Over time they developed styles of composition that laid the foundations for the more formal structures of later Tracing Boards.

Ultimately, as the cloths became more intricate – and more expensive to produce and maintain – the brethren began to pay attention to their preservation. Initially they were hung from rollers on the wall to protect them; next they began to be stretched over frames and hung on the wall, laying the foundation for the later progression into creating them as paintings.

However, while creating beautiful, lasting tools to illustrate lectures and talks, the wall hangings did not meet all the Craft's needs: the floor cloths that replaced the original chalk drawings had served another purpose.

While meetings were held in temporary spaces, it was often necessary to create a space, suitable for the Lodge work, within rooms that were intended for other purposes. The ceremony and ritual of the Craft requires a certain form – known as the 'form of the Lodge'. Where the temporary spaces of the travelling Masons of the Middle Ages didn't provide this form, the brethren created the shape they needed – partly with the floor drawings, and later with the placement of the cloths on the floor around which the brethren assembled, learned and taught. As the cloths evolved and were stretched or mounted they were, in some Lodges, laid on a central trestle or table, around which the brethren would assemble.

A remnant of this practice is seen in modern Lodges in the form of the tiled or painted section of floor in the centre of the room.

By the end of the 18th century, this form of Masonic art moved on again.

Lodges were becoming unsatisfied with the makeshift nature of the cloths. The 'form of the Lodge' had been lost from many designs; in some cases the stories and symbols of the three Degrees had been combined into single cloths for reasons of practical need. What remained, however, was the most important element – the symbolism contained within the imagery.

Next step was the creation of sets of boards designed for permanent use within individual Lodges, a progress that was, in hindsight, quite logical. As a vehicle for expression they offered artists from outside and within the Craft opportunity to explore styles, composition and interpretation of the narrative for instruction in the Three Degrees.

Devices that are common to the imagery in the tracing boards are found also as integral components of Lodge rooms. They form a language understood by Masons for understanding and teaching the Craft, and for assigning rank, or Degrees of the Craft, attained by members of a Lodge as they progress through levels of learning. These visual devices fall loosely into six different groups: tools, stones, architecture, nature, codes or diagrams and mystical symbols.

The tools

The tools relate originally to the Craft of stonemasonry and within Freemasonry, as explained in Chapter Seven, they can be divided into three main groups. There their moral and spiritual teachings were outlined: here we see them as interpreted by the creative artist.

The first group includes the working tools of the Entered Apprentice at the First Degree: the gavel, the chisel and the gauge. To the artist, they represent passion and the capacity to energise a situation; education and the ability to analyse; and the intellectual capacity to determine how much of these to use, and when to use them, thus creating a balance.

The next group, specific to the Second Degree, includes the tools of the Fellow Craft, seen as tools of testing. They are the plumb-rule, the level and the square. To the Masonic artist, the first relates to the use of licence, the second to the use of restraint and the third defines the relationship between licence and restraint.

The tools of the Master Mason, the third group, are design tools. The pencil, representing creativity, the tool that makes the drawing; the skerrit – a string on a reel – constrains the pencil, representing occasions where we should constrain creativity; and the compass is the instrument of proportion that keeps creativity and restraint in balance. The three sets can be seen to contain elements of a complementary and contradictory nature, always with an element in the form of the third tool, about balance.

The stones

Stones can be found in various shapes, sizes and stages of preparation. Ashlars were the foundation stones of King Solomon's Temple in Jerusalem. In Masonic usage we find two ashlars in particular, the Rough Ashlar and the Perfect Ashlar. The Rough Ashlar is the chunk of stone, roughly quarried, that is ready to work. It symbolises the Entered Apprentice who is at the beginning of a learning journey that is seeking refinement. The Perfect Ashlar is ready to be used in a building. It has been worked, cut and polished to fit a particular position, and represents the individual after he has worked to improve himself.

Architecture

Architectural motifs are logical extensions of stones. The ancient lore of modern Freemasonry in the Middle East is centred on the Temple of King Solomon in Jerusalem, completed in 960 BCE. In a Masonic context, the temple represents the body, the mind, the spirit.

That temple was a holy space, dedicated to God. So, according to Masonic teaching, is the 'temple' of the body, mind and spirit dedicated to the path of learning, improvement and striving for betterment through the Craft.

The Three Orders of Architecture are represented by three historical columns, Ionic, Doric and Corinthian, meaning, in turn, Wisdom, Strength and Beauty.

Nature

Elements of the natural world abound in Masonry. Stars, clouds, terrestrial and celestial globes, the Sun and the moon can all be found on the tracing boards, represented in Lodge rooms and on various accoutrements and regalia. They represent themselves and the universal human need to connect with the universe. For example, a sprig of acacia features on the tracing board illustrating the story of the Third Degree, symbolising the ever-present hope for divine guidance and protection.

Codes, diagrams and mystical symbols

Seven different liberal arts and sciences are celebrated and commemorated in Masonry, originating from Classical Greek and Roman teaching: grammar, rhetoric, logic, arithmetic, geometry, music and astronomy. In this context, they represent education and its attendant values. Plato's suggestion was that education was something that could lift the mind above the mundane and routine, and enable the individual to comprehend the ultimate aim of philosophy – a fuller understanding of God.

Elements from this group of disciplines that can be found in Masonic imagery include musical notes, geometry diagrams, mathematical equations, passages of text in myriad languages and encrypted codes. Some are common enough that the non-Mason will recognise them; for example, יהוה, often transliterated as *Yahweh* or *Jehovah* and known to Jews as the unspeakable name of God. This is translated throughout the Judeo-Christian world variously as Adonai, Our Lord, or simply, God. Other symbols are cryptograms that have been buried in history or created from combinations of archaic codes specifically to embed information within an image.

The use of the term mystical is loose, encompassing symbols of an other-worldly nature. Angels are representative of the watchfulness of God, known in Masonry as the Great Architect and represented by the Renaissance image of the 'All-seeing Eye' used for the Great Seal of the new United States in 1776 and first used in Masonry more than 20 years later.

Concepts such as the Three Graces appear sometimes in human form, and sometimes in more abstract ways.

Composition

Throughout the vast and complex range of Masonic artwork, symbols frequently come in groups containing significant tensions. The tools come in sets of three, with two opposing or contradictory pieces held in balance by the third. Ashlars are in pairs, one rough and one smooth and perfectly finished, representing the individual at the beginning and at the end of his journey.

The Masonic Lodge is the building where the work of the Craft takes place. The Operative Lodge, on the other hand, is a small building found on every building site, which was where the craftsmen met, ate, and did some types of work. In Masonic tracing boards the Temple and the Masonic Lodge, representing complexity, ritual and completeness are offset by the Operative Lodge that houses the everyday, the mundane and the ordinary.

The Masonic artists put these different forms side by

side within symbolic frameworks so they are ritualised and commemorated, giving the tracing boards extraordinary power as teaching aids, as well as works of art. To the Mason, they offer a heightened awareness of differences within similarities, so it becomes impossible for them to pass unnoticed. Part of the work of passing through the Three Degrees requires acceptance of contradiction and oppositional factors in the human condition.

Example: Richard Reid

One very early set of tracing boards held in the Museum of Masonry at the Sydney Masonic Centre was created by Richard Reid in 1827. They were painted in oil and gilt on stretched canvas. (See colour section.)

The board of the First Degree depicts the elements of instruction in a realistic and straightforward style. The work has a chequered, tessellated border, echoing the tessellated floor in the lower third of the composition. This represents the interior of a Lodge, the mosaic pattern reflecting the diversity of creation. Four tassels in the corners of the board signify the four cardinal virtues of Temperance, Fortitude, Prudence and Justice. The space on the floor is busy with objects and elements of the story, bounded by the three columns of Wisdom, Strength and Beauty.

The floor seems to float out over a distant landscape of bare hills, under a lowered and somewhat threatening sky. The clouds break in the top quarter of the work revealing in the centre the all-seeing Eye – the Deity – with downward streaming rays of light illuminating the central space between the columns. The Eye is flanked by the Sun on the left and the Moon and Stars on the right, messengers of the Great Architect's Divine Will. They are balanced by terrestrial and celestial globes directly underneath on the far edge of the floor.

Directly under the Eye is the Volume of Sacred Law supporting the ladder – representing Jacob's ladder and the hope of ascending to God through learning. The Three Graces, shown here in classical human form, are present to assist in the acquisition of virtues.

The Rough Ashlar rests at the foot of the Doric column on the left and the Perfect Ashlar is at the base of the Corinthian column. The tools of all Three Degrees of Masonry are present in the composition suggesting, perhaps, that the journey is ongoing for all candidates, that lessons learned at each stage are not to be forgotten as they progress further.

The second tracing board of this set is a balanced and symmetrical formal composition. The Temple, occupying the upper three quarters of the board is of austere Georgian style. It is flanked by two columns, traditionally representing the pillars of fire and smoke that accompanied the Israelites' wanderings in the desert in their search for the Promised Land. At the top of each column is a sphere which, although lacking detail, represent the terrestrial and celestial spheres. The winding staircase is guarded by the Junior Warden, who requires a password to indicate that the candidate has accomplished the necessary tasks and is properly motivated to travel this next stage of learning.

Climbing the stairs is a continuation of the mystical journey begun with Jacob's ladder. At the top of the staircase is the Senior Warden, guarding the entrance to the Middle Chamber. The Middle Chamber is representative of the soul, so this is a journey that takes the candidate deeper into the self.

The bottom of the composition is a separate landscape, depicting the story of Jephthah the Gileadite, who led an army against the Ammonites (Judges 11:1 – 12:7). After succeeding, he was forced to battle the Ephraimites, who wanted to share in his spoils. In the course of the battle, many Ephraimites were slain, identified through their inability to pronounce a password Jephthah had given his soldiers – the origin of the Word required to ascend the winding staircase. In the foreground of the landscape is a single ear of ripe wheat, a symbol of wisdom and enlightenment. It also represents a process of maturation.

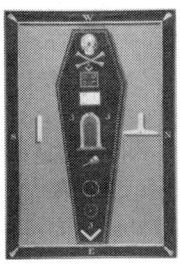

Reid's third board is starkly simple. The lesson of the Third Degree is how to die. The black coffin is central, with a grey background. The four tassels are here again, suggesting that the cardinal virtues are necessary attributes to carry an individual through a metaphoric death of self to become an enlightened being.

The tools of the Fellow Craft and Master Mason are also present, making a link between the Second and Third Degrees. The skull, crossbones and coffin represent mortality. They are balanced by the sprig of acacia at the top of the coffin, which refers to the immortality of the soul. The porch and doorway is a reference to the entrance to the Holy of Holies, the inner sanctum of Solomon's Temple.

Example: Richard John Harris

Also in the collection at the Museum is a set of boards by John Harris, one of the most popular creators of tracing boards.

Harris was a miniaturist, draftsman and facsimilist. He was initiated into Freemasonry in 1818 and almost immediately became interested in tracing boards. His designs were quickly adopted, becoming very popular and their general acceptance led to their use as the basis for many later commercial designs. This set was painted in 1845 in oil on canvas.

The Harris boards offer an enormous contrast to the Reid set. Harris uses much more veiled imagery, and tends to reinterpret earlier imagery in a more allegorical style.

The First Degree board has a tessellated border with plump, opulent tassels in the corners. The chequered floor, instead of floating, occupies the width of the picture plane, and disappears into a horizon of clouds. Light streams from the Sun in the top left hand corner of the piece, and from the seven-pointed star placed diagonally below it, which replaces the more traditional All-Seeing Eye as a symbol of the Great Architect. A full moon hovers serenely in a star studded sky.

The entire work is composed around a single vanishing point, focused on the cup at the base of the ladder. This powerful treatment draws the eye immediately to the centre of the image, then up the ladder towards the star (the ladder presented as a staircase of light with no visible means of support).

The Sacred Book of Law sits on a light-bathed plinth adorned with twin columns. Faith is represented by the chalice and hand, Hope by the anchor part-way up, and Charity in the form of a heart. The Rough Ashlar sits in the lower right side of the composition, the Perfect Ashlar is slightly left of centre at the bottom. The tools of all three Degrees are stacked around the bases of the columns, suggesting a readiness to be collected and used.

The second board is a marked departure from the austerity of Reid's Georgian Temple. The architecture of the Temple is a mix of Middle Eastern styles, heavily ornamented. Again, Harris has used a single vanishing point, this time converging within the open doorway leading to the inner sanctum. Unlike Reid's, the view is from *within* the Temple, creating a sense of immediacy and expectation not evident on the earlier board. The Junior Warden at the bottom of the staircase has his back to the viewer, watching through the doorway and over the landscape. The narrative of Jephthah's story is assumed knowledge, the landscape lacking the figures of Reid's depiction. However, the ear of wheat is prominently placed just outside the portico.

Harris's third board has none of the restraint of Reid's almost monochromatic work. In this board, as in the rest of the set, the style is exuberantly coloured in high key tones, reflecting a Victorian taste for florid ornamentation that is very different from the restrained Regency style of the Reid boards.

For example, the backdrop to the coffin is a glowing orange with a maelstrom of clouds in the upper third. The heavily black-bordered coffin shape becomes a work within the work, framing a lifelike skull and crossbones and a colonnaded approach to the Holy of Holies, the Hebrew inscription, ל קדש יהוה, translating literally as 'holy to God'. The tools are all here, bringing together the Three Degrees and suggesting that while the journey has been taken, all the elements of the individual are carried for all time. The acacia sprig, on the top of the coffin, has its base in a small heap of soil, making a very clear statement about the continuity of the soul, rather than the more symbolic message given in Reid's work with the sprig floating amorphously above the coffin.

The enormous popularity of Harris's boards is demonstrated by other sets in the Museum painted by different artists, using his designs.

One set painted in 1845, known as the 'Emulation' set after a particular style of ritual, is compositionally identical, and elements of the detail are the same as the Harris boards, but the painting style has been simplified and has naturalistic decorative motifs on the borders rather than the traditional checks.

Another small set, the Zetland boards of 1877, is made up of small copies of the Harris boards. It is named after the Earl of Zetland who was Grand Master of the Hong Kong Lodge at the time they were made. Like the Emulation boards, these lack the vivid luminosity of the original Harris boards, although as they carry all the elements required to tell the stories, they are perfectly serviceable Masonic tools in themselves.

This raises the issue of their merit as art pieces, which is a completely separate discussion from that of their purpose. Where there is a clear purpose for the works, it seems that their artistic worth is, perhaps, of secondary consideration. However, when it comes to placing them within the official language of art, there are different criteria. The main difficulty is whether it's even possible to include them within a particular genre: the way they straddle religious and secular art makes this very complex.

Defining a religion means being able to attribute to it a deity, a text and a people. Masons require that their members believe in a Supreme Being, but as they come from myriad religious backgrounds it can be argued that there are many different deities, depending on the creed. One definition of religion in the Macquarie Dictionary is 'the quest for the values of the ideal life, involving three phases, the ideal, the practices for attaining the values of the ideal, and the theology or worldview relating the quest to the environing universe'. So it could be said that Masonry fills a certain level of the criteria to meet the definition.

When related terminology is broken down and explored, this becomes a stronger possibility. 'Religious', as used to describe this genre of art, could be defined as 'appropriate to religion or to sacred rites of observances'. 'Ritual', another term that can definitely be applied to Masonic practices, carries, among others, this definition: 'a prescribed or established rite, ceremony, proceeding or service'. So, again, perhaps it could be said that Masonic practices *do* fall within the parameters that would allow the tracing boards, with their attendant ritual purpose, to be included in the canon of religious art.

Whether or not they can or should be included in the canon makes no difference, of course, to the place they hold within Masonic practice. They are teaching tools that are still being used. People within Masonry continue to create them, based on the principles of past designs, but using any number of new media and technologies. They remain a vehicle of expression for artists within Masonry, as do the doctrines of the many religious practices of modern Masons for artists moved to create religious art. Within the Craft of Masonry, they are just one aspect of a rich arts tradition that includes architecture, music, literature and decorative and fine art.

John Oxley
(1783–1828)

John Joseph William Molesworth Oxley was born in Yorkshire in 1783. He worked as a coastal surveyor in the Navy, was appointed as Surveyor-General of New South Wales in 1811 and then began exploring the country.

Governor Macquarie instructed him to map the course of the Lachlan River. With George Evans and botanist Alan Cunningham, Oxley followed the river for two months in 1817 until he reached impassable marshes and returned to Bathurst.

He tried again in 1818 along the Macquarie River. The team travelled through the area, now Tamworth, naming the river that runs through it after England's Prime Minister, Robert Peel. When they reached the Hastings River they followed it to the mouth and named the area Port Macquarie.

In 1820, Oxley published *Journals of Two Expeditions into the Interior of New South Wales* giving the first detailed description of the Australian inland he had explored. Incorrectly assuming that much of the inland was barren, Oxley returned to coastal surveying, making several trips along the coast.

He travelled with Hamilton Hume and James Meehan from Liverpool to Jervis Bay, NSW. In 1823 he explored the area around Moreton Bay, Queensland, seeking a site for a new penal colony. He explored the Brisbane River, naming it after Governor Brisbane, and recommended a new settlement there.

Exploration was not Oxley's only achievement. He organised land sales in the colony, was a keen supporter of cultural life, a sheep breeder who won prizes at agricultural shows and a founder of the Bank of New South Wales. He served on the first Legislative Council and remained Surveyor-General of New South Wales until his death in 1828.

He is remembered by the Sydney suburb, Oxley Park, Oxley Highway, Oxley Wild Rivers National Park and in a statue on a facade of the Lands Department Building, Bridge Street, Sydney.

John Oxley was a member of the Lodge of Social and Military Virtues No. 227, Irish Constitution. Several Lodges are named in his honour.

Earle Page
(1880-1961)

The fifth of 11 children of a blacksmith, Earle Christmas Grafton Page was born in Grafton, NSW and would grow up to be Prime Minister – for 20 days.

Earle Page studied medicine at Sydney University before joining a medical practice in his home town. In 1904 he became one of the first Australians to own a car. In World War I he served as a doctor in the First Australian Infantry Force and during his later years in politics, became known as 'the Doc'.

Described as a man of 'boundless energy and fertile ideas', Dr Page successfully contested the 1919 Federal election as a representative of the Farmers and Settlers Association. The following year, along with 10 other members elected on similar tickets, he formed the Country Party and emerged as its Parliamentary leader the following year.

After the 1922 elections, Page used Country Party numbers to influence the governing Nationalist Party to replace its leader, Billy Hughes, with Stanley Bruce and to accept the Country Party as its partner in a Coalition government. Dr Page became Deputy Prime Minister to Bruce and Treasurer from 1923–29. In 1925 he was credited with having the shortest-ever official stay in Britain – just one day – before again becoming Deputy Prime Minister following the 1934 election. He was knighted in 1938.

When Prime Minister Joseph Lyons died in office in 1939, Dr Page was sworn in as Prime Minister, a position he held for 20 days prior to the election of Robert Menzies.

Earle Page was initiated into Freemasonry at Lodge Prince Leopold No. 87 in Grafton on December 4, 1917.

Vic Patrick
(1920–2006)

Vic Patrick has been called the best Australian boxer never to have won a world title.

Born Victor Patrick Lucca in 1920, he had modest beginnings, growing up in Sydney in the Depression. He became an Australian legend, earning enough from boxing to buy a hotel at Woolloomooloo, Sydney.

In 1940, preparing for his first fight, his equally famous trainer, Ern McQuillan, asked his name. 'Lucca,' said Vic. 'That's Italian, isn't it?' asked McQuillan, 'We can't have you fight as Victor Lucca, there's a war on.' Australia was fighting Italy and Italians here were being interned as enemy aliens.

All who knew Vic Patrick ... he later adopted the name by deed poll ... were impressed by his skill and stamina in the ring, but also knew him as a quiet, dignified man and a top sportsman.

Despite his Italian origins and the war, Australia loved him. Once he started fighting – he had a debut run of 20 wins, 19 by knockout – he was a hero and a winner. The Australian Lightweight and Welterweight Champion retired to referee bouts at the old Sydney Stadium – the 'Old Tin Shed' at Rushcutters Bay which was Sydney's main entertainment venue.

Patrick and his wife, Nancy, led a modest lifestyle, perhaps as a consequence of Vic's tough time in the Depression. They had two daughters, Anne and Vicky. At his funeral in 2006, Vicky remembered her father as 'unlike a boxer – certainly not one cut from contemporary cloth. Dad was a placid man; he never raised his voice and didn't like those who did'.

Victor Patrick was initiated into Freemasonry at Lodge Fellowship, No. 623 on January 28, 1942.

Frederick Peters
(1836–1937)

Senior Australians remember the penny ice-cream – a small scoop of ice-cream on a tiny cone. It was all families could afford in the 1930s.

American expatriate, Frederick Augustus Bolles Peters, was the man behind the ice-cream. Born and raised in Michigan, USA, he became a travelling salesman for a Boston drug company at age 18, then for Union Manufacturing Company of Toledo, Ohio, where he quickly rose to sales manager.

Working for a New York company which exported bicycles to Australia, Peters feared the business was failing and came to Sydney. Here he met and married his wife, Daisy (the first of four marriages) at the Hotel Australia in 1897.

As Peters predicted, the company failed. He returned to America, then came back to Sydney in 1899 as an agent for several American firms including the Union Manufacturing Company of Toledo, for which he had worked previously. In the early 1900s he started manufacturing Peters' Pile Cure – an ointment – also claimed to be effective for skin irritations, burns and eczema.

Peters enjoyed his expat lifestyle but remained involved with the American community in Sydney. From time to time he became homesick, and in particular longed for American ice-cream, not then available in Australia.

To remedy this, he leased rooms at a Paddington ice factory and in August, 1907 he started Peters' American Delicacy Company Limited. With catchy slogans such as 'Health Food of a Nation' – which lasted until the 1970s – Peters made his ice-cream a household name.

Made from his mother's recipe, it was an instant hit with Australians and by 1929 he had companies across the country. The Redfern factory became the largest in the British Empire, producing 1,000 gallons of ice-cream an hour.

Frederick Peters retired as managing director of the company in 1936 and died in 1937. Peters' Ice Cream was bought by the multinational, Nestlé, in 1996, but its ice-creams are still locally made under the Peters Ice Cream logo.

Frederick Peters was initiated into Terre Coupee Lodge No. 204, Grand Lodge of Indiana on December 27, 1890.

Chips Rafferty
(1909–1971)

John William Pilbeam Goffage – aka Chips Rafferty – was one of Australia's most significant actors. During his 30-year career (1940s-1970s) he starred in many feature films, working with greats such as Richard Burton, Marlon Brando and Elvis.

Born in 1909 in Broken Hill, NSW, Rafferty spent his childhood towering over everyone else. At 13 he was already a six-footer, and often teased for it. 'Chips' came from long, lean and gangling English comic, Cornelius Chips.

After his father's death, Chips, aged 16, became a miner, kangaroo shooter, drover and sheep shearer. His first acting gig was as an extra in *Ants in His Pants* in 1938. He was only 'on' for five minutes but his comedic talent and laconic bushman appeal branded him 'the typical Aussie'.

Charles Chauvel's *40,000 Horsemen* made the young man a star, but his name, John Goffage, didn't fit. 'Chips' seemed fine – 'Rafferty' arrived when he said, 'What sort of Rafferty Rules business is this anyway?'

In 1941 Rafferty enlisted in the Royal Australian Air Force, entertaining the troops. During his service he made the film *The Rats of Tobruk* (1943), the only Australian feature film made during the war.

After World War II many war films were made. British director Harry Watt came out to make *The Overlanders* with Rafferty. *Bush Christmas* (1947), *The Loves of Joanna Godden* (1947), *Eureka Stockade* (1949) and *Bitter Springs* (1950) followed, all starring Rafferty.

Rafferty made his first American film in 1951, *Kangaroo* (shot in the Flinders Rangers), then headed to the States with Bud Tingwell to make *The Desert Rats*.

He wrote and produced many films for his own company and with Lee Robinson set up Television Enterprises, buying the Cinesound studios at Bondi Junction.

Rafferty campaigned tirelessly for the Australian film industry. He appeared in *The Sundowners* (1960), *The Mutiny on the Bounty*

(1962) and the television series *Wackiest Ship in the Army* (1965). His last film, *Wake in Fright* (1971), was an Australian production, praised by critics but not successful here.

In 1971 Rafferty was awarded an MBE for his service to the performing arts. His contribution and commitment to the Australian film industry will never be forgotten. His picture appeared on an Australian stamp in 1989. In 2006 Broken Hill City Council named its Entertainment Centre in his honour.

Chips Rafferty was initiated into Freemasonry at Lodge Literature No. 500 UGL of NSW in 1957.

 ### George Reid
(1845–1918)

George Reid was Australia's fourth Prime Minister. A strong and, unlike Barton, unshakeable supporter of free trade, Reid's personality, politics and principles made him an electoral winner in New South Wales. A great supporter of public education, he was a member of the NSW Parliament for 20 years, Premier for five years and Leader of the Opposition in the new Federal Government.

The only Prime Minister to be a member of the Free Trade Party, Reid was in office for 11 months from August 18, 1904. That may seem a short term by today's standards, but his government was the second longest serving of the first seven Federal governments.

He was knighted in 1911 and further honoured in 1916.

It was under Reid's leadership that the act setting up the Commonwealth Conciliation and Arbitration Court was passed. As an avid imperialist, Sir George Reid was later Australia's High Commissioner to London and, remarkably, a member of the British House of Commons for the last two years of his life.

George Reid was initiated into Freemasonry at Lodge Centennial No. 169 United Grand Lodge of New South Wales on November 16, 1896.

CHAPTER TEN

Masonic music

The fact that Freemasonry is open to people from many backgrounds means it has proved attractive to a wide range of creative individuals: artists, writers, musicians, architects and others in what, these days, is being called 'the creative class'. That, in turn, has led to the development, over hundreds of years, of a rich culture of creativity in Freemasonry around the world.

The specific celebration of the seven liberal arts and sciences – grammar, rhetoric, logic, arithmetic, geometry, music and astronomy – creates a culture within Masonic groups in which artists can feel accepted and encouraged to pursue their work. The products of their creative genius are also embraced: the objects, artwork, buildings and music made by many Masons are part of the Lodges to which they belong and, in some cases, part of the wider community of Freemasonry.

As the Craft opens up to the world of the 21st century, this artistic heritage is becoming available to a wider audience for the first time. The study of Freemasonry and Masonic culture, including music, could well become a hot topic in its own right.

Music, as a component of ritual, has been used by religious and secular people throughout the ages. Emotionally, we respond to both melody and harmony in conjunction with ritual itself. It is also a means of bringing a group of people together and making the ritual experience inclusive. People who would not normally sing will join in with a well-known hymn as part of a church service. The chanted memorial prayer *El male rachamim*, the only music at a traditional Jewish funeral, brings the mourners together in a moment during the burial service that has not changed for centuries.

Indeed, the therapeutic benefits of music are only just being fully understood in our times, as psychologists and others explore the impact of music on the human psyche, whether it is enjoyed actively or passively. Once again, modern science is confirming ancient wisdom.

Music has been a fundamental part of Freemasonry for hundreds of years. Australian Lodge rooms have always featured some form of organ and a dedicated organist. Songs and hymn-like works are sung by Lodge members as part of ceremonies, while accompanying and incidental instrumental music contributes to make a reinforcing environment for rituals.

The requirement for music has drawn on the talents of the brethren and outside sources. There have been musicians who have been influenced by Masonry and Masons influenced by musicians. Some Masonic composers and performers have made music specially for Masonic ceremonies; in some cases, Masonry has informed their music while not being specifically Masonic; and in other cases the Masonic composers and performers seem to have kept their music entirely separate. There is a great deal of academic discourse about these differences: nonetheless, the journey of the Freemason is a journey of personal growth and development. It must be difficult for any observer to judge precisely how the inner development of each composer is manifested in the beauty of his music.

As Masons come from such diverse backgrounds, the music reflects this breadth, drawing on many religious and cultural influences. In addition to the creation and appropriation of music for Masonic purposes, the works of

185

Masonic composers have found a place within the canon of general music.

Masonic composers

In the classical world, Mozart (1756–1791), Johann Christian Bach (1732–1782), Franz Joseph Haydn (1732–1809), Luigi Cherubini (1760–1842), Samuel Wesley (1766–1837) and Jean Sibelius (1865–1957) were all Masons.

Haydn and Sibelius appear to fall into the category of composers who kept their Masonry and composing separate from each other. It is thought that Sibelius' great nationalistic work, *Finlandia*, 1899/1900, has some Masonic overtones, although that has never been conclusively proved. What is clear is that its richness and depth and power are the product of a highly developed, highly creative composer.

Bach, Cherubini and Wesley were all known for their dedication to sacred music, being church organists. Wesley particularly, is a well-known composer of hymns. Here again, it's easy to see the link between the spirituality of the music and the spiritual journey of Freemasonry. And we'll see more about Mozart shortly.

From Sousa to Louis via Gershwin and Glenn

In more contemporary music, the familiar names of John Philip Sousa (1854–1932), George Gershwin (1898-1937), Irving Berlin (1888–1989), W. S. Gilbert (1836–1911) and Arthur Sullivan (1842–1900), Louis Armstrong (1901–1971), Glenn Miller (1904–1944), and Smoky Dawson (1913–2008) also number among the Masons. Of these, the first is perhaps the least well-known ... an American composer of marches that are more widely recognised than the name of their creator.

John Philip Sousa (1854–1932) himself embodied the diversity that characterises Masonic music: he was born in Washington DC to parents of Portuguese, Spanish and Bavarian origin. Like other famous musicians, he started his musical career at an early age, learning to play the violin when he was six.

When he was 13, his father, a trombonist in the Marine Band, enlisted his son in the US Marine Corps as an apprentice, to keep him from joining a circus band, so it's hardly surprising that Sousa should have become king of the march. Probably his best known work is *Stars and Stripes Forever*, the national march of the United States, although fans of *Monty Python's Flying Circus* may know him better for *The Liberty Bell*, which was played as the credits rolled after each episode of that classic series. *The Gladiator March* is another popular favourite, and the US Marine Corps still uses *Semper Fidelis* as its official march.

The Magic Flute

Probably the music most widely associated with Masonry is Mozart's highly successful opera *Die Zauberflöte* (*The Magic Flute*). The story of this one work alone would make an interesting chapter in the history of the culture of the Craft, if only because there is much debate about whether or not it was written to tell a Masonic story, whether or not it was written as Masonic music.

But what I found especially interesting, in researching this material, is that it was also written at a time and in a place where the subject of Freemasonry was something of a political hot potato. (You might expect a music-lover born in Vienna to know more about its history, but of course my education was in Australia, and clearly it didn't get quite this far.)

This curious fragment of the story began in 1731, when Francis, Duke of Lorraine, was initiated as a Freemason in the Austrian Netherlands. Five years later he married Maria Theresa and soon afterwards became Emperor and joint ruler of the Austrian Empire of the Hapsburgs.

Maria Theresa, a conservative Catholic, was firmly opposed to the wave of new ideas that broke over Europe during the Enlightenment, and this attitude included a strong opposition to Masonry. In 1764, she issued an Imperial Decree forbidding the practice of Freemasonry – although apparently this decree was largely ignored. My research didn't establish whether her husband was required to give up his membership of the Craft, though this does seem likely!

In 1765, Francis died and his son, as Joseph II, became joint ruler with his mother. Joseph was not a Freemason, but had a benign interest in the fraternity, so when Maria Theresa died in 1780, her decree died with her.

However there was still pressure from conservative members of the clergy. In 1781 Joseph decreed that no spiritual or secular orders were to submit to a foreign authority outside the Empire, which led to the establishment, in 1784, of the *Grosse Landesloge von Österreich* (The Grand Lodge of Austria), with 62 Lodges. This was the year that Mozart was admitted as an initiate: a brand new member of a brand new Lodge.

Stanley Sadie notes in his biography of Mozart that 'The society was essentially one of liberal intellectuals, concerned less with political ideals than with the philosophical ones of the Enlightenment, including Nature, Reason and the brotherhood of Man'. This description of the fraternity was reflected in the membership of the Viennese Lodges which included nobility, senior army officers, leading businessmen, and intellectuals of the city.

Further pressure from the clergy led Joseph to issue a decree, in 1785, ordering the consolidation of Lodges – and government scrutiny of their membership lists. This was the year Mozart became a Master Mason, and also the year in which he wrote *Gesellenreise* K 468, a song for the installation of a new journeyman. A cantata for tenor and male chorus, *Die Maurerfreude* K 471 (*The Mason's Joy*) followed in the following month.

It was a busy year for Mozart. The deaths of two Masonic brethren, Duke Georg August of Mecklenburg-Strelitz and Count Franz Esterhazy, prompted the composition of *Maurerische Trauermusik* K 477/479a (*The Masonic Funeral Music*).

The Magic Flute, K 620, was Mozart's last finished work, completed in the year of his death, 1791. Mozart lived long enough to see the opera performed in Vienna and conducted the first performance himself. The poster outside the theatre announced 'The Magic Flute, a grand opera in two Acts by Emanuel Schikaneder ... The music is by Herr Wolfgang Amade Mozard[!], Kapellmeister ...' Herr Schikaneder, who did indeed write the libretto, based on a fairytale by Wieland, was also a Mason.

Mozart arranged for his parents to see the opera and was delighted by their praise, as he reported to his wife. He even played games with the conductor, one famous evening, by contributing unexpected music from the wings during a performance. His last letters show how much he enjoyed its rapid success with audiences.

Mozart did not live to see the suppression of Masonry ten years later by the Emperor Joseph's nephew Francis II, who believed that all secret societies, including Freemasonry, were working against him. In fact, it seems the Lodges had seen this coming and closed voluntarily in the previous year: Freemasonry did not return to Austria until 1918.

The story of the opera

The Magic Flute is the dramatic story of the young prince Tamino, who loses his way during a hunt and encounters the Queen of the Knight, via three ladies he meets in the forest. The Queen tells him that her beautiful daughter, Pamina, is being held captive by the wicked Sarastro, and starts him on a mission to find her. She gives him a magic flute intended to protect and sustain him in his quest.

Along the way Tamino meets the bird-catcher, Papageno, who becomes his companion on the search. The two are assisted by three boys, who, they are told, will guide them. Papageno is given a magic chime of bells.

Meanwhile Sarastro, who is leaving on a journey, leaves instructions for Tamino to be received at the gates of the temple and questioned ... it is time, he says, for him to become an initiate.

The two heroes become separated. Papageno finds Pamina, and tells her that rescue is on the way. Tamino, with the three boys, arrives at a grove with three temples, each with a word above the door: Reason, Wisdom and Nature. They tell him that he is now within reach of his goal but he must remain steadfast, tolerant and discreet.

Tamino tells the keeper of the Temple of Wisdom that he is seeking Love and Virtue. He claims that Sarastro is an evil villain – but he is asked how he knows this. Unable to tell Tamino the whole story, the keeper of the Temple merely hints that there is more going on than he has been led to believe, and that Sarastro is not an evil man.

Sarastro arrives, with Pamina and Papageno, and orders that the two men be tested in the Temple for their virtue, discretion and charity. The priests vote to accept Tamino as a candidate. His success is rewarded by Sarastro who commends him for his steadfastness but announces that Tamino must be tested with further trials.

Tamino prepares for his initiation through these trials of fire, water, air and earth. If he can overcome his fear of death he will be enlightened. Pamina arrives and begs him to take her with him. The guards praise her bravery and agree, and they pass through the gates together.

A comical sub-plot involving the bird-catcher and his beloved is not detailed here, as the story of Tamino's search for enlightment and his initiation are the focus of the Masonic interest.

Many people believe the opera tells a Masonic story, others simply accept that it speaks of deep wisdom. And perhaps its greatness is just that: those who enjoy the opera are free to enjoy it at the level at which it reaches them.

As another famous Freemason of the day, Johann Wolfgang von Goethe, said: 'It is enough that the crowd would find pleasure in seeing the spectacle; at the same time, its high significance will not escape the initiates.'

An expert's interpretation

The renowned Swedish director, Göran Järvefelt, wrote the following program notes for his production of *The Magic Flute* for The Australian Opera in 1986.

Gods of Light

Now marching down the road of morning
The sun is on his way.
His eyes flash out a joyful warning:
The wise must win the day.
O peace look kindly on our striving,
The hearts of peaceful men reviving.
Then all the world is paradise
And men may all be gods of light.

These are the words of the three boys, at their appearance just before Pamina's attempted suicide and at the start of the finale of Mozart's opera The Magic Flute. *Their vision is apocalyptic, their better world actual and imminent.*

Yet how often is the same opera, with its wide-eyed vision, portrayed as trivial pantomime or solemn mumbo-jumbo? At one extreme it is a fairy-tale about nothing, an incomprehensible plot redeemed by wonderful music. At the other it is a holy, sacred ritual, all movements subdued in an aura of saintliness. Both these views, and the sometimes uneasy mixture of the two, ignore the opera's continued vitality, its sense of the actual. For this opera is about us today. In our technocratic, materialistic world, it has become even more actual. For that reason, this production avoids reference to ancient Egypt and to the omens. It seems instead to concentrate on people as real and psychologically true.

The story is a quest or awakening. It shows the journey from darkness to light, from unconsciousness to consciousness, from being unaware to becoming aware.

The journey is undertaken by four characters – Tamino and Pamina, Papageno and Papagena; these four stand for us. They wander, in order to become full human beings. They must go through the trials of the opera – their suffering, their longing – to develop all their latent talents. The trials exist to bring alive these qualities and senses.

The trials that beset the four characters should in turn provoke us also to develop. Their purpose is to enable the participants

191

to reach the highest step of human beings – to love, to feel responsibility for each other and the whole human race. This means not just the wish to be loved, but to love in return, not just the wish to be understood but to understand. These are the highest aims to fight for. They are neither easy, nor will everyone reach them. Hence the trials in Mozart's opera, the different steps on the road to the goal described by the three boys.

It is possible to see this story in terms of the human beings who enact it, and it is possible to see it in allegorical terms as the different steps in a pilgrimage of the soul ...

Wisdom is only of value, if you use it. Tamino has to develop his talents, if he is to fulfil his destiny. He must undergo the trials, to conquer his fear of death. Only then can he become part of the unknown. That is what Mozart says and what his opera wants us to do. If these things happen, then human beings will be like gods. It is our task to develop God in ourselves.

Sarastro has picked out three boys from among the people, for their great talents. He sends them to schools, and teaches them wise words and phrases. They belong to the future: it is they who pronounce the credo of The Magic Flute.

'Nobility of heart'

As we said in the introduction to this chapter, music will always be an important component of Masonic life, as it is for all ritual based communities. The diversity of Masonic communities will continue to contribute to a richly diverse music practice within the Craft. And composers and performers who are Masons will also, no doubt, continue to have their work explored for its Masonic significance.

What is useful to remember is that those responsible for the making of the music were highly respected men, as is shown in the words of Brother Karl Friedrich Hensler, the Viennese theatre director, in the words of his eulogy for Mozart:

The death of Mozart is an irreparable loss for Art. His gifts, recognised since childhood, made him one of the wonders of this era. Europe knew and admired him. The Princes loved him and we can call him 'my brother'. But, while it is evident that we should honour his genius, we must not forget to celebrate the nobility of his heart. He was a conscientious member of our Order. His brotherly love, his devout and whole nature, his charity, the joy he showed when one of his brothers benefited from his goodness and talent were his immense qualities that we praise in this day of mourning.

Mervyn Richardson
(1893–1972)

Born at Yarramalong NSW in 1893, Mervyn Victor Richardson had a poor education. He was apprenticed to a jeweller, then became a signwriter. In 1916 he helped his brother, Archibald, build a low-winged monoplane, powered by a radial engine with contra-rotating propellers.

The brothers were filmed demonstrating the machine at Mascot, Sydney – but it crashed later that day.

In the 1920s, Mervyn was a car salesman, designed a coupé body for the locally assembled Austin 7, then set up New South Wales Motors with a showroom in William Street. The business failed in the Depression.

By the early 1930s Mervyn, his wife, Vera and son, Garry, lived in one room at Strathfield. In 1941 the family moved to a house in Concord. When Garry started a lawn-mowing business in 1948, Mervyn made two reel-type mowers for him. Richardson continued building mowers in his backyard, registering the name Victa Mowers in 1950. By 1952 he had built and sold 60 reel-type mowers, with imported Villiers engines.

He hit upon the idea of putting a Villiers engine on its side to drive a set of rotating blades. Within hours he had assembled the prototype Victa Rotary lawnmower: scrap metal, billy-cart wheels, a jam tin petrol tank. Amazingly, the contraption cut fine grass with precision, ploughed through long grass and weeds.

By 1953, Richardson's staff of six produced 60 mowers a week. By 1957 Victa had sold 100,000 mowers, some overseas. In 1966 Number 1,000,000 rolled off the line.

What was so special? Why was an entire routine devoted to Victa in Australia's Olympic Games 2000 Opening Ceremony?

The Victa was brilliant and timely. Previously, mowers had revolving cylinders – like cotton reels on their sides. The Victa Rotary introduced a horizontal disk with blades attached. Spinning very fast, it worked on uneven ground and rough backyards.

Victa levelled the hilly bits – dumped the soil into the hollows. In time you had a lawn instead of just a backyard.

An advertising agency came up with the slogan: 'Turn Grass into Lawn'. Victa did that ... for thousands of first-home owners.

Mervyn Richardson was initiated into Freemasonry at Lodge Wentworth, No. 89, on February 6, 1945.

James Rogers
(1873–1961)

A superb horseman, bushman and crack rifle shot, James Rogers lived on the land in New South Wales and Victoria before joining the Victorian Mounted Rifles in 1898. The following year he enlisted and embarked for South Africa as a private in the 1st Victorian Mounted Infantry Company. In 1900 he was seconded as a corporal to the Provincial Mounted Police, Orange River Colony. Later that year, instead of returning home with his regiment, he joined the South African Constabulary (SAC) as a Sergeant.

In June 1901, Rogers was serving with the SAC's No.6 Troop led by Lieutenant Frank Dickson. The troop was part of a 200-man column patrolling Thaba 'Nchu in search of Boer forces. North of Hout Nek, the column came under Boer sniper fire. Six men, including Dickson and Rogers, waited in ambush and, after surprising the Boers, were themselves attacked on their way back to join the column.

Dickson's horse was shot. Sergeant Rogers rode back, helped his friend up behind him on the horse and carried him to safety. He returned twice to rescue two other men whose horses had bolted, then caught two of the escaped horses and led them back.

Sergeant Rogers was awarded the Victoria Cross on April 18, 1902, following his return to Australia. In late 1914 he was commissioned in the 3rd Light Horse Brigade Train, Australian Army Service Corps, Australian Imperial Force. The following year he was seriously wounded at Gallipoli and evacuated to Egypt. He resigned from the army in 1922 and resumed farming. Following his death in Concord Repatriation

Hospital on October 28, 1961, he was cremated with full military honours in Melbourne.

James Rogers was initiated into Freemasonry at Lodge Robbie Burns No. 88 Victoria on November 11, 1913.

Caleb Soul
(1817–1894)

Soul Pattinson Chemists have filled prescriptions for Australians for over 130 years. The business evolved from a one-roomed chemist shop opened by Caleb Soul in 1872.

Born in London in 1817, Caleb Soul spent 18 years in the drug manufacturing industry in England and America, moving to Sydney in 1863. Seeing a market for imported pharmaceuticals, he opened his first pharmacy in Pitt Street, Sydney with the slogan, 'All goods sold at New York and London prices'. He called it Washington H. Soul, incorporating his son's name.

The business was an instant success and soon required larger premises. The new pharmacy included a ladies only department, run by a trained nurse. This was a 'first' in Australia and hugely popular. It also featured a milk bar and soda fountain which became a social hub.

When the pharmacy was destroyed by fire in 1886, Soul rebuilt on the same site, calling it the Phoenix Building, decorated with a phoenix on the front facade. This building stands today and is one of the busiest Soul Pattinson stores.

Lewy Myall Pattinson, living in England at the time, read about Soul's success and in 1881 came to Australia to investigate. He met Soul and decided there was room in the market for a similar business, opening his first pharmacy in Balmain in 1886. Pattinson's business was run just like Soul's but the two became friends and never opened in direct competition.

When Soul died in 1894, his son Washington carried on. Meanwhile Lewy Pattinson's business continued to prosper. In 1902, Washington decided to retire and invited Pattinson to buy him out. Pattinson re-branded the company, Washington H. Soul Pattinson and Company out of respect for his old friend and it became publicly listed.

By 1937 Soul Pattinson's retail outlets expanded rapidly with over 15 pharmacies opening in New South Wales. Today there are more than 80 nationwide, still bearing the names of the men who created the company.

The quality they instilled in the business has continued through four generations and the company continues to be managed by the Pattinson family.

Caleb Soul was initiated into Freemasonry at the New Concord Lodge No. 181 in London on November 28, 1860.

Hugo Throssell
(1884–1933)

One of 14 children, Hugo Vivian Hope Throssell was the son of a storekeeper and local politician, George Throssell, who became Premier of Western Australia for three months in 1901. With the outbreak of war Hugo and his brother Frank Eric (Ric) joined the 10th Light Horse Regiment, with Hugo commissioned a Lieutenant.

Landing at Gallipoli in August, 1915, Lieutenant Throssell was in the historic charge at the Nek where nine officers and 73 men of his regiment were killed within minutes. His chance to avenge his comrades came at Hill 60 – a battle that had been raging for a week with heavy losses. A moonlight raid on August 29 by the 10th Light Horse was designed to take a long trench, part of which was held by Turkish troops. As a guard, Throssell killed five Turks while his men constructed a barricade across their part of the trench.

A fierce bomb fight began. More than 3,000 bombs were thrown by both sides during the night, with unexploded bombs being picked up and hurled back over the barricade. Towards dawn the Turks made three rushes at the Australian trench but were stopped.

Wounded twice, Hugo Throssell was at one stage in sole command, repeatedly yelling encouragement to his men. For his actions he became the first Western Australian to win a Victoria Cross in the war. While in hospital in England, Throssell was promoted to Captain.

At the second battle of Gaza, Hugo Throssell was again wounded and his brother, Ric, was killed. On the night of Ric's disappearance, Hugo crawled across the battlefield under enemy fire, searching for his brother amongst the dead and dying, whistling with the signal they had used as children.

After the war Throssell married Australian author, Katharine Susannah Prichard, and settled on a farm near Perth. In the Depression he joined the search for gold, but to no avail. When another money-spinning scheme also proved unsuccessful, he shot himself in November 1933. Friends blamed his melancholy on an attack of meningitis at Gallipoli. He was buried with full military honours in Perth.

Hugo Throssell was initiated into Freemasonry at Lodge Bulwer No. 1068 England on June 15, 1917.

Charles 'Bud' Tingwell (1923–2009)

A favourite of stage, screen and television, Charles William 'Bud' Tingwell played many characters, but none so well loved or fondly remembered as he has been himself.

He acquired the nickname 'Bud' before he was born, when friends at the Coogee Surf Club teased his pregnant Mum, asking 'What's budding in there?' which became 'How's the bud today?' before being shortened to 'Bud'.

Bud developed an early love of film and radio. His radio career began as a cadet announcer/panel operator for Sydney radio station, 2CH, making him the youngest radio announcer in Australia at the time.

In 1941 he joined the Royal Australian Air Force. Sent to the

Middle East, he completed 75 missions in Spitfire and Mosquito aircraft as a photographic reconnaissance pilot.

After the war Bud won his first film part, playing a control tower officer in the film *Smithy*, a part he won on the proviso that he wore his own uniform.

Bud played lead roles in many Australian films including *Always Another Dawn*, *Captain Thunderbolt* and *King of the Coral Sea*. A feature role in *The Desert Rats* saw him working with Richard Burton, James Mason and Chips Rafferty in 1952. He was offered a seven-year contract to stay in Hollywood but declined and returned home to continue working in Australian productions

In 1956 he left for England, where he spent 16 years as a star of film, television, theatre and radio before again returning to Australia in 1972 and the role of Inspector Reg Lawson in *Homicide* – Australia's most popular TV drama.

An accomplished director, Bud was later responsible for many other shows including *The Box*, *The Sullivans* and *Cop Shop*. His death in 2009 marked the end of an era in Australian show business.

Charles Tingwell was initiated into Freemasonry at Lodge Carinya, No. 785, on January 27, 1950.

CHAPTER ELEVEN

Another book about Freemasonry?

Literature Review by Dr Bob James

Alarm bells went off in many Masonic jurisdictions around the world when it became known that Dan Brown's next book after *The Da Vinci Code* would be about Freemasonry.

Such was the power of the Brown publishing phenomenon, it was inevitable that whatever he turned his attention to would come under close and searching attention. What might happen to Freemasonry in such a situation? Could the organisation handle the attention? What should be the response?

Members of the Australian media began asking local Grand Lodge officers months ago to comment on the closely-embargoed manuscript. They received the obvious response: 'We have no comment' and the time-honoured rebuke: 'Freemasonry does not engage in public debate as an organisation. And we certainly have nothing to say about a work of fiction we have not seen and know nothing about.'

The Da Vinci Code was a work of fiction, too, but so engaging was the story-telling and so compelling the issues raised that it was argued over as though it was, just possibly, true. This was the author's greatest skill – the situations, the puzzles seemed plausible, the characters and the events seemed at least possible.

Freemasonry is no stranger to intense scrutiny. Indeed, the first published 'revelations' appeared in London in the 18th century not long after what became the United Grand Lodge of England first met in 1717. Continuously since then, Freemasonry has contended with wave after wave of ill-informed criticism and wild conjecture.

Dan Brown has not created but has taken advantage of an already long-running phenomenon. Part of the conundrum of Freemasonry, of course, is that it has fascinated and intrigued many people for such a long time. Without appearing to do anything Freemasonry has attracted attention, and because it has rules about its members not telling non-Masons what goes on behind the Lodge room doors, speculation has been rife.

This current surge in interest began to take shape over thirty years ago. In 1985, when journalist Stephen Knight's book *The Brotherhood* appeared in the UK, it suggested that the Grand Lodge of England had attempted to prevent him getting reliable information and had perhaps even attempted to block publication. He quoted a Grand Lodge 'Quarterly Communication' issued in June, 1981 which included the reminder for all brethren:

> *We have nothing to hide and certainly nothing to be ashamed of, but we object to having our affairs investigated by outsiders…(We) have found that silence is the best policy. Comment or correction only breeds further enquiry and leads to the publicity we seek to avoid … Remember the Antient Charge, 'Behaviour in the Presence of Strangers, not Masons': You shall be cautious in your words and carriage, that the most penetrating stranger shall not be able to discover or find out what is not proper to be intimated.*[i]

This was a policy founded on pragmatism and has much to recommend it to any publicity-shy organisation. To his credit,

---

i   S Cox, *Cracking the Da Vinci Code*, Harper Collins, 2004, p. 70.

Knight explained that the suggestion that Freemasonry, the organisation, had attempted suppression of his book was, in fact, an example of a personal decision taken by a publisher sensitive to the wishes of his father:

> *If the incident does not demonstrate the direct power of Freemasonry, it does offer a vivid example of the devotion that Freemasonry so often inspires in its initiates, a devotion that is nothing less than religious.*

There are perfectly good and innocent reasons for the secrecy and the oaths of loyalty which sustain the barriers between 'insiders' and 'outsiders'. They are nothing more than the barriers between those 'in the know' and those not, also operating in the worlds of commerce, politics and sport. People pay their membership fees and expect to gain some benefit in return, a benefit which justifies the expense and which gives them a mark of belonging to something 'special' and different.

Freemasonry has been spectacularly successful in achieving an aura of being 'something special'. It was never, of course, doing nothing, but just what it was doing has often been the stuff of legend and rumour rather than hard historical research. In the Masonic case, too, it has seemed to observers that there were secrets within secrets, some known to every initiate and others known only to the highest reaches of the organisation. So, whatever Freemasons said was never enough. There always seemed the possibility that there was something more.

But is the current surge in public interest any different? I think it is, for a number of reasons, the main one being that while a policy of strict secrecy may have served its purpose over the preceding three centuries, it is proving unsustainable in the changed circumstances at the beginning of the 21st.

For its first century or so, Freemasonry wrote little down about its inner workings and relied on word-of-mouth for ceremonial continuity. This brought its own problems, not least of which was variations in the rituals from Lodge to

Lodge. Nowadays, either because of the many 'exposés' or because of publishing programs set in motion by Grand Lodges, conformity is insisted upon, in rites, regalia and in responses to outsiders such as enquiring journalists, who may or may not be genuinely interested in the truth.

Knight said he had set out to answer two questions: Does Freemasonry have an influence on life in Britain, as many people believe? And if so, what kind of influence and in which areas of society? He was thus concerned with the possibilities of improper influence in public life in the present and the very recent past. That he had to ask these questions at all shows how successfully the barriers have been maintained but takes us also to the heart of the Masonic dilemma – in secrecy is privacy. But as the outside world has changed, unless Freemasonry also changes, the gap between the reality and the perception becomes so wide that it no longer charms and intrigues but rather appears quaint, comical and eventually irrelevant. The message of Freemasonry remains as it has always been but to communicate that in the modern world requires much more openness and transparency than has ever seemed necessary before.

Freemasonry is being asked new questions across a range of issues and because there are already many books in print, readers, despite the acknowledged barriers, have access to more genuine information, including, importantly, illustrations of many of the key artefacts, such as aprons. They therefore start from a very different point from their counterparts of, say, the time of the French Revolution when Freemasonry was coupled with anti-Government groups such as the Illuminati and blamed for the terror and mayhem convulsing Europe.

Publication of *The Brotherhood* created a local fire-storm of outrage and forced the English Grand Lodge to become more pro-active in its dealings with the non-Masonic public. One long-term consequence has been an acceptance that education of the brethren themselves has been far less than it needed to be. But it is a further part of the Masonic conundrum that the reading public has turned out to be much more interested in the centuries-long history of Freemasonry than the alleged corruption and influence-peddling of recent times.

So, the intellectual context into which Dan Brown has inserted himself involves a better-informed and infinitely more serious debate about important religious and social questions than previously. The bookshelves have a broader range of titles from which to choose, from the scholarly to the puerile, from the deadly dull to the quirky and bizarre.

Scholarly readers in the 1960s and '70s would have noted titles by Francis Yates on the Hermetic tradition, the Enlightenment and the Rosicrucians, and, perhaps, the plea by J.M. Roberts in 1969 that Freemasonry make itself more research-friendly than it had been, since its archives, akin to the Vatican or the KGB, represented storehouses of untapped resources for the better understanding of all our histories.[ii] These urgings had already begun to detonate inside the decision-making offices of English and American Freemasonry before the volumes of paper-back blockbusters began to appear in the 1980s, but further proddings were required.

In 1982, Baigent, Leigh and Lincoln published *The Holy Blood and the Holy Grail* and it is their approach to the 'secrets of Freemasonry' rather than *The Brotherhood* which has spawned follow-ups and long-term media attention. The Italian P-2 conspiracy around the Banco Ambrosiano deflected attention away from English courts and public officials to the Vatican and the role of secret societies in religious conflicts and even to the origins of Christianity itself.

The three co-authors of *HBHG*, as it's come to be known, were wanting to show that descendants of Jesus Christ and Mary Magdalen had made it to the south of France and inspired, if not promulgated the Cathar heresies and the Knights Templar. In 2004, Simon Cox described this book as 'The international best-seller, from which a great deal of the background to *The Da Vinci Code* is drawn':

---

ii   JM Roberts, 'Freemasonry: Possibilities of a neglected topic', in *English Historical Review*, 1969.

Although today's Priory of Sion researchers continue to dispute the veracity of the historical information contained within the book, there is a general agreement overall that Holy Blood, Holy Grail has, for better or for worse, been singularly responsible for unleashing revolutionary religious and historical concepts that had never been publicly examined before.[iii]

When their next book, *The Temple and the Lodge* appeared in 1989, Baigent and Leigh laid down more of the template Dan Brown would later follow by linking the Knights Templar, the Stuart Royal Family, Rosslyn Chapel in Scotland and the founding fathers of the United States of America:

It is in America that our story comes full circle, for it is there that the Knights Templar have received the most fulsome public homage to be paid them anywhere in the world. This homage takes the form of a youth organisation sponsored by Freemasonry, the Order of De Molay, established in Kansas City, Missouri, in 1919.[iv]

Freemasons, behind closed doors and in in-house journals such as *Ars Quatuor Coronatorum* which has been in continuous production since 1886, had long debated possible connections between their organisation, apparently formalised in 1717 in London, and earlier events, but Baigent and Leigh considered themselves pathfinders:

Historians – especially Masonic historians – had long sought either to prove or disprove, definitively, the alleged survival of the Templars in Scotland after the Order had been officially suppressed elsewhere ... (They) had found no conclusive evidence one way or the other.[v]

They claimed to have found the key evidence in Scottish graveyards and churches. For example:

Inside the chapel of Kilmory stood just such a (Templar) cross, dating from before the fourteenth century ... (Inside) the church

---

iii   S Cox, *Cracking the Da Vinci Code*, Harper Collins, 2004, p. 70.

iv   M Baigent & R Leigh, *The Temple and the Lodge*, Cape, 1989, p. 355.

v   M Baigent & R Leigh, 1989, as above, p. 27.

lay a fourteenth century graveslab incised with a sailing galley,
an armed figure and another Templar cross. Above the head of
the armed figure ... was carved a Masonic set-square.[vi]

In 1991 they claimed another 'sensational exposé', that of
a conspiracy to keep hidden from public gaze many of the
Dead Sea Scrolls on the basis that these ancient documents
provided a view of the origins of Christianity not favoured
by the guardians of mainstream opinion:

The Dead Sea Scrolls offer a new perspective on the three great
religions born in the Middle East. The more one examines those
religions, the more one will discern not how much they differ,
but how much they overlap and have in common – how much
they derive essentially from the same source.[vii]

They were not the only authors claiming startling new inter-
pretations of this long span of history, equally important to
the Christian churches and to Freemasonry. Two Freemasons,
Knight and Lomas, in 1996 achieved commercial success
with *The Hiram Key*, in which they asserted they had found
'the secret scrolls of Jesus' under Rosslyn Chapel in Scotland,
a building they claimed was 'a detailed reconstruction of
Herod's Temple'. These 'facts' they said, linked the Egyptian
Pharoahs with Jesus, the Knights Templar and Freemasonry,
a bridge they then turned to the defence of the Protestant
Reformation and secular democracy:

The attack on the Templar Order by a greedy and unimportant
French king proved to be the first vital step in the long process
of releasing the Christian world from the prevailing principle of
intellectual castration, exercised by the Vatican, and allowing
it to build a civilisation driven by a desire for knowledge and a
recognition of the worth of the individual.[viii]

---

vi   Baigent & Leigh, 1989, as above, p. 34.
vii M Baigent & R Leigh, *The Dead Sea Scrolls Deception*, Cape, 1991,
     p. 340.
viii C Knight & R Lomas, *The Hiram Key*, Arrow, 1996, p. 381. In 2004 this
     was followed up with *The Book of Hiram*, also published by Arrow.

In the following year, another team, Picknett and Prince, claimed to have trumped all previous efforts:

> *We owe a debt of gratitude to all these writers for the light they have shed on our shared areas of investigation, but we believe that all of them have failed to find the essential key to the heart of these mysteries.*[ix]

In *The Templar Revelation* they claimed to have proved that not Jesus Christ but John the Baptist and Mary Magdalen were the founders of 'a secret underground religion' which, connecting Leonardo da Vinci, the Turin Shroud, the Knights Templar and the Freemasons, located the 'secret guardians of the true identity of Christ' and thus the true foundations of the established Christian churches:

> *We believe that, on the whole, the heretics have a case worth making. Certainly, grave injustice has been done to the historical figures of John the Baptist and Mary Magdalene, and the time to set the record straight is long overdue. Respect for the Female Principle and the whole concept of sexual alchemy needs to be understood if Western mankind has a hope of entering the new millennium free from repression and guilt.*[x]

Needless to say, such a rich brew has continued to ferment in fevered imaginations and to throw up yet more titles. In the United States, particularly, a number have come from Christian fundamentalists attempting to claw back the Biblical 'home ground'. Others, by initiated Masons, have claimed to be designed to help the general public find a stress-free way through the many controversies. The more useful include *The Complete Idiot's Guide to Freemasonry*, *Freemasons for Dummies*, and *The Everything Freemasons Book*, but even these should be treated with caution. Inevitably, for an organisation holding to both ancient and modern beliefs, findings of genuinely new research are, at times, being uncritically mixed with recycled 'facts' from the titles

---

ix   L Picknett & C Prince, *The Templar Revelation*, Bantam, 1997, p. 16.
x   Picknett & Prince, 1997, as above, p. 480.

which are being superseded. Some of the US-generated titles are unreliable for even though they mean well and canvass many possibilities they remain full of words like 'perhaps' and 'maybe' and are therefore useless to searchers after solid information. For example:

> *As Secretary of (the US) Congress for fifteen years, Thompson witnessed the birth and struggle of the new nation and recorded its transactions for posterity.* ***It is possible*** *that the wisdom he gained from the Native Americans and his Rosicrucian friends in the Ephrata community provided him with the insight he needed to establish the final design of America's Great Seal.*[xi]
> [My emphasis.]

A similar, but somewhat better effort is *Solomon's Builders* which concentrates on Washington, the town, and the influences exercised upon its planners by Freemasons, one of which the author claims 'invented the United States.'[xii]

Away from the limelight, the work of serious research was continuing and, riding to some extent on Dan Brown's coat-tails, some of it was being more widely published than would have been the case without his assistance and that of other best-sellers. A book that falls between the merely sensational and the well-researched is John Robinson's *Born in Blood*. Released in 1989 and again claiming to reveal 'the lost secrets of Freemasonry', this effort centred on 'certain unexplained aspects' of the Peasants Revolt in 1381, a long-standing staple of English schoolboy history. Robinson claimed

> *that far from being a spontaneous uprising which happened to involve 100,000 low-born Englishmen spread throughout the country, it was in fact secretly organised by the Knights Templar.*[xiii]

Again, links from this medieval history to 'modern' society and the Freemasons were claimed:

---

xi   R Hieronimus, *Founding Fathers, Secret Societies*, Destiny Books, 1989, p. 92.
xii   C Hodapp, *Solomon's Builders*, Ulysses, 2007, p. 105.
xiii J Robinson, *Born in Blood*, Guild, 1989, cover notes.

More than six hundred years have passed since the suppression of the Knights Templar, but their heritage lives on in the largest fraternal organisation ever known. And so the story of those tortured crusading knights, of the savagery of the Peasants Revolt, and of the lost secrets of Freemasonry becomes the story of the most successful secret society in the history of the world.[xiv]

Also straddling the academic/popular divide has been Margaret Jacobs, a Californian academic with a solid background. Following the path of Francis Yates into the pre-1717 world of alchemy versus rational science, she has followed books on the Enlightenment and early scientific culture with a more-popular style in *The Origins of Freemasonry*. She has broken new ground by exploring female membership of European Freemasonry and by using as source material Masonic almanacs and pocket diaries. Noticeably shorter than the 'blockbusters', her book concludes with a pithy reference to the continuing issues of race and gender confronting Freemasonry but also with a positive note:

The Lodges naturalised constitutional practices, nationally organised and representative assemblies, voting and speaking before such assemblies. For these practices and habits opponents of the French Revolution blamed the freemasons, claiming that they conspired to cause it. In reality the Lodges may be said to have pushed European mores, at least at home, ever so slightly in a democratic direction.[xv]

An earlier title which has not received the public attention it deserves is Stevenson's *The Origins of Freemasonry: Scotland's Century, 1590-1710*, published in 1988. The value of this work is that it directs attention away from London and the English Grand Lodge to Scotland and the operative Lodges of stone masons. Margaret Jacobs wrote approvingly:

---

xiv Robinson, 1989, as above, p. xix.
xv M Jacob, *The Origins of Freemasonry: Facts and Fictions*, Uni of Pennsylvania, 2006, p. 132.

The early history of how English and Scottish guilds of stonemasons evolved into the freemasons of the eighteenth century is still incomplete, but in broad outline the story is now basically understood…Among the earliest Scottish records – so brilliantly illuminated by David Stevenson – we see all of these traditions attracting learned gentlemen, some also drawn to the new science.[xvi]

Another important, even earlier title deserving of greater recognition is *Travelling Brothers*. In this case, the trail of artisans forced to go 'on the tramp' for work is followed from the medieval stonemasons to the trade societies of the industrial revolution.[xvii]

A third is Petri Mirala's *Freemasonry in Ulster 1733-1813* which, because it is new research about northern Ireland, is of great significance to the earliest Masonic Lodges in Australia. The last in this group I want to mention is *The Mythology of Secret Societies* by Oxford academic J.M. Roberts, which could usefully be read by the authors of many of the blockbusters of recent times:

The mythology of the secret societies has many different specific embodiments, religious and non-religious, liberal and conservative but it is always an example of the 'puppet' theory of politics. It claims that the real makers of events are not the statesmen who strut before the public, but secret directors who manipulate them. The freemasons, the Jesuits, the Carbonari, the Comintern have all had the blame placed on them at different times.[xviii]

These titles have acted as signposts to a necessary new approach to Masonic history. They have helped to convince Grand Lodge administrations that the old approach – secrecy at all costs – is no longer viable. They have forced a recognition that historical claims which cannot be verified should not be made.

---

xvi   M Jacob, 2006, as above, pp. 5-6.

xvii R Leeson, *Travelling Brothers*, Allen & Unwin, 1979.

xviii J Roberts, *The Mythology of Secret Societies,* Secker & Warburg, 1972, p. 29.

More than fifty years ago Francis Yates asserted that most of the 50,000 titles then available about Freemasonry in English-speaking libraries were useless because their claims could often not be verified.

In 2007, a Masonic scholar and key-note speaker at an international conference organised by and for Freemasons summarised a growing northern-hemisphere consensus by arguing:

In the light of what has been said, it may have become clear that we have entered a new phase, one in which much of (Masonic) history needs to be re-written.[xix]

He went on:

Of course, we will have to cover the complete scope of all the fields which influenced or were influenced by Freemasonry. We surely need more and better studies of guilds, confraternities, chivalric and knightly orders … but also of friendly societies, Masonic 'spin-off' societies and Trade Unions. This is a major shift in internal emphasis and it will be quite some time before the new principles are fully implemented but already a number of crucial decisions have produced positive outcomes. The Canonbury Centre in London and the Centre for Research into Freemasonry and Fraternalism at Sheffield University under the guidance of Andrew Prescott have built a solid platform, including a number of important publications.[xx]

He also assisted with the organisation of the two international conferences on the history of Freemasonry in Edinburgh in 2007 and 2009. The papers presented on these occasions illustrated the depth of the change and the Degree to which Masons and non-Masons are starting to work together.

---

xix J Snoek, 'Researching Freemasonry: Where are We?', Working Paper Series, Sheffield Centre for Research into Freemasonry and Fraternalism, 2007, p. 19.

xx See as one example only: M Scanlan (ed), *The Social Impact of Freemasonry on the Modern Western World*, Vol 1, Canonbury Papers, Canonbury Masonic Research Centre, 2002.

Another key individual in these developments is Bob Cooper, Curator and Librarian at the Scottish Grand Lodge. His books on Rosslyn Chapel, the Templar Church in London and on Freemasonry are highly recommended.[xxi]

An example of the new approach that is of direct interest to Australians is *Builders of Empire* by North American researcher Jessica Harland-Jacobs, published in 2007.[xxii] She introduced her key arguments with a letter John Stephen, Sydney Magistrate and Worshipful Master of the newly-created 'Lodge of Australia' wrote in 1827 to England's Grand Lodge requesting a Charter for the new Lodge. She argued his request was a clear example of Freemasonry's place at the heart of British imperial achievement and of the brotherhood's impulse to be ultra-respectable, to be a supporter of the legal status-quo and to be free from controversy:

> *Stephen realised that this brotherhood had a role to play in strengthening the British Empire. The growth of Freemasonry in the Australian colonies would serve to create 'an eternal bond of union which will more closely connect this colony with England than any other that can possibly be devised'.*[xxiii]

Stephen, indeed, went on to chair meetings of seven of the colony's prominent business and professional men which celebrated the brotherhood and as the Lodge Executive, inducted the first new candidates into its mysteries. Overall, Harland-Jacobs' argument has three arms:

i) Freemasonry, from 1717, identified with the ideals of the Enlightenment, including universal brotherhood, sociability, tolerance and benevolence;

ii) Freemasonry was central to the building and the cohesion of the British Empire;

---

xxi   R Cooper, *The Rosslyn Hoax?*, Lewis Masonic, 2006; *Cracking the Freemasons Code*, Random House, 2006; 'The Revenge of the Operatives?', in A Prescott (ed), *Marking Well*, Lewis Masonic, 2006.

xxii J Harland-Jacobs, *Builders of Empire Freemasonry and British Imperialism, 1717-1927*, Chapel Hill, 2007.

xxiii Harland-Jacobs, 2007, as above, p. 1.

iii) By the 19th century, it had altered in character and become noticeably more Protestant and an 'unquestioning ally of the (British) imperial state.'

Moving from cosmopolitan tolerance of diversity in the 18th century, to being stoutly loyalist in the 19th, she argues, necessarily involved Freemasonry abandoning its claim to be politically neutral, the continuing rhetoric thereafter that neither politics nor religion was a fit Lodge topic, exposing Freemasonry to the charge of hypocrisy.

Unfortunately for the important role assigned to him by Harland-Jacobs, in 2006 an Australian researcher, Carol Baxter, concluded in her account of what she called 'the Jane New scandal' that not only had Stephen precipitated the events which had brought her convict heroine to disgrace and ruin, but that he'd been an inveterate liar and opportunist well before he met the woman who became his 'irresistible temptation.'[xxiv]

Baxter showed that in 1829, as he prepared to open what was the first English Masonic Lodge in Australia, Stephen had continued his adulterous relationship with Jane, who was a convicted shoplifter. He'd worked to undermine the colony's Governor, he'd forged court documents and engaged petty criminals to smuggle her out of the colony away from her husband and out of the reach of the death penalty which had been recorded against her. Clearly Stephen was not the person Harland-Jacobs thought he was. Why not? Did he deceive her? Did she deceive herself? Did Freemasonry deceive her?

Harland-Jacobs and Baxter together illustrate the sorts of new questions confronting Freemasonry in the 21st century. The benefits are potentially huge for the organisation but the dangers in getting it wrong are equally great. That is why it was considered necessary to produce the present volume but, in Australia, it must be only the first step in a whole new approach.

---

xxiv C Baxter, *Irresistible Temptation*, Allen & Unwin, 2006.

TIME AND TIDE WAIT FOR NO MAN
by Dr Bob James

I've been asked to put down some thoughts on the particular voyage of discovery which has brought me, at age 68, into Freemasonry. The person making the request was not to know that one of my earliest memories is that of my mother, of Irish Catholic extraction, sounding off in the 1940s and 50s at 'the Masons' and their darkly suspicious doings.

He was not to know, either, that my father was, apart from his trade union commitment, a conscientious non-joiner who instilled in all his family habits difficult to shake. He was a non-drinker and affable comradeship was, for him, a foreign land. Whether he, or my older brothers would have turned out any differently, or been any better off if they had joined Freemasonry at a time when class and religious tensions remained strong is doubtful. The truth is that, back then, they would not have been seen as suitable.

Six decades later, with an eye made keener by experience, I see the Craft very differently from the way my parents did: but then, Freemasonry has changed a great deal in the interim, too.

I'll leave others to express opinions about the uniqueness of Freemasonry's spiritual message or the timelessness of its moral appeal. It is, first and foremost, in Freemasonry's belated recognition that it is a social phenomenon that I perceive its attractions and its capacity for renewal.

Viewed historically, Freemasonry is a modern fraternity which has evolved as the Enlightenment, the Industrial Revolution and, now the Information Age, have hammered and chiselled all of us into shapes we could neither predict nor prevent. The old world has not been entirely replaced and it is into that tension between medieval mysticism and rational enquiry that Dan Brown casts his stones and where Freemasonry now faces its most challenging times.

Swimming against the tide by joining rather than leaving Freemasonry, I am now willingly caught up in the latest waves of change which, beginning in Europe and North America some two decades back, are now set to break slowly but heavily on local shores. It is entirely coincidental but it seems my personal search for meaning and for historical 'truth' mirrors this tsunami with which Freemasonry is now faced.

I first observed fraternal ideas in trade union banners some 25 years ago. In my ignorance I referred to the bee-hives and the doves and the temples displayed there as 'Masonic' and tempted a black-eye from wharfies and other stalwart sons of toil by putting that word in the same sentence as 'trade union' when asking why their banners showed these symbols. Whatever their responses, the mounting evidence clearly showed that consideration of all fraternities as parts of a single context was the key to my and to their understanding.

So, though I had hated History when I left high school and teachers' college behind, my circumnavigation of the known world had resulted in my returning to it, but under my own terms. The PhD I was doing at Newcastle University eventually turned into a look at parades and the communities that produced them.

What I also found myself doing increasingly was rescuing 'the evidence' – regalia, photos, jewels, certificates, minute books, even Lodge furniture and large marching banners – from mouldy basements, garbage skips and op shops, and writing my own version of Australian history to accommodate them.

It seemed that no-one in Australia had previously considered the connections between the labour movement and Freemasonry, and the established frameworks in which Masonic history and other genres were set did not work. Even a new definition of 'fraternity' was required to highlight disregarded and misunderstood elements. Delving into the standard Masonic histories had disclosed the obvious connection, the operative stonemasons, but had uncovered numerous other fraternities, including the extremely important Friendly Societies and those based on religious affiliation, such as the Loyal Orange, Hibernian and Holy Catholic Guild societies. These added to the sense of being on the right track but also added to the complexity of the undertaking.

The more I searched, the more I found, and the more I was confronted with the fact that the present-day members of fraternal societies did not know their own history, and by and large, did not care. Freemasons and trade unionists appeared to care, often making a great show of their heritage, but was it real or strategic?

Many false starts later I felt I had a workable definition of fraternalism and a viable historical framework. After two decades, I felt I understood why my mother had ranted against 'the Masons' and why members of other working class communities strongly supported them. I was in a position to identify Ned Kelly's sash, to understand why Francis Greenway had been horse-whipped, and to explain why certain umpires were selected to stand in Test Cricket matches and others were not.

It was a warts and all history of Australia, acceptance of which was not going to be straightforward.

I had, by then, left Labour history behind and been initiated as two kinds of Odd Fellow, and as a Druid. I had been made the official custodian of Rechabite memorabilia and been elected on to the Board of Management of the Grand United Friendly Society Health Fund. The 'bobalogue' of fraternal items in my care ran to over 200 pages.

Consideration of a new history could not be separated from a new approach to the display of that history. It was useless thinking of Freemasonry, for example, as an organisation devoted to learning and to changing men for the better without taking on board the real-time processes of conservation, publishing and distribution. Since my whole life had been spent in the education industry it again seemed I was destined to be in the thick of it.

Keeping this part of the story brief, almost the last action of the GUFS Board before it became part of the Australian Unity group of companies in 2005 was to vote $300,000 for the Australian Centre for Fraternal Studies which I then established in conjunction with the Newcastle Regional Museum.

It soon became clear that despite having a history in Australia as long as that of the Freemasons, the various Odd Fellows, Foresters, Druids and Rechabites had succumbed to government legislation and were now 'financial instruments', not brotherhoods practising or teaching mutual aid. They had little in the way of written history and were not sufficiently curious to consider indulging my 'fantasies'. As private health funds they saw no reason to associate themselves with the care and display of strange ritual items or arcane symbols.

The seed money quickly ran out and was not replaced. The Centre closed and I retreated into more and purer research, the results of which were derided in this country but were increasingly in demand in Europe. I first made acquaintance with fraternal enthusiasts at a conference at Manchester in 2003, and was invited to give the keynote address at the 2004 'We Band of Brothers' conference at Sheffield where Professor Andrew Prescott was setting up the Centre for Research into Freemasonry, the first of its kind in the English-speaking world. I've subsequently given papers at the 2007 and 2009 International Conferences on the History of Freemasonry at Edinburgh which has been the main focus of the shockwaves about to reach these shores.

It was in 2007 that I first heard scholars of authority say that Freemasonry had to re-examine its past and all its previous assumptions about itself in order to survive. *Further, that it had to remove the barriers to rigorous research and see itself within a broader historical context.*

Looking at what I've written here might seem to invite a charge that I entered into Freemasonry in 2008 only in order to satisfy some long-held interests which have nothing to do with the Craft and which had been frustrated elsewhere.

Rather, the reverse is closer to the mark. Being my father's son, I would not have considered coming 'inside the tent' except for the indications that Freemasonry, alone among significant fraternities, *was prepared to acknowledge previous shortcomings and, trusting to an inner resilience, to try charting a new, more realistic future. Of all the fraternities which I've studied, some of which I've also looked at from the inside, Freemasonry is the only one which so far has shown itself to have sufficient integrity and sufficient self-belief to look its detractors squarely in the eye and, without pulling down new shutters, make a serious attempt at its own re-invention.*

Only time will tell how thorough and how successful the effort will be.

John Treloar
(1928–)

John Treloar never won Olympic gold, but was still one of Australia's greatest athletes and, in his time, one of the fastest sprinters in the world. Born in 1928 in New South Wales, his interest in athletics started when he won the Roseville Public School championships at age 11. He then attended North Sydney High where, coached by Arthur Henry, he only ever lost the 100 yard sprint on one occasion.

Treloar played rugby union and cricket for North Sydney High. He could also jump – both high and long – but finally decided to concentrate on sprinting, winning his races at University with his brilliant finishing speed.

Selected as a member of the Australian Athletics Team for the 1948 Olympic Games in London, Treloar competed in the 100 yards, 220 yards and 4 x 110 yard relay, reaching the semi finals of both the 100 and 220.

In 1950 Treloar made history when he became the first Australian to win gold medals in sprint events for the 220 yards (21.5 seconds) and 100 yards (9.7 seconds) at the Commonwealth Games in Auckland. He also won gold in the 4 x 110 yard relay with the team finishing in 42.2 seconds making him a triple gold medallist at the games.

Chosen again for the athletics team, Treloar represented Australia at the 1952 Olympic Games in Helsinki. He was part of the closest finish in Olympic history – placed sixth in the 110 yard final, but only 0.1 of a second behind the winner. The Olympic gold went to American Lindy Remigino, with three other competitors also finishing on the time of 10.4 seconds, and fifth and sixth place-getters coming in at 10.5 seconds.

While Australians have won medals in the men's sprint competition at the Games, none has come as close to the winning time as Treloar.

John Treloar was initiated into Freemasonry at Lodge Frank McDowell, No. 362, on March 4, 1948.

Fred Walker
(1884–1935)

Fred Walker is best remembered for creating the popular spread, Vegemite – an Australian icon for 86 years (so far).

Walker was born in Melbourne in 1884 and was educated at Caulfield Grammar School. In 1899 he joined J. Bartram & Sons, produce and export merchants, where he learned about canning and refrigeration.

In 1903, aged only 19, he started his own import-export business, Fred Walker & Co, in Hong Kong to manufacture Bonox, the beef extract still produced today.

After time in the army (1908-1919) Walker established his business in William Street, Melbourne. In 1922 he hired a young chemist, Dr Cyril Callister, to develop a spread from brewer's yeast, the richest known source of Vitamin B.

Walker needed a name for it and decided to ask the public – running a competition with a prize of £50 for the winner. His daughter, Sheila, selected the name Vegemite and it was launched in 1923. There are only two kinds of people … you either love Vegemite … or hate it: but its success is undoubted.

Walker continued making other products and in 1925 teamed up with American businessman, James L. Kraft, to manufacture processed cheese in Melbourne, establishing Kraft Walker Cheese and Co. A caring employer, Walker encouraged staff to take up further study, introduced first aid facilities, a staff canteen, a workers social club and morning tea breaks.

Before World War II the British Medical Association officially recognised the benefits of Vegemite and the Australian Medical Journal recommended it as a food rich in Vitamin B. It was rationed during World War II but by war's end it could be found in nine out of ten Australian households.

The 'Happy little Vegemites' jingle sung by healthy, smiling children is one of Australia's best-remembered advertisements. Most Australians know the words. First launched on radio in 1954, it moved to TV in 1956 and in 2003, when Vegemite turned 80, it was re-launched.

Australians continue to love Vegemite – buying 22 million jars every year.

Fred Walker was President of the Melbourne Rotary Club from 1933 to 1934 and a director of the YMCA. He died in 1935 of heart disease.

Fred Walker was initiated into Freemasonry at Austral Temple Lodge No. 110, Victorian Constitution, on July 9, 1919.

Blair Wark
(1894–1941)

Described as a man who 'liked the wind in his face and lived the life of three men', Blair Anderson Wark demonstrated military interests from an early age.

In 1915 he was appointed to the AIF and embarked for Egypt with the 30th Battalion. By the time he reached the Western Front in June, 1916, he was a captain and company commander. Although a risk-taker himself he was protective of his men's safety, often moving ahead of his troops when encountering heavy fire.

After being wounded in the battle of Fromelles, Wark returned to active duty with the 32nd Battalion. He was recommended for a Distinguished Service Order (DSO) for his conduct during that battle and at Sunray Trench in March, 1917. No award was made then, but he was promoted to Major the following month. However he did win a DSO later in the year for his conduct on the front line east of Ypres, as well as for previous courage and devotion to duty.

In September 1918, aged 24, he was given temporary command of the 32nd Battalion in operations against the Hindenburg line. When the advance was held up by machine-gun fire near Bellicourt, he recruited a passing tank to deal with the problem. Major Wark also attached 200 leaderless Americans to his command before rushing a battery of 77mm guns, capturing four guns and 10 men. With two others, he later surprised and captured 50 Germans near Magny-la-Fosse.

On October 1, Major Wark 'dashed forward and silenced machine-guns which were causing heavy casualties'. Awarded the Victoria Cross, he returned to Australia with a new bride in 1919. He became a principal of Thompson & Wark, quantity surveyors, as well as director of a number of companies, a councillor of the National Roads and Motorists' Association and a life governor of the Benevolent Society of NSW.

In 1940 he was appointed to the 1st Battalion, assuming command in July as a temporary Lieutenant-Colonel. He died suddenly of a heart attack while bivouacked at Puckapunyal, Victoria.

Blair Wark was initiated into Freemasonry at Lodge Lane Cove No. 338 on November 8, 1921.

William Wentworth
(1790–1872)

William Charles Wentworth – explorer, poet, journalist and politician – was born at sea in 1790, en route to Norfolk Island. The family moved to Sydney in 1796 and after his mother died in 1800, Wentworth and his brother were sent to school in England.

Returning in 1810, Wentworth was appointed Provost-Marshal. A determined, adventurous young man, he, together with Lawson and Blaxland, explored inland New South Wales in 1813, extending the colony's pasturing land and making the first crossing of the Blue Mountains.

Back in England in 1816, Wentworth studied law at Cambridge. In 1819 he published the first book written by an Australian: *A Statistical, Historical, and Political Description of the Colony of New South Wales*.

Wentworth was admitted to the bar in 1822, returned to Sydney in 1824 and with Robert Wardell, published the first privately-owned newspaper in Australia, the *Australian* (no connection with *The Australian* of today).

Wentworth wanted the English political system for Australia, campaigned for responsible self-government and used his newspaper to attack Governor Darling's initiatives so vigorously that Darling tried to have the paper shut down.

In 1827, Wentworth inherited his father's wealth and bought Vaucluse House in Sydney's eastern suburbs, where he lived for 25 years.

He campaigned for legal reforms including the successful introduction to the colony of trial by jury. In 1842 the British Parliament granted self-government and Wentworth was elected to Parliament.

In 1853 he chaired the committee which drafted a new Constitution for New South Wales. Wentworth developed the first real system of primary education in New South Wales and worked to establish the University of Sydney. His name is remembered by Wentworth and Wentworth Falls and the Federal Division of Wentworth and in Canberra by the Wentworth Falls waterfall and Wentworth Avenue, Kingston.

Wentworth returned to England in 1855, where he died in 1872.

Australia Post recognised Wentworth on stamps – in 1963 in recognition of the Blue Mountains crossing and in 1974 on the 150th anniversary of the publication of Wentworth's first newspaper.

William Wentworth was a member of Lodge Amis Incorruptibles of the Orient de Paris in 1818.

John Whittle
(1882–1946)

Born at Huon Island near Gordon, Tasmania, John Woods Whittle enlisted as a private in Tasmania's 4th (2nd Imperial Bushmen) Contingent, which reached South Africa in April 1901. He saw action in the Boer War before returning to Tasmania in 1902, where he enlisted in the Royal Navy as a stoker.

In 1915 he transferred to the AIF as an acting Corporal and by 1916 was in France with the 12th Battalion, where he was wounded in action. Shortly after this John Whittle was promoted to Sergeant. Early the following year, he won the Distinguished Conduct Medal for bombing an enemy machine-gun post during the German withdrawal on the Hindenburg line.

In April, 1917, the 12th Battalion carried out a diversionary attack on the village of Boursies, with Whittle leading his platoon in the initial assault. Following fierce resistance and German counter-attacks, Sergeant Whittle steadied his troops until support arrived. The battalion advanced close to Lagnicourt but, on April 15, was surprised by a counter-attack and forced from the trenches to make a stand on a sunken road. Whittle saw Germans bringing up a machine-gun: 'Rushing alone across the fire-swept ground', he attacked the enemy with bombs, killing the crew and capturing the gun.

John Whittle received the Victoria Cross for his heroism at both Boursies and Lagnicourt.

Wounded twice during 1918, Whittle returned to Australia to settle in Sydney and, with other VC winners, took part in a recruitment drive. Falling on hard times during the Depression, he made a desperate plea in 1932, stating: 'I have been trying to struggle on for some time, but the children [of which there were six] are badly in need of boots and clothing for the winter, and I cannot get any work.' Within a month he had been employed.

Whittle was one of only two Australian VC winners of World War I who had been in permanent service before the war.

John Whittle was initiated into Freemasonry at Lodge Sydney St Andrew No. 7 on November 1, 1923.

CHAPTER TWELVE

Crafting the future

by Jan Lee Martin

FREEMASONS

This book has now reviewed the history and culture of Freemasonry – ancient, medieval and modern. It has also described the present activities of a fraternity that is teaching good men how to live better lives; and working in various charitable activities aimed at helping others to be happy.

But what of the future? Will the Craft simply accept that the future is unknown? And if so, does it risk watching the decline of Freemasonry – like so many other service organisations – as emerging generations live their lives in front of screens instead of people?

It might be argued that it has no choice.

On the other hand, a professional futurist would insist that it has. We create the future through the choices we make in the present, whether we think about it or not. The great challenge – and the great opportunity – is to create the future we want, by making our choices consciously.

As I write these words, that's not quite a simple as it sounds. The challenges that face us have never been greater. Our 'unconscious civilisation', and its greedy over-use of the world's natural resources, has led us to the unwilling realisation that we need to do something special now to avoid catastrophe. There is every reason to fear that our grandchildren and theirs will not enjoy the easy prosperity that we in Australia took for granted in the late 20th century.

At the same time there are signs of a global awakening, a growing impatience with traditional political processes in the face of the challenges that we already know are on the way. Perhaps, instead of easy prosperity, our grandchildren and theirs will respond to the crises we now face by creatively rebuilding the world in a more sustainable, more just, more mature way.

That sounds like the sort of approach that Freemasonry might teach.

If building a cathedral was the big challenge for the men of the first millennium – and building cities the big challenge of the second – could building a new, green, sustainable world be the big challenge of the third millennium?

Well ... actually ... it already is.

So who will meet this challenge?

Millions of citizens, all over the planet, are already uniting to protest too-slow political responses to the undeniable reality of climate change which, converging with population growth and peak oil, will threaten the supply of food and water in vast areas of the world. Others are protesting inadequate responses to the poverty and starvation we already have; to continuing violence to women; the growth of slavery; organised crime and other major issues.

Many more are engaged in the active design and production of alternatives – alternative energy, alternative access to water, alternative food production and distribution, alternative economic systems; alternative approaches to peace; and more. Social research provides evidence of growing demand for just such sensible responses, perhaps as a result of the re-awakening interest in personal growth and spirituality.

Will it be enough? Can we create a new world in time?

It's no wonder Dan Brown chose to use his latest thriller to draw attention to the need for new wisdom. This is the stuff of high drama – the greatest drama of human history. In the words of the ancient Chinese curse, we are heading for 'interesting times'. 'Can we grow up in time?' he might ask, breathlessly.

Futurists are asking the same question: can we move on from the denial and distraction of the 20th century to the emotional and spiritual maturity that we need – before we lose the opportunity to make thoughtful choices?

Whatever happens, there's no doubt that our descendants of the 22nd century will be enthralled by stories of the stupidity, the ingenuity and perhaps the heroism of their ancestors in this period of dramatic change.

Even Mr Brown's spooky speculations about thoughts as matter, and the conscious use of intention, don't seem too far-fetched to those of us who have been watching the pioneering expeditions of modern science. This is the kind of learning we need. I joined the Institute of Noetic Sciences in the 1980s, and though I've not had time to stay close to their work, I have great respect for the experts exploring these frontiers of science.

Never before has humanity faced such a shared challenge; never before could it have contemplated a shared response. Yet as Dr Willis Harman, then president of the Institute, wrote many years ago, what we need most is simply a change of mind. Ultimately, it is the inner journey of the individual human that will determine the success or failure of our communities and our world.

So what will happen? Does anybody know? How will we cope?

What can a futurist tell us?

Futurists explore the future. They use sophisticated tools and methodologies to help them identify trends, assess probabilities, speculate about possibilities and, most of all, help others understand the implications of their own choices.

With these tools, they explore the outer world, scanning the growing noise of our global society for signals of deep change. And they explore the inner world, exposing and challenging the mental habits that have created our present realities – the realities that we fail to see because we are immersed in them, as the fish fails to see the water.

Challenging ourselves and the way we think is the best way to free ourselves, to unlock the future we expect and help us to imagine better futures instead. That's how William Wentworth challenged the 1850s reality of the penal colony in New South Wales with his vision of the democratic society that he believed was both desirable and possible. He imagined a better future for New South Wales.

So one of the futurist's most powerful tools is the practice of scenario development – using the results of rigorous research and scanning to imagine alternative futures and turn them into stories. Some of these alternative scenarios should be positive, some negative. Some might be probable, some merely plausible, some barely possible.

Whether they are achievable or not, alternative scenarios of future outer worlds have the effect of flexing participants' inner worlds … opening up the windows through which they see their surroundings, helping them to challenge what they once took for granted, to see more possibilities, think about probabilities they hadn't considered before. And this process has a very practical benefit in helping them recognise early signals of real change, because they have already explored and mapped a range of possibilities.

In short, scenarios help us to create new stories for ourselves – and that is a powerful way to create new futures. All too often we fail to challenge our stories. We dutifully live out the stories we have been told, or the stories we tell ourselves from habit.

Like other tools, stories have great power if used well.

Stories help us to share knowledge. They help us to work together to meet the uncertainties of change. Stories give us strength and coherence. And stories also *create* change. They fire the imagination. We create the future through the stories we imagine. How can we create the future – how can we create anything? – if we can't imagine it first?

We really, seriously, need to create new stories for the future.

What, then, will be the story of Freemasonry in a future that desperately needs the kind of leadership it can teach?

As it considers the changes occurring in the world around it, will it remember the words of Charles Darwin – the son and grandson of Masons? He said: 'It is not the strongest species that will survive, nor the most intelligent, but the one most responsive to change.'

Will Freemasonry imagine new and better futures for itself by responding to change, and by making conscious choices about the kind of future it wants?

That, of course, is a decision for the leaders chosen by members of the Craft. However there seems little doubt that their choices, whatever changes they may involve, will be aimed at the unchanging goal of helping good men lead better lives. That, as I understand it, is the core purpose of Freemasonry.

And consciously choosing to lead better lives, according to philosophers, psychologists and mystics from east and west, north and south, past and present, not only fosters good health and happiness, but is the logical direction of human evolution.

Here again we encounter the theme of learning, personal growth and higher consciousness that is so much part of Freemasonry's venerable story. Again, it brings together the wisdom of ancient traditions with modern science in an exciting convergence that is now engaging the sciences of chaos and complexity, quantum theory and systems theory, psychology, neurology and other disciplines in the exploration of consciousness.

Professor Ervin Laszlo, founder of the Club of Budapest, argues that our inner growth and development is more than just an individual journey: it is the next great phase of evolution.

The past 10,000 years of human history have been a period of 'extensive evolution', he says: centuries of conquest, colonisation and consumption. Humanity has extended its power and influence in space and time. It has sought control and domination of the other, the outside, the external. The next phase must be one of 'intensive evolution', with a new value system, a new ethic, a new culture and even a new civilisation. It will be about communication, connection and comprehension.

That is exactly the kind of shift increasingly being reported by social researchers. Many studies of changing values are tracking shifts away from the mindless materialism that has dominated recent decades in western societies (and increasingly in others). This research supports Professor Laszlo's suggestion – and Willis Harman's hope – that we are now at one of those 'hinges of history' where big changes emerge from deep shifts in our inner states of being. The challenges that face us, including global warming, energy migration, population overshoot and more, will accelerate this changing depth of focus.

Perhaps we are learning at last that in spite of all its lovely toys, in spite of the improvements of technology in health, transportation, productivity, personal comfort, entertainment and more, the world of materialism does not make us happy.

Leading better lives, according to sage and scientist alike, is the road that leads to happiness. And happiness is the logical outcome of human evolution.

Today, the art of happiness has become a science as more and more universities and scientists establish centres for the study of happiness – what it is, and how it is achieved.

One famous study of how happily people live out their lives was reported by the Harvard professor George Vaillant in his book, *Ageing Well*. He described social maturation as 'the sequential mastery of a series of life tasks'. It's interesting to compare the tasks we have mastered, as humans, with those that are yet to come.

So what next, would a futurist say? Well, she would probably say that her work is not about prediction. Instead, futurists monitor change, look for patterns, explore alternatives, learn about implications, speculate about possibilities. But she might suggest that the Craft imagine some alternative scenarios like the examples that follow this chapter.

Will any one of these scenarios answer our original question: what next for Freemasonry? Of course not. Scenarios are merely tools for exploring possibilities, stretching the imagination – and to remind us that we can play an active role in creating the kind of futures we want. The ones offered here are quick examples (and by way of disclaimer, I draw your attention to the editor's notes on how quickly this book was produced. This chapter, including the scenarios, was prepared in a matter of hours – but it does draw on many years of study and experience.)

A professional approach to the future of Freemasonry would certainly invite members to identify the drivers of change, imagine their own sets of alternative future scenarios, introduce them to the tools to do so, point them to relevant data, and show them how to use various methodologies to imagine and create new futures – as an artist might use his colours and tools to imagine and create the result he wants.

Whatever that turns out to be it seems likely that, for as long as it lives, the ancient and honourable Craft of Freemasonry will continue to support men in their journey of evolution, toward living consciously, living better lives, and creating happiness for themselves and others.

But perhaps, in these challenging times, it might also imagine an exciting new story for itself – shaping a goal of such power that it acts as the 'strange attractor' of chaos theory, and draws millions of men all over the planet into the task of creating that new world we need so badly.

Remember that excellent quote from Leon Carter, in Chapter 4? 'We should stand tall, and profess our faith in our organisation. We should salute the past, celebrate the present and inspire the future.'

This futurist couldn't agree more. And when you've done all that, how about *building* a new future? Isn't that what Masons do?

The challenge, and the opportunity, have never been greater.

SCENARIO 1:

Heading for 2115...

FREEMASONS

Good morning and welcome. It is my great pleasure today, as Grand Master, to open this celebration of 50 years of Applied Freemasonry.

This audience is familiar with the many achievements of the Craft … the care of the aged, the support of the needy, developmental support for the very young, our pivotal role in the turbulent shift to natural capitalism, and so on. So let us look beyond these achievements, to what they represent.

Human beings are tribal. We need our families, our communities, our societies to survive and thrive. Healthy humans in healthy societies can achieve a great deal, and they can be happy. But as our recent ancestors learned during the Metacrisis, unhealthy humans – whether physically, mentally, emotionally or developmentally unhealthy – are both the cause and the consequence of unhealthy societies.

So I am honoured today to salute the Freemasons of Australia, whose intervention in the early 21st century reversed this negative feedback loop. Ironically, this occurred as a result of the near-mortal illness of the Craft itself.

Historians among you will know the story of Jason, Grand Master of the United Lodge of Australia in 2015. It was his vision – his recognition of the challenges *and the opportunities* of the future – that rescued Freemasonry from a serious decline from the post-war heights of membership. That was due to the twin impact of the Craft's self-imposed secrecy and the wider society's plunge into denial and distraction as the world moved toward its great civilisational crisis.

Jason understood that never before had there been a greater need, nor a greater opportunity, to offer humanity the wise teaching of the Craft. He anticipated the collapse of the industrial economy; the breakdown of government; the rise of pandemics; the evacuation of the cities; the shortage of food and water; and other impacts of the Metacrisis. As a Mason who had studied the Craft he also understood that the only hope of human survival, let alone happiness, would be to use the creativity of our brethren from many cultures to strengthen our communities. Thus was born the Creative Code of Civilisation, the practical application of Masonic, and other ancient and modern wisdom, in a simple set of principles to guide the leaders of all communities, from families to meta-tribes.

Jason's impressive intellect was matched by his powerful skills as an orator. Thus he was able to communicate effectively the challenges of the present, the threats to the Craft, and his vision for the future. A key to his success was the use of graphics to communicate in a world drowning in information: the practical visual tool that he and his brethren developed to nurture healthy societies in the new, nature-based economy.

The story of Jason and his CCC has become one of the guiding legends of post-industrial civilisation. That's why we have borrowed from it to develop our new shared vision for the Craft of the future …

SCENARIO 2:

In case they find me ...

I must keep this message short – I do not have much blood to spare. But the words must last, so spare it I will. By the time this hide is discovered, surely the dark forces will have self-destructed. Then perhaps you will be able to share this story of the heroism of a band of brothers called Freemasons.

Freemasonry was already more than 2000 years old when the clouds of the Metacrisis began to gather. As the lands dried out and the cities were flooded, populations starved and died of thirst, governments fell. Soon the only systems still working were those of organized crime. Its revenues from illicit trade were already, by 2010, twice the value of all the military budgets in the world put together. As economic crisis cut into their traditional businesses the networks began to use their power openly, even in the formerly affluent west – from murder in the suburbs to sweatshops and sex slavery. Corruption of government officials bled the strength of official structures until they took on the porosity of sponges.

During these dreadful times there remained only the slightest hope of a future return to civilisation – and that is the story I must tell. There was a group of men called Freemasons. Their society's philosophy was to help good men lead better lives, and to be happy.

I hope to survive long enough to emerge from this cave into a world of humanity returned, where I can tell this story in all its glorious detail – detail of ceremony and rite, of story and metaphor, of symbol and sign. Freemasonry was a rich culture, and that is what allowed it to survive as a strong underground movement during the Rule of the Godfathers. Now, as never before, the trust between its brethren meant the difference between life and death.

The Freemasons organized hidden settlements where children could be kept safe, and taught the principles of living consciously. Protected by elaborate camouflage from satellite observation, these settlements taught the children how to live with nature, using solar energy, wave power for desalination, sustainable harvesting from native bush and so on. And, even more important, they taught the children how to live with each other – in peace and principle – and how to be happy.

Some of these settlements were discovered, usually by chance, or betrayed by other citizens in fear of their own lives. When that happened, the children and their carers were taken into slavery or worse. But many of them survived, and as generation followed generation these multicultural tribes of Freemasons became the only remaining cohesive societies across Australia.

You will know what has happened after that. I don't. I have been in this cave for 15 years because my settlement was one of those betrayed in 2035. My visible mutilation will identify me as a Mason and until I am stronger I dare not emerge. But I am working on that. Meanwhile I can tell this story. I will write more when I can risk losing more blood ...

SCENARIO 3:

Once upon a time ...

FREEMASONS

Life cycles of 21st century cultural organisations (04 08 50)
Welcome back to this fascinating topic. Our context is the sudden end of the American Empire and the resulting global fragmentation. As you know, these events resulted from climate change, the end of capitalism, peak oil and human population overshoot among other things. Although that was a tumultuous time for those who lived through it, the beneficial outcome for humanity was the rebirth of regions as our basic societal building blocks. The holo-logue holds more details ... including notes about sub-causes such as species extinction, ocean acidity, loss of arable lands and so on and so forth.

Today we begin to examine the cultural aspects of this shift with the example of a men's society called Freemasonry. This society – they called it a Craft – was born many centuries before the Christian era, and flourished for many more before waning and dying. Our question is: was it ever a sustainable system, or was it inevitably destined to a 'natural' lifecycle of birth, maturity and death?

You might choose to argue the latter. Or you might argue that its death was not necessary. Using complexity theory, you could explore the fractal effect ... the life cycle of the branches (called Lodges) of this organisation, within the life cycle of the larger groups to which the Lodges belonged, within the life cycle of their nations, the post-Christian civilisation, and so on. Or you could use living systems theory to explore why this social phenomenon didn't breed in the way natural living systems breed. After all, the life cycle isn't really just birth/maturity/death is it? Most organisms breed at maturity, and if we accept the contemporary view of organisations as living systems, perhaps they too could breed.

As usual, you will find all the references you need in the holo-logue. Those of you who decide to explore that last approach might want to search for examples of the work of this fraternal organisation and ask yourselves whether the charitable groups that they created could be considered 'offspring' and whether, as in nature, those might outlive the parent.

Another approach would be to locate the question within the context of spiritual growth. Although the Craft fiercely disclaimed allegiance to any one religion, its teachings were consistent with many of the religions of the period and its life cycle could be compared with theirs. On the other hand, Australia's own emerging global leadership was attributed to the creativity of its multi-cultural populace: how important was that in a fragmented world?

As always, you get double credits for being *really* creative and developing your own approach. Please do not exceed 20k or ten frames. Otherwise, the only requirement is that you be thoughtful and inclusive, balancing your analytical approach with creativity and humanity. I look forward to viewing the results …

SCENARIO 4:

Welcome to Hapibanc ...

It is a great pleasure for me to welcome our annual intake of outstanding happiness graduates to join the team at Hapibanc. Nobody understands better than you do the philosophy that underpins our operation and the reasons for our success. That's why you're here, and we look forward to working with you throughout your careers in the happiness profession.

But we must remember that success, as an ancient philosopher said, is the first step on the ladder to failure. As we enjoy our success, and the fun we have making it happen, should we consider what changes could contribute to some future failure of this hugely successful initiative of Freemasonry?

To do that properly we must revisit the past. I know – you studied the history of the Great Transition at E-uni, but nonetheless I want to make sure you all understand some of the underlying theory as you begin a new stage of your personal journey.

Scientists of the 20th century first identified the 'butterfly effect' of chaos theory – otherwise known as sensitive dependence on initial conditions. Their metaphor describes the major impact that a small change can have on a complex system through the escalation of positive or negative feedback loops. Thus, said those early systems scientists, the flapping of the wings of a butterfly over Brazil could eventually create a hurricane over China.

Freemasonry's Hapibanc was just such a butterfly. Its establishment in 2015, as the old global economy of predatory capitalism was still collapsing, occurred at a moment in time when a convergence of positive change would lift the gentle wind of its wings into stronger breezes of social change. Its instant success as a community bank dedicated to the pursuit of health and happiness was quickly followed by other successes, and the outcome was Australia's repositioning in the emerging global creative economy as the world's centre of excellence in happiness.

We were already identified as having a high proportion of cultural creatives – among the top few countries in the world in this category well before 2000. Thousands of people were engaged in the happiness economy even before it was named – from permaculturalists to physical trainers, psychotherapists to solar engineers. The young people on which the economy depended were choosing to do work that was healthy, fulfilling and good for the planet. Investors wanted their money to work for the good of the community. Regulators, after the debacles of 2008 and 2012, had tightened control of profiteering. For all these reasons and more, organizations were choosing social responsibility. It was Freemasonry's good fortune that it read these signals and recognised the growth potential of the new economy, as well as its alignment with the values of the Craft itself.

As the age of materialism gave way to the age of creativity, Australia had an unparalleled opportunity to recognise, value and protect resources that could deliver an exciting future – helping the world to learn how to be happy. And, as usual, Freemasonry was right there in the lead, helping to make it happen …

ACKNOWLEDGEMENTS

In the Prologue of this book I took liberties with Dan Brown's Prologue to *The Lost Symbol*. Mr Brown began with the words 'The Secret is how to die'. He is right, that is the basis of the Third Degree in Freemasonry, but I added the thought that the moral lesson in the Degree is that if you live a useful, ethical life and make a contribution to society, then you have no reason to fear death. '**The Secret is how to Live**'!

Let me now pay tribute to Dan Brown once more. Having read his new book since I began working on this one, I can now say that he has been more than fair to Freemasonry. One could argue with a fine point or two of his treatment of the Craft in his novel … and I am sure that many a critic will do so. But in essence he applauds the universality and inclusiveness of Freemasonry. And he recognises the fact that Freemasons have high moral principles and that the Craft treats all men as equal, welcomes every race and religion into its brotherhood and does not insist that there is only one way to live your life or to meet your death.

In *The Lost Symbol* Dan Brown bookends his opening words 'The Secret is How to Die' with a final word which elegantly summarises what Freemasons regard as a central tenet of the Craft. That word is **Hope**. Well done, Mr Brown. In the final word of *It's No Secret* let me express the hope that it has achieved its aims; that readers will have found what they wanted in these pages and that some will continue to read and to experience. Australia's Freemasons will welcome all enquiries, greet good men as potential candidates and continue to develop those who are already members of the Fraternity and all who may now wish to join.

Compiling this book has been as instructive as it was pleasurable. Members of the Board of The United Grand Lodge of NSW and ACT are commended for their foresight and confidence in supporting the production of this book, which it is hoped will contribute to the future success of Freemasonry in Australia.

Masonic colleagues who have contributed ideas and material have been encouraged by Dr Greg Levenston, Grand Master of the United Grand Lodge of New South Wales and the Australian Capital Territory. Dr Greg wrote the Foreword for the book and opened all the doors into Freemasonry. He is one of a number of Grand Masters around Australia who have recognised that the Craft needs to let in some light, show what it is and what it does for our community and to emphasise that *It's No Secret.*

Grand Secretary, Kevin McGlinn, provided constant support and contact with contributors to the book. Past Assistant Grand Master, Chris Craven, suggested contents and selected material from the archives of the Masonic Museum and from his amazing memory. His assistance was invaluable.

Many leading members of the Craft, and others, have helped with this book. Grateful thanks to John Armfield, Warwick Boyling, Andrew Brown, Leon Carter, Ian Cox, Tony Craig, Grahame Cumming, Andre Fettermann, Paul Foster, Stephen Green, Doug Grigg, Douglas James, Roland Keller, Tony Lauer, Mark Mansour, Noha Sayed, Alex Shaw, Michael Ward, Susan Williams and more.

My thanks to Sir James (Jim) Hardy, Past Deputy Grand Master, whose love for the Craft proved a dead-heat with his love of sailing and a good red wine.

A very special vote of thanks to Dr Bob James, a foremost expert on the history of the world's fraternities. He tells us in the book why he chose to join Freemasonry. Bob James researched and contributed the chapters on Masonic Architecture and the Literature Review. The latter provides a list of recommended reading about the world's great fraternities, available in libraries and websites.

The initial idea for the book came from Richard Lazar. His determination and enthusiasm for the project and for the task of communicating and demystifying Freemasonry to the media and the general public kept us all going at full speed.

Many other wonderful colleagues worked on the book. In particular, special thanks are due to John Tuffin, an experienced journalist and public relations counsellor, good friend and a non-Mason. John was deliberately chosen to reflect a journalist's view on the subject from the general public's perspective. His interviews feature in the book but his efforts behind the scenes in pulling together content material were greatly appreciated.

Three contributing writers, Jane Llewellyn, Marion Newall and Karen Finch helped with excellent research and writing and their interest in the topic brought the added benefit of a female perspective.

Cover designs were created by Neil Redding of Creative4Sight. Gary Lawrence and Andre Fettermann took some great photographs for the book. Midland Typesetters designed and typeset the book and Graham Austin provided illustrations and drawings.

My thanks to Richard Alleley, CEO of PMP Limited, to Ben Jolly, General Manager of Griffin Press, a PMP company and to Craig Davidson from The Scribo Group, Australia's largest book distributor.

A final vote of thanks to Jan Lee Martin who sub-edited the text, corrected and re-wrote, but more importantly, contributed the final chapter.

Jan Lee Martin is one of Australia's leading futurists. She brings a woman's view and a futures perspective. She applies a deep understanding of the tools and methodologies of futures studies and in the final chapter suggests some scenarios for the future of Freemasonry. Jan's imaginative scenarios were produced in double-quick time to meet the deadline of the book. Normally this kind of scenario work would take many months to develop, but we sought to include some thoughts for the future of Freemasonry and not just to dwell on its past.

As prediction is not what futurists claim to do, Jan has merely compiled some ideas to stimulate further thought and to point to some possible and probable outcomes for the Craft, based on her knowledge of global trends and her many years as a consultant, speaker and writer on the subject of alternative futures.

In the interests of Masonic transparency I wish also to reveal that Jan has watched me go off to Lodge for the past 25 years and despite this … despite everything … has remained my wedded companion throughout.

I love the idea that a woman gets to say the last word about Freemasonry … at least in this book.

Peter Lazar

History of Freemasonry in Australia

No one has captured the rich history of Australian Freemasonry in such detail as Grahame H. Cumming, past Assistant Grand Master of the United Grand Lodge of New South Wales, in his book *The Foundations of Freemasonry in Australia*. Published in 1992, the preface to this enlightening work quotes American Freemason, author and humourist, Samuel Clemens (better known to the world as Mark Twain), who visited Australia in 1895.

> *Australian history is almost always picturesque; indeed, it is so curious and strange, that it is itself the chiefest novelty the country has to offer, and so it pushes the other novelties into second and third place. And all of a fresh new sort, no mouldy old stale ones. It is full of surprises and adventures, incongruities, and incredibilities; but they are all true, they all happened.*

Australian Freemasonry is proud to have its own strong story interwoven through those surprises and adventures, incongruities and incredibilities. And, as Australia continues to develop, there will be more to tell, as the stories woven through these pages demonstrate.

The stories of Australia's first Masons are told in Chapter 4, because these men were truly carrying the light of leadership. For a start, they had left their homeland for unknown parts, in an age when that was no air-conditioned, catered, comfortable hop in a jet. On arrival they not only had to make a new home for themselves: they also had the task of creating a brand new community and a brand new nation. As in the United States, the principles of Freemasonry informed the work of those early brethren – perhaps better described as some of the fathers of our nation.

As we saw, their work began in the first settlement of New South Wales, but slowly and steadily Freemasonry spread beyond the founding settlement. As early as 1807, a letter to the Commandant of Norfolk Island, Freemason Captain John Piper, confirmed the brotherhood was alive and well there. The letter expresses 'gratitude for the patronage and generous protection which we in our collective capacity as Free and Accepted Masons have experienced under your authority', and is signed by two free settlers, James Mitchell and William Atkins, as well as Thomas Lucas, a marine private in the first fleet and a master carpenter. A Lands Department survey shows a Masonic building there in 1814.

In 1821, Australia's oldest permanent Masonic Lodge, the Australian Social Lodge, considered the establishment of other Lodges within the colony. When approached, the Grand Lodge of Ireland granted permission for new Lodges. To help carry out their plans, the Leinster Masonic Committee was established and soon formed the Leinster Marine Lodge of Australia in February 1824. Between 1834 and 1843 they set up five more Lodges: The Tasmanian Operative Lodge, Hobart (1834); the Australia Felix Lodge, Melbourne (1840); the Windsor Social Club, Windsor, NSW (1841); the Auckland Social Lodge (later Lodge Ara), Auckland, New Zealand (1842) and Lodge Fidelity in Sydney (1843).

Gaining autonomy

A Provincial Grand Lodge under the English Constitution was inaugurated on May 10, 1849, in the presence of 200 Masons.

Although the Leinster Masonic Committee had many of the powers of a Provincial Grand Lodge, it did not have full authority or status, and again wrote to the Grand Lodge of Ireland seeking to establish a Provincial Grand Lodge. The authorities in Dublin would not at first sanction Provincial Grand Lodges outside Ireland, but not to be deterred, the committee made four more attempts and the Grand Lodge of Ireland finally permitted the establishment of a Provincial Grand Lodge in Sydney on December 27, 1857.

In the wider community, Australia's free settlers sought some measure of political self-determination from the early days of the 19th century. As a result, the British Parliament passed the New South Wales Act in 1823 and a Legislative Council was established in Sydney the following year. The Freemasons also sought local control of their affairs and, although the three Masonic British Constitutions (England, Ireland and Scotland) agreed to the Provincial Grand Lodges, the Australian Masons sought complete autonomy.

The campaign to form a Masonic union was led by Irish and Scottish Past Masters and The Most Worshipful The Grand Lodge of New South Wales of Ancient, Free and Accepted Masons was inaugurated in December 1877.

James Squire Farnell, the former Provincial Grand Master of the Irish Constitution, became the first Grand Master and Premier of New South Wales just 15 days after his installation. This new Grand Lodge was bitterly opposed by the three British Grand Lodges which refused it recognition. Despite this animosity, the new Grand Lodge prospered, and in 1884 opened the Masonic Hall in Castlereagh Street, Sydney – headquarters of the Craft in New South Wales until 1972.

By 1885 the last Irish Lodge in NSW had returned its warrant to Dublin and transferred its allegiance to the Grand Lodge of NSW.

The arrival of Lord Carrington as Governor of NSW brought new developments in 1885. Lord Carrington was a Freemason and a past Grand Warden of the United Grand Lodge of England. Masonic unity was still under discussion at the time, and a meeting was called to 'agree upon such united action as may restore harmony'. Although only seven attended the first meeting, the second attracted 50 Masters and Past Masters, who agreed to the formation of a committee called the Party of Union.

Meanwhile, the Earl of Carnarvon, Pro-Grand Master of the United Grand Lodge of England, arrived on a visit to New South Wales. On January 20, 1888, the members of the Party of Union were entertained by the Earl at Government House and a basis of union was prepared and signed by Lord Carrington. The District Grand Masters, meanwhile, had indicated their willingness to resign in favour of Lord Carrington. This cleared the way and the long-awaited union came about at a meeting held in the Great Hall of the University of Sydney on August 16, 1888, with Lord Carrington elected as the first Grand Master. More than 4,400 Masons were present when Lord Carrington was installed as Grand Master of the United Grand Lodge of New South Wales of Ancient, Free and Accepted Masons on September 18, 1888.

Colonising Australia

Freemasonry followed in the footsteps of settlement around Australia.

New South Wales

The first colony historically takes pride of place for establishing the first permanent Masonic Lodge in Australia in 1820 – the Australian Social Lodge. The ceremony of dedication and installation was conducted on August 12 at the Golden Lion Tavern opposite the King's Wharf on the western side of what is now Circular Quay in Sydney. During the first year, membership rose from 12 to 27.

The Governor of New South Wales at the time was Freemason Lachlan Macquarie. As many convicts were being emancipated, free settlers began raising issues regarding the convicts' new status. The question of whether emancipated convicts could become Freemasons was also a question under discussion in the Australian Social Lodge. Finally, it was decided to seek advice from the Grand Lodge of Ireland. The ruling, given in 1822, read: 'That an individual becoming free by pardon or expiration of sentence, possessing a good character, may and would be eligible to become a member of a Masonic Lodge.'

Any person who had been initiated in Britain was also eligible to affiliate after emancipation. One Mason accepted under this ruling was the convict architect, Francis Greenway. Explorer Hamilton Hume was initiated into the colony's second oldest Lodge, the Leinster Marine Lodge of Australia, which was formed in February 1824 at Hills' Tavern in Sydney's Hyde Park.

Benevolence has always been one of the prime values of Freemasonry. In 1834 a Fund of Benevolence was established, and quickly followed by a proposal to establish a school to educate the children of needy Masons. This was the origin of the Freemasons' Orphan Society. In 1880, scholarships to the University of Sydney were available to the children of Masons with the necessary qualifications.

The first Scottish Lodge was the Sydney Lodge of St Andrew. The members of this Lodge had some standing and in 1857 paid for the return of a widow and her large family to Scotland. A substantial sum of money was provided to help her set up a new home on her arrival.

In 1853, Edward Hargraves, the man credited with the discovery of gold in Australia, joined the Leinster Marine Lodge.

Although it was now clear that more and more outstanding men were being attracted to Freemasonry, the issue regarding the admission of emancipated convicts was still unresolved. The Leinster Marine Lodge had a by-law to preclude ex-convicts: '… however good his character may be, or however trifling his original offence might have been, from being initiated or becoming a member of this Lodge.'

When the Australian Social Lodge objected to the Grand Lodge of Ireland about this by-law, the Grand Lodge ordered that: 'The said rule or by-law be expunged and be of no effect; being unmasonic …'. And that was the end of the matter.

The early military connection with Freemasonry continued when a number of officers formed a Lodge which later broadened to become the United Services Lodge of New South Wales.

Tasmania

The next colony established after the settlement of Sydney was Tasmania. The settlers first met Freemasonry through a number of travelling military Lodges, notably the 40th Regiment Lodge, which involved itself with local residents in 1827–28. The first of the civilian Lodges was the Tasmanian Lodge (Irish Constitution) which commenced in 1828 with meetings held at the Macquarie Hotel, in Hobart Town.

Two more Irish Lodges were established in 1832 and 1834 – the Brotherly Union Lodge and the Tasmanian Operative Lodge. One of the outstanding early members of the Tasmanian Operative Lodge was Captain Robert Wyndham Lathrop-Murray who served with fellow Mason, the Duke of Wellington during the Irish rebellion. Captain Murray became father of every Lodge in the colony and nearly every Mason was initiated by him, or those he had instructed, during his stay.

Tasmanian Union was the first English Constitution Lodge. Formed in 1844, it convened its first meeting at the Freemasons' Hotel, Hobart. The first Scottish Lodge was consecrated at Launceston in 1876 and named St Andrew.

Autonomous Masonic government was uppermost in the minds of some leading Masonic members and in 1888, a meeting of the three Constitutions in Launceston resulted in a unanimous agreement, to form a union and bring a Grand Lodge into being.

By 1890 all was in readiness for the Lodges of the three Constitutions to amalgamate and a Launceston convention of delegates from every Lodge determined to erect the Grand Lodge in Hobart. Richard Deodatus Poulett-Harris, the former headmaster of Hobart High School, was installed as Grand Master of the Grand Lodge of Free and Accepted Masons of Tasmania on June 26, 1890. The new Grand Lodge commenced with 22 private Lodges and 864 members.

Victoria

The first recorded Masonic activity in Victoria was a meeting in 1839 – less than five years after the founding of Melbourne. There it was resolved that: 'the time has come when Freemasonry should be officially represented in the Port Phillip District and that the proposed Lodge should be called The Lodge of Australia Felix' (Felix being Latin for happy.)

This Lodge grew rapidly and by 1841, 39 members had signed a petition to form a Scottish Lodge. The first Scottish Lodge to be formed in Australia, The Australasian Kilwinning Lodge, opened on May 13, 1844.

In 1860 the Lodge of Australia Felix circulated a letter suggesting the formation of a Grand Lodge. But it was not until 1883, 23 years later that a meeting at the Protestant Hall carried a motion to establish the Grand Lodge of Victoria. After a long fight for recognition by the three British Grand Lodges, the Grand Lodge of Victoria was inaugurated on March 20, 1889.

Sir William John Clarke was installed as Grand Master in the Melbourne Town Hall on the following day. One of Victoria's social leaders, Sir William was an extremely wealthy man and generous benefactor to a wide range of charities. In the latter part of the 1880s he saved the state's Masonic community from embarrassment by taking over a £50,000 mortgage on the Masonic Hall in Melbourne.

South Australia

In 1840 Adelaide became the first Australian settlement to be designated a city. South Australia's Grand Lodge of Free and Accepted Masons, established in 1884 – four years ahead of NSW – occupies pride of place at the head of the list of Grand Lodges of Australia and New Zealand.

Among the free settlers of South Australia were a number of Masons determined to continue their activities in their new land. They set the necessary procedures in motion to set up a Lodge in the colony prior to leaving England, and The South Australian Lodge of Friendship was consecrated in London, not Adelaide, in October 1834.

It was a very long time before the next meeting was held in the assembly rooms of Black's Port Lincoln Hotel, Adelaide on August 11, 1838.

Scottish Freemasonry appeared in 1844, with the formation of the Adelaide Lodge followed the next day by the initiation of Revd. Robert Haining and the laying of the foundation stone of his church. Reporting on the ceremony, *The Register* newspaper said that: 'The novel spectacle of the procession caused considerable sensation among both the white and native population of all ranks and ages and many hundreds were present at the imposing ceremony.'

During 1851-52, the Lodges of South Australia experienced great difficulties as a result of the mass exodus to the Victorian goldfields. In *History of Adelaide,* Freemason Thomas Worsnop wrote: 'Everyone who could go away left the place. Shops were shut up and "gone to the diggings" was the announcement frequently seen on the shutters of the abandoned places of trade. It is estimated that somewhere about 16,000 persons left the colony.'

The most prominent Irish Mason was Sir James Penn Boucaut, a Judge of the Supreme Court and three times Premier of South Australia. Irish Freemasonry grew steadily and the Alfred Masonic Hall was established by 1867. Revenue from the hall was devoted to a benevolent fund.

A number of meetings were held to form a Grand Lodge of South Australia and 108 Masons formed themselves into a Masonic union to help with this task.

On April 17, 1884 the Grand Lodge of South Australia was opened and Samuel James Way installed as its first Grand Master. Way became Chief Justice in 1876, Lieutenant Governor the following year and Chancellor of Adelaide University in 1883. He was made a Baronet in 1899. The new Grand Lodge, which gained full recognition, began with 20 English, six Scottish and five Irish Lodges.

Northern Territory

The Northern Territory forms part of the Masonic jurisdiction of the Grand Lodge of South Australia, with Port Darwin

Lodge being the first formed in 1896. Other Lodges have subsequently been established at Katherine, Tennant Creek and Alice Springs.

Western Australia

Freemasonry came to the most remote settlement in 1842, when less than 2,000 people populated the colony. Both the Governor, John Hutt, and the Colonial Secretary, Peter Brown, were Masons, who, along with several other citizens, held a meeting at Government House on September 1, 1841. The Lodge of St John (English Constitution) began in Perth on April 4, 1843. Meetings were held at Leeder's Tavern, which the owner later renamed the Freemasons' Hotel.

Twenty years were to elapse before another Lodge was formed, during which time the transportation of convicts provided the necessary manual labour for Western Australia's growth and expansion. The discovery of gold also accelerated development, allowing Freemasonry to prosper as the population expanded. This was particularly evident in the country, where new Lodges were formed at Geraldton, Bunbury, York, Albany, Northam and Roeburne.

As late as 1894, all Lodges in Western Australia belonged to the English Constitution. However within a few years both Scottish and Irish Lodges were established, thereby complicating the formation of a Grand Lodge for Western Australia.

Nonetheless, on February 27, 1900 the Grand Lodge of Western Australia came into being with 37 constituent Lodges. The impressive installation ceremony was held in the ballroom of Government House and attended by some 2,000 Masons.

Thirteen Lodges continued to be chartered by Scotland and even as late as 1943, 15 Scottish Lodges continued to be governed by their respective District Grand Lodges.

Queensland

The year Queensland became a separate colony – 1859 – also saw the establishment of the first Masonic Lodge, making the Craft as old as the state itself.

There were 12 foundation members in the North Australian Lodge (English Constitution), the first meeting of which was held on July 13, 1859, at the Freemasons' Hotel, Brisbane. Among those initiated into the Lodge at its first meeting was John Petrie, first Mayor of Brisbane.

Irish Freemasonry came to Queensland with the opening of the St Patrick Lodge of Queensland. Scottish Freemasonry began with the St Andrew Lodge, with the first meeting held in 1864. From the mid-60s onwards, the Scottish Lodges grew and were strengthened by engineers and other workers brought out from Scotland to help establish the Queensland railways.

With Queensland being a vast area twice the size of New South Wales, the state's inland Masonic development followed the construction of the roads and railways. Consequently, in true pioneering spirit, Queensland Freemasonry needed to be highly resourceful when spreading to new areas. For example, Charters Towers Lodge, founded in 1875, furnished the Lodge room with upholstered packing crates while using cedar table legs to fashion some Masonic regalia.

It was not until 1920 that a conference of three representatives from each Grand Lodge met to establish the United Grand Lodge of Queensland, formed in 1921 with 281 Lodges.

Papua New Guinea

The United Grand Lodge of Queensland has jurisdiction over Lodges in Papua New Guinea. The first of these was formed under the English Constitution at Rabaul in 1919.

Other Orders and Degrees

The structure of Freemasonry and the variety of orders associated with the Craft can be confusing to the non-Mason. This variety is a logical outcome of hundreds of years of continuity: as with a growing tree, slight initial divergences become, over hundreds of years, almost independent limbs. But they remain part of the mother tree – and so it is with Freemasonry. Indeed this diversification demonstrates one of the great strengths of Masonry, its ability to embrace diversity and to remain true to the shared goals and objectives of its members.

Nonetheless it must be made clear that there is a single parent trunk, which is the Ancient and Accepted Order of Freemasons. In this Order, there are three degrees – which have been explained at some length in this book – of Entered Apprentice, Fellow Craft Freemason and Master Mason. The Degree of Master Mason is the highest degree in Freemasonry.

Members of the philanthropic club, the Shrine, call themselves 'Shrine Masons', for example, and members of the Scottish Rite call themselves 'Scottish Rite Masons'. However it is only because they have completed the three Degrees of Freemasonry, and continue to be members of a Lodge, that they can call themselves Freemasons.

Details of the various associated Orders are available from books and websites. In this book, we felt it was enough to share with you the chart from the website of the Grand Lodge of British Columbia and Yukon. It's all there … except I should add that the placing of degrees on the chart is not intended to show relative ranking. As the Canadian site points out, these other bodies 'confer additional—not higher—degrees. The use of this numbering system has left the erroneous impression that their additional degrees are in some way superior to the first three degrees. There can be nothing further from the truth.'

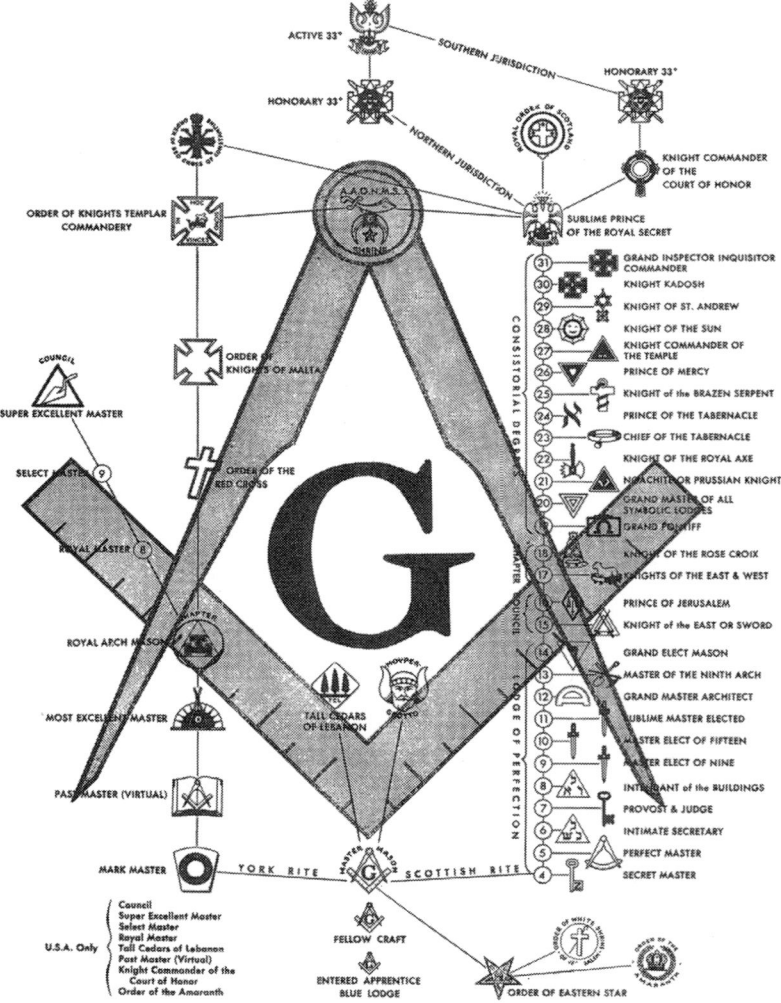

Thanks to the Grand Lodge of British Columbia and Yukon for permission to use this chart (www.freemasonry.bcy.ca)

Women Freemasons … The Order of the Eastern Star

This organisation had its origins in eighteenth century France, then spread to other parts of Europe. The objects were 'to associate in one common bond the worthy wives, widows, daughters and sisters of Freemasons; to secure to them advantages from a moral, social and charitable point of view, and from them, the performance of corresponding duties'.

The Australian Order of the Eastern Star commenced in 1912 in Queensland and Chapters can now be found around Australia. More information can be found at http://www.mastermason.com/oes-ugcofa/.

Women's Freemasonry also exists in other forms. For example, here is how Wikipedia describes the Order of the Amaranth.

Order of the Amaranth is a Masonic-affiliated women's organization founded in 1873. As in the Order of the Eastern Star, members of the Order must be age 18 and older; men must be Master Masons; and women must be related to Masons as wives, mothers, daughters, widows, sisters, nieces, aunts, et cetera, or have been active members of the International Order of the Rainbow for Girls or Job's Daughters International for more than three years and be recommended by a Master Mason.

Amaranth was based on Queen Christina of Sweden's court. Christina had created the 'Order of the Amarantha' for the ladies and knights of her court. In 1860, James B. Taylor of Newark, New Jersey drew upon this order to create a new fraternal society. In 1873, Rob Macoy organized Taylor's society into the Order of the Amaranth, part of a proposed Adoptive Rite of Masonry. Eastern Star was to be the first degree, and until 1921, Amaranth members were required to join Eastern Star first.

In the Order's teachings, the members are emphatically reminded of their duties to God, to their country and to their fellow beings. They are urged to portray, by precept and example, their belief in the 'Golden Rule' and by conforming to the virtues inherent in TRUTH, FAITH, WISDOM and CHARITY they can prove to others the goodness promulgated by the Order.

In France from 1902 there has been a system of mixed Lodges, also called Co-Masonry. In 1909 The Honourable Fraternity of Antient Freemasonry was founded in London. Its first Grand Master was a man, but since 1912 its Grand Masters have all been women.

While the United Grand Lodge of England acknowledges the regularity and sincerity of women's Freemasonry it does not recognise the order officially.

Similar organisations for young people

A movement associated with Freemasonry that is suitable for boys, called DeMolay, originated in Kansas City, in the USA, more than 80 years ago. It is based upon the lessons and values of love of God, home and country. According to its Australian website (www.demolayaust.org) DeMolay is an organisation 'dedicated to preparing young men to lead successful, happy, and productive lives. Basing its approach on timeless principles and practical, hands-on experience, DeMolay opens doors for young men aged 12 to 21 by developing the civic awareness, personal responsibility and leadership skills so vitally needed in society today. DeMolay combines this serious mission with a fun approach that builds important bonds of friendship among members in more than 1,000 chapters worldwide.'

A similar movement catering for girls is called The International Order of the Rainbow for Girls (IORG). It also originated in the USA. IORG operates in Australia with three Assemblies in NSW (Sydney, Cumberland & Illawarra, and Blacktown); and Assemblies in Adelaide, Bundaberg and Cairns.

For more information go to http://www.geocities.com/nswrainbow/

Script for the Son et Lumière at Sydney's Grand Lodge Centre

FREEMASONS

A sound and light presentation can be viewed by the public at the Grand Lodge Centre, corner Goulburn and Castlereagh Streets, Sydney. Inside a newly refurbished Lodge Room, the Son et Lumière presentation can be seen during office hours. Arrangements can be made by calling 61 (0)2 9284 2800. Visitors can also view the Masonic Museum with its excellent displays of Masonic regalia, working tools, hand painted antique tracing boards, display of Masonic Aprons from around the world and more.

———————

Music (from Mozart's 'Magic Flute') Group enters and takes seats ...
Lights dim to as dark as possible ... music under

Female voice: In the beginning, the Great Architect created the heavens and the earth. And the earth was without form and void and darkness was upon the face of the deep ... And the spirit of God moved upon the face of the waters and God said 'Let there be light ... and there was light ...

The Star above the Master's chair is illuminated ... the stars of the canopy come on ...

Male voice: Having been restored to the blessing of material light, let me beg you to observe that light was ever an object of attainment in all ancient mysteries. It was then as it is now the symbol of Truth and Knowledge, a fact of which we must never lose sight when we consider the nature and significance of Masonic light.

Slide of the exterior of Grand Lodge Centre ... segues to interior of the various Lodge Rooms (empty) ... final one: the Green Lodge Room (also empty)

Female Voice: When a candidate expresses a desire for light he seeks not only that light which removes his physical darkness but also that intellectual light which brings to his view the sublime truths of Morality and Virtue which it is ever the object of Freemasonry to teach ...

Male Voice: These words and ideas are taken from the ritual of the first degree in Freemasonry ... a fraternity which has existed from time immemorial ... in the next few minutes ... let us take you through a journey which explains why in all ages the greatest and wisest of men have been promoters of this Ancient and Honourable Fraternity ... *voice fades ...*

... famous historic buildings are projected and alternated as in a traditional slide show ... Parthenon, Notre Dame, Roman and Greek buildings, pyramids ... and architectural features such as flying buttresses, various forms of columns, gargoyles...etc...

Boy's Voice: Hullo Mister ... Sir ... ... are you the foreman?

Foreman's Voice: Yes I am

Boy's: What are you building here ?

Foreman: ... it's a great Temple for the King ... what can I do for you?

Boy: ... are there any jobs going?

Foreman: Maybe ... have you worked on a building site before?

Boy: No ... but I reckon I could learn ... especially if there's any work with stone ...

Foreman: We have some groups of stonemasons on the job. One's from France, there's one from Spain and there's a Lodge from Rome … go and see the Master Mason on one of those and see if he'll give you a job … maybe take you on as an apprentice …

Boy: What do you have to be able to do ?

Foreman: Well if they accept you, they'll teach you how to make rough boulders into building blocks … how to shape them … set them into the building… make sure they're level and square … But in addition they'll expect you to behave 'on the level' and deal 'on the square' with all the people you work with.

Boy: That sounds great …

Foreman: And if they accept you, you will develop skills which will enable you to become a Craftsman and finally a Master Mason.

More slides of world buildings – changing to more modern buildings

One day, you will be able to travel with your Lodge to new countries … see the world … and find employment wherever great buildings, churches, palaces … are being built.

Boy: How would I get work in a place where I can't speak the language?

Foreman: The Lodge will teach you special signs … give you words which will get you work even in foreign countries … because the foreman or the architect on the job will know from those handshakes and words how skilled you are as a mason … but even more importantly, that you are honest and a good man who can be trusted in whatever you do.

Boy: What sort of signs? What do you mean 'symbols'?

Foreman: Well let's look at some signs and symbols in this lodge room …

Light illuminates the G suspended from the ceiling at the centre of the building ...

Foreman: What do you reckon that stands for?

Boy: ... 'G' ... maybe ... God?

Foreman: Well ... you're right of course ... in Freemasonry ... we recognise that there is a Supreme Being ... in English speaking countries that would be 'God' ... but because Feemasonry is open to all good men ... because it's a brotherhood ... also called a Craft ... which allows for any man to join ... no matter what race or religion or any other distinctions ... it doesn't matter whether he's a plumber or a doctor or a bus driver ... we don't care how wealthy or poor he might be ... but we do want our members to be decent upright people ... men who believe in a Higher Power, a Supreme Being ... and to make that point ... Freemasons call that ... 'The Great Architect of the Universe'

The light on the 'G' is dimmed ... and another lights up the Master's chair ...

Boy: Is that His chair??

Foreman: (laughs softly) ... No ... that is the chair for the Master of the Lodge. Notice the carved symbol on the front ... that is the square ... the most common implement used by stonemasons and builders of all kinds ... and used by Freemasons to remind members to act 'on the square' to all ... Freemasons use the tools of stonemasons as symbols of how we should lead our lives ... each of these has deep meanings which we teach to the brethren ... to stress to them the great principles of morality and virtue which all good people should value in their lives ...

Light dims on Master's chair and square ... light up on Senior Warden's chair ...

Foreman: Now that stonemason's implement is called the level and it's the symbol on the front of the chair for the Senior Warden in a Freemason's Lodge

Boy: What's a Senior Warden?

Foreman: He's the Master's right-hand man ... and the level is a symbol which stands for equality ... makes the point that everyone in a Masonic Lodge is equal ... that's one of the reasons why Freemasons wear dinner suits when they go to Lodge ...

Boy: I've seen them going to Lodge ... looking like a flock of penguins ... with their little black bags ... *(pause here to allow for possible audience reaction)* ... my mates reckon they wear the dinner suits to make out that they're better than other people ...

Foreman: ... well, I guess that's one of the many misunderstandings about the Craft ... the real reason that it was decided we should wear black ties was because in earlier times, the wealthier members could be distinguished from the less well-off because of the clothes they wore. ... so it was decided that dinner suits would make all the brethren look the same ... and the dinner suits also made a Lodge meeting seem a bit more important than going out for a night with friends ...

Light dims and a spot illuminates the altar and the Volume of the Sacred Law

Boy: Gee ... is that a Bible ...?

Foreman: Yes it is ... Freemasons call it the Volume of the Sacred Law ... and depending on which country the Lodge is in ... or which religion most of the members belong to ... that book could be the New or the Old Testament ...or maybe the Koran ... whatever ... indeed in some Lodges, they have more than one Sacred Book open on the altar. That just underlines the Masonic view that a man is not judged by which particular religion he follows but by his behaviour towards others, how he lives his life ... his basic values ... the essential ingredients that make a good man ...

Light dims and a spot illuminates the first Tracing Board ... a slide of the Tracing Board also appears on the screen ... the slides then also show the second and third tracing boards...

Foreman: Now that is what Masons call the First Tracing Board. The symbols you see there demonstrate what an apprentice Freemason learns in his initiation into the First Degree of Freemasonry and during his early period in the Craft. All those symbols ... the columns ... the winding stairs ... the tessellated pavement ...

Lights come on to illuminate these features in the Lodge room

carry valuable lessons with them and they are all designed to 'make good men better' ... which is one of the key objectives of the Craft. The lessons are taught by the officers of the Lodge in special ceremonies ...

Boy: So do you have to go through those ceremonies ... ?

Foreman: Yes ... they are really quite wonderful events. The officers and members of your Lodge perform a very moving and ancient ceremony for each of the three Degrees of the Craft. The new Masons usually remember those occasions for the rest of their lives ...

Boy: Is the initiation scary?

Foreman: Candidates tend to be nervous because they don't know what is involved ... but once they realise the good intentions of the Craft and the values we believe in, they tend to relax and enjoy what they are about to learn ...

Boy: So what about the goat?

Foreman: (laughs) ... let's get this straight once and for all ... there is no goat! ... It's another of those urban myths that people like to laugh about ... and it's come about because Masons have been so secretive about their beliefs and activities. In fact that secrecy has been quite harmful to the Craft. People who aren't Masons wonder what the secrecy is about … and as you know, if someone is keeping secrets from you, you suspect their intentions …

Boy: Yes, I've wondered why Masons don't talk about what they do … if it's all so good …

Foreman: That's part of the tradition … which goes all the way back to the building of King Solomon's Temple thousands of years ago …

Slide of the Temple is thrown on to the screen…

… in those early days, and later in the early Craft Guilds when there were no diplomas or other documents to prove that a mason or a carpenter had the required skills, they used the secret handshakes and secret words to distinguish the Apprentice, the skilled Craftsman and the Master Mason.

Slides of handshakes, diplomas, degrees …

Because those skills were highly prized, anyone who had them didn't reveal the secret words because they didn't want other workers claiming to be qualified when they didn't actually have the learning and the skill which the genuine stonemasons had. Today we have diplomas and other documents … but in Freemasonry we have kept those traditional secrets as part of the history … The handshakes and words are actually the only secrets we aren't prepared to tell you until you have shown enough interest to join the Craft … but all that I've told you can be found in many books in libraries or on the web …

Boy: So I could get all this information without becoming a Mason?

Foreman; You could, but it would have much less meaning for you to read all that from a book or a computer screen. You'd learn about some of the great earlier Masons … world leaders, great composers … the music you heard as you came in was by Mozart … one of the most famous Masons of all time …

Music up from The Magic Flute …

his opera 'The Magic Flute' contains direct references to Freemasonry … Mozart was a devoted Mason … as were Haydn and Sibelius and Gilbert and Sullivan … and among the more modern composers … Glenn Miller, Irving Berlin and Count Basie and great performers like Louis Armstrong …

Music segues into Armstrong's 'It's a wonderful world' … slides show some of the famous Australian Masons …

and Australia's 'Smoky Dawson' was a Mason too… and while I'm running hot … Australia had great explorers … like Matthew Flinders, Oxley and Wentworth … we had 16 VC winners … great sportsmen such as Don Bradman; Ian Craig, one of our Cricket captains; Sir James Hardy the Americas Cup skipper; Merv Wood, the Olympic Gold Medallist for rowing; John Treloar, the sprinter. Ten of Australia's 25 Prime Ministers were Masons; vice-regal representatives; leaders of industry; inventors; architects; doctors and on and on … At one time there were 140,000 Masons from all walks of life in NSW alone. They all saw the value of Freemasonry and gained greatly from their participation.

Boy: That's amazing … why would you keep all <u>that</u> secret?

Foreman: Yes, you might well ask that … It's been a tradition that we don't give Masonry a 'hard sell'. Instead we wait until our sons or our friends ask us about it. Maybe we've overdone that too… but today we're determined to change and to stop hiding ourselves … our members are being encouraged to talk about Freemasonry, to wear Masonic lapel badges and to have conversations …

Slides of social situations, men wearing badges, talking over a drink

… which we think will encourage people to ask us questions. We'll answer honestly and openly … and that will lead to new members wanting to learn more …

Then, if they join, they'll find there is real magic ... real value in actually experiencing the ceremonies. And I can tell you it has made a difference to me in how I live my life. I think you'd get great pleasure and value from it too ...

One of the really great things about Freemasonry is the friendships we form and the good work we do together ...

Boy: So what happens?

Foreman: Well at most Masonic meetings, there is some serious business like the usual things in any organisation ... we keep records, there is a Secretary whose job it is to keep Minutes ... a Treasurer who looks after Lodge funds ... a Caring Officer who visits members who are sick or in need ... though once you become a member most Masons do that sort of thing ... concerning ourselves about our brethren ... then we usually do some Degree work for the new members ... and afterwards we have supper ... most Lodges make small charges for the meal and refreshments.

Slides of scenes in the South

We call it the South ... and there's usually some fun ... a toast or two ... some jokes ... a bit of singing ... some music ... entertainment nights and other social events to which ladies and friends are invited ...

Boy: So what else do I need to know?

Slides of lodge centres ... welcoming scenes

Foreman: There are Lodges in nearly all parts of Australia ... 580 of them ...with about 30,000 members ... and providing you are known to have a good reputation, you could join any one you like ... and then you can visit any Lodge anywhere in the world and you'll be made welcome. You'll have 'brethren' wherever you go.

Boy: So even if I can't speak the local language, I could go to a Lodge and hope to find someone who speaks English who would invite me in?

Foreman: That's right! There are 164 countries where you can try that ... and, don't worry, there are about 5 million Masons around the world ... and there's usually someone who speaks English ... and whether they can or not, they'll all welcome you as a brother.

Slides of charities supported by Masonry ...

Foreman: And you'll be proud of the work Masons do in society. Over centuries Masons have supported benevolence ... formed and operated charities ... in Australia and New Zealand we have about 100 Masonic retirement villages ... People who want to live in them don't have to be Masons ... They are all comfortable without being lavish ... and they're affordable. We have special funds for orphans, widows and others in need ... and the Craft makes generous contributions to bushfire appeals and to other needy purposes.

Slide showing where to get more information

Female Voice: As you have passed through the ceremony of your initiation, allow me to congratulate you upon your admission to our Ancient and Honourable Fraternity. Ancient no doubt it is having existed from time immemorial ... Honourable it must also be as it tends to make all those so who are strictly obedient to its precepts. *(voice fades)*

Male Voice: Indeed, no institution can boast so solid a foundation as that on which Freemasonry rests - the practice of every social and moral virtue - and to such an eminence has its credit been advanced that in all ages the best, the greatest and the wisest of men have been promoters of the art ... (voice fades)

Foreman: But that's enough for now ... maybe if you decide to join, you'll one day welcome other members into your Lodge ... the main thing is to remember to enjoy your life ... live it on the square ... to help others ... we see Masonry as 'doing good and being happy' ... it's the pursuit of happiness and we urge all people to 'be happy and confer happiness' ...

Slide of hands shaking … words over read 'Be happy and confer happiness'

Music up on something joyful by Mozart … or Glenn Miller's 'Tuxedo Junction' … or reprise Louis Armstrong 'It's a Wonderful World'.

Peter Lazar
26 October 2009